Early Intervention for Deaf and Hard-of-Hearing Infants, Toddlers, and Their Families

Early Intervention for Deaf and Hard-of-Hearing Infants, Toddlers, and Their Families

Interdisciplinary Perspectives

EDITED BY MARILYN SASS-LEHRER

OXFORD
UNIVERSITY PRESS

OXFORD
UNIVERSITY PRESS

Oxford University Press is a department of the University of
Oxford. It furthers the University's objective of excellence in research,
scholarship, and education by publishing worldwide.

Oxford   New York
Auckland   Cape Town   Dar es Salaam   Hong Kong   Karachi
Kuala Lumpur   Madrid   Melbourne   Mexico City   Nairobi
New Delhi   Shanghai   Taipei   Toronto

With offices in
Argentina   Austria   Brazil   Chile   Czech Republic   France   Greece
Guatemala   Hungary   Italy   Japan   Poland   Portugal   Singapore
South Korea   Switzerland   Thailand   Turkey   Ukraine   Vietnam

Oxford is a registered trademark of Oxford University Press
in the UK and certain other countries.

Published in the United States of America by
Oxford University Press
198 Madison Avenue, New York, NY 10016

Library of Congress Cataloging-in-Publication Data
Early intervention for deaf and hard-of-hearing infants, toddlers and their families :
interdisciplinary perspectives / edited by Marilyn Sass-Lehrer.
pages cm. — (Professional perspectives on deafness: evidence and applications)
Includes bibliographical references and index.
ISBN 978–0–19–995774–3
1. Deaf children—Services for.   2. Hearing impaired children—Services for.
3. Deaf children—Education.   4. Hearing impaired children—Education.
5. Hearing disorders in children—Diagnosis.   6. Hearing disorders in infants—Diagnosis.
I. Sass-Lehrer, Marilyn, 1948-
HV2391.E266 2016
362.4'20832—dc23

To the many outstanding professionals all around the world devoted to providing infants and toddlers who are deaf or hard of hearing and their families with the tools necessary for a great start.

CONTENTS

PART II EARLY INTERVENTION PRACTICES

FOREWORD

WORKING WITH FAMILIES OF DEAF AND HARD-OF-HEARING INFANTS AND TODDLERS: IS IT A SMOOTH DANCING EXPERIENCE?

The readers of this book may ask themselves what early intervention for deaf and hard-of-hearing infants, toddlers, and their families may have to do with dancing. Before I come back to this question, I have some thoughts at the outset that I would like to share.

This book is a "must-have" for every professional who is working with families of deaf and hard-of-hearing infants and toddlers, as well as for students who plan to work in this field. This book may also be of interest to families who want to know what they can expect when an early intervention provider is knocking on their door after the confirmation that their child is deaf. Whoever reads this book is offered a masterpiece of ideas regarding challenges and opportunities in early intervention. The principles described in this book are based on a comprehensive survey of recent empirical data and on a strong foundation of the practical expertise of the contributors to this book (hearing professionals, deaf professionals, and parents). The integrative combination of theory and practice makes this book especially valuable.

When Marilyn Sass-Lehrer invited me to write a foreword for this book, I was, at first, somewhat reluctant. As we are all busy people, I was doubtful that I would find time in my tight schedule to do this job. Today, I am so happy that I accepted this invitation. My initial plan was to read one chapter at a time when I had a moment between my other engagements. But things happened in a very different way. After I read the first chapter I could not stop, and so I finished my reading of the whole book the evening after I started it! I even gave a copy of the book manuscript to a German mother of a deaf child who I have known for many years. After reading the book, she told me that this was the information she was looking for when her deaf child was identified as being deaf many years ago. She then asked if it would be possible to write something similar for early intervention in Germany.

Now back to the dance analogy. I found a citation in a book I have that also concerns families of young children with special needs (McWilliam, 2010a). One mother describes a situation far too familiar to many families who have just received confirmation of a "disability" for their child. It is often not easy for parents to immediately engage in collaborative relationships with professionals. This mother compared her situation to an invitation to a dance, in which one of the dance partners may be very unsure if he or she is willing to dance:

> Here you are, the professional, eagerly awaiting your new dance partner. Your arms are stretched out inviting us, parents, to enter your world. . . . We, as parents, having not chosen this dance, are usually not as eager to join you. We may approach you not with open arms but with tightly folded ones clutched to our chest. … We may feel reluctant, ambivalent, and often unwilling. For one thing, if we choose to join you, we have to acknowledge that our child has special needs. We have to acknowledge that we are entering your world—one that is initially unfamiliar and frightening.

> Entering into our partnerships with you demands that we let go
> of our dreams and begin to build new ones. (Fialka, 2001, p. 22)

Professionals who read this book (and who follow its pivotal guidelines) will be well prepared to encourage families of children who are deaf or hard of hearing to build new dreams! The focus on an intensive collaboration of professionals and families, and of professionals with each other—one of the core concepts of this book, helps parents and professionals find a way to share a common language and to be on the same page:

> Priorities for parents and professionals often differ. It is as if we each have on our own set of headphones and are listening to our own music, with its own tune, words, and rhythm. There's the mother song, the father song, the speech pathologist song, the neurologist song, and the teacher song. Sometimes the only song we can momentarily agree on is "Hit the road Jack, and don't you come back no more!" (Fialka, 2001, p. 26)

After learning that their child is deaf, parents often feel confused about their roles and competence: "Do I have to teach him or her language? If so, how will I do that? I know nothing about what it means to be deaf. Do I have the strength to cope with this new situation?" If professionals want parents to accept their dance invitation and collaborate with them, they have to be able to develop relationships with families and their children, have excellent communication skills, and know how to be a good dance partner. As stated in the preface of this book, it is also essential for professionals to understand people who are deaf and hard of hearing. Professionals, both hearing and deaf, need to understand Deaf and Hard-of-Hearing communities and understand the varying perspectives and experiences on being deaf in a predominantly hearing world.

Readers of this book will be provided with much theoretical and practical information at a hitherto unprecedented level of expertise and detail. We learn that for children who are deaf or hard of hearing early access to language (regardless of which language modality is used) is essential and must be supported by parents (and other members of the family) who learn to communicate sensitively and responsively with their child.

Implementing this has implications for the supportive manner in which professionals serve families and requires early intervention providers to make internal and external resources available to the families.

McWilliam (2010b, p. 2) described the values necessary to provide effective early intervention: The first value he addresses is providing services to children and families in the context of everyday routines rather than in sessions; the second value includes working with families in a family-friendly manner rather than instructing them on what to do with their (deaf or hard-of-hearing) child; and the third value discusses the importance of concentrating on family quality of life not only on child competence.

Five practices are necessary, according to McWilliam (2010b), to implement these values into the everyday life of families. These practices are "assessing informal and formal supports, assessing functional needs in everyday situations, coordinating services, using home visits to provide support, and consulting collaboratively with child care providers" (p. 2). Behind these practices are some very simple, but very important, key principles of a family-centered philosophy of early intervention for families with deaf or hard-of-hearing infants and toddlers (McWilliam, 2010c, p. 208). We must note that it is the family that has the most powerful influence on the child, and that professionals can only indirectly influence the family. Furthermore, children learn throughout the day, and so early intervention cannot be limited to weekly sessions (in which the parents observe how the professional "works" with the child and then later try to imitate the interactions with their child). The real intervention takes place between visits and so professionals have to give families the support and guidance they need to help them manage and make the most of any opportunities they have to interact with their child during the week. This short digression into the work of McWilliam has been necessary to remind the reader of this book that there is a multitude of support to fulfill the expectations of family-centered early intervention!

A foreword is not the place to discuss the various chapters of the book, so instead, I encourage the reader to appreciate on their own the value of each of the chapters! Perhaps I could sum this up by saying that I got caught up by the core messages that emerge from each of the book chapters. The authors make clear the underlying empowerment philosophy expressed in the wording of many passages: Family-oriented early intervention is a process that encourages the parents of a child who is deaf or hard of hearing to take their affairs into their own hands. They encourage parents and other caregivers to discover their own strengths and competencies and to take these seriously; and they support and encourage parents to appreciate the value of solutions they have worked out on their own (Hintermair, 2014). Professionals, from an empowerment philosophy, try to work together with parents on a level playing field. I have found many passages in this book in which this attitude of respect for the face-to-face experience with parents can be perceived and felt. For example, in Chapter 3 the authors stress that it is important to establish a partnership with parents that reflects sharing power *with* the family and not power *over* the family as this would be the case in a professional-as-expert model. The authors make clear why a "one size fits all" does not work, and why each family needs to find the way that will best suit their child and family. I also like the arguments made by the authors in Chapter 6 that assuming a universal "timeline of readiness" for every family is an unrealistic perspective for working with families with children who are deaf or hard of hearing. Families are different, and need professionals who will discover through dialog what suits them best at different points along their way as they learn how to cope with their situations. Finally, I appreciate the importance of the message that families should not lose sight of outcomes beyond language, including aspects such as a sound self-esteem or good social relationships with peers, or complex thoughts and ideas.

I have to stop at this place. But I can promise the readers of this book that they will find innumerable examples similar to the few singled out by me. All arguments by the authors in this book support a holistic family-centered perspective on deaf education. I will conclude with a statement by Irene Leigh (2009). In her seminal book on deaf identities she has written that after an intensive examination of the available material on this topic it is as clear as day for her that there are many ways to be Deaf, deaf, or hard of hearing. To create and to nurture this rich diversity starts in early intervention. Therefore, I wish that many people will read this book; they will learn a lot about diversity and, in particular, they will learn to view diversity as something very positive. Nothing better could happen for deaf education!

Manfred Hintermair
Heidelberg, May 1st, 2015

REFERENCES

Fialka, J. (2001). The dance of partnership: Why do my feet hurt? *Young Exceptional Children, 4*, 21–27.

Hintermair, M. (2014). Psychosocial development of deaf and hard of hearing children in the 21th century. Opportunities and challenges. In G. Tang, H. Knoors, & M. Marschark (Eds.), *Bilingualism and bilingual deaf education* (pp. 152–185). New York, NY: Oxford University Press.

Leigh, I. (2009). *A lens on deaf identities*. New York, NY: Oxford University Press.

McWilliam, R. A. (Ed.) (2010a). *Working with families of young children with special needs*. New York, NY: The Guilford Press.

McWilliam, R. A. (2010b). Introduction. In R. A. McWilliam (Ed.), *Working with families of young children with special needs* (pp. 1–7). New York, NY: The Guilford Press.

McWilliam, R. A. (2010c). Support-based home visiting. In R. A. McWilliam (Ed.), *Working with families of young children with special needs* (pp. 203–230). New York, NY: The Guilford Press.

PREFACE

This book explores, among other things, the complexity of perspectives that families and professionals bring to early intervention for infants who are deaf or hard of hearing. So let me begin by sharing my own perspective and how my experiences have brought me to the writing of this book. My passion for the field of early intervention has been a natural progression from my first area of academic interest, sociology, to my second area of study, deaf education. This led to my doctoral studies in the field of early childhood education. My formal education represents many years of study, but it pales in comparison to the education I received from the people with whom I have worked throughout the years.

My real learning began with the children and families I worked with in elementary school, in preschool, and in parent–infant programs in schools and programs for deaf children. My understanding of what it means to be deaf or hard of hearing deepened when I arrived at Gallaudet University. My mentors have been the many undergraduate and graduate students I have taught, as well as my colleagues and friends. Without them, I would not be the professional I have become.

As a hearing person, I will always be an outsider to the Deaf Community and am indebted to my friends and colleagues who have coined the expression "ally to the Deaf Community," giving status to my work and giving me a sense of belonging in the Community. I strongly believe that it is not possible to provide effective services to children or their families without understanding, if only as an ally, the life experiences of people who are deaf or hard of hearing.

Melding the real life experiences of families, garnered from both practice and research, with my appreciation of the rich cultural and linguistic heritage, strengths, and abilities of people who are deaf or hard of hearing has not always been easy. Conflicts inevitably arise as we try to navigate the minefield of child rights, family rights and responsibilities, legislation and policy, and community involvement. The field of early intervention is the place in which the differences in beliefs and philosophies about what is best for children who are deaf or hard of hearing collide. Early intervention is the perfect training ground for learning how to collaborate with others whose values, experiences, and perspectives are different from our own.

I am proud to have been affiliated with programs that have prepared many outstanding professionals to work with infants, toddlers, and their families. These programs emphasized interdisciplinary perspectives and encouraged students to keep open minds and open hearts. As an early believer in the value of collaboration, I have been determined to provide training that includes courses and practicum experiences taught and facilitated by professionals from disciplines outside of the field of education, for example, audiology, speech-language pathology, counseling, and social work, and by parents and other caregivers. The results of this interdisciplinary "experiment" yielded high marks from learners, while sometimes raising eyebrows from my colleagues who were skeptical of what professionals from other disciplines might offer to the preparation of early education specialists.

My conviction concerning the importance of interdisciplinary training for early intervention professionals led to the creation of the Deaf and Hard of Hearing Infants Toddlers and their Families (ITF) Interdisciplinary Graduate Certificate Program. My colleague, Beth S. Benedict, and I developed an innovative blended program (online and face-to-face) to provide teachers, audiologists, speech-language pathologists, counselors, psychologists, and social workers with the knowledge and skills they would need to practice their respective crafts in early intervention programs. The program was designed to infuse best practices in early intervention with an appreciation of the language, cultural experiences, and life experiences of deaf and hard-of-hearing people. As such, it has served as the groundwork for the topics and perspectives included in this book.

The compilation of these 10 chapters, with their multiple authors and points of view, exemplifies the importance of collaboration. The authors are experts in different disciplines and often possess divergent philosophical perspectives. Each chapter is written by an interdisciplinary team that have academic backgrounds in fields such as audiology, speech-language pathology, medicine, education, counseling, psychology, and social work. The authors are parents of deaf or hard-of-hearing children, professionals who are deaf, hard of hearing, or hearing, and other experts from the United States and beyond. The book illustrates how the collaboration of professionals with different areas of expertise is essential to the whole of what professionals working with infants, toddlers, and their families need to know.

Few people would argue that collaboration and interdisciplinary teamwork comprise the right approach for working with families and their infants and toddlers. As researchers, faculty, program administrators, and consultants, the authors of this book were challenged to create chapters that reflected their respective areas of expertise and demonstrate how collaboration works. This experience came naturally for some and proved challenging for others. Our academic disciplinary differences proved to be only the tip of the iceberg. Our diversity, as in all teams, is also reflected in our different life and work experiences; our values, beliefs, language, and traditions; our communication and working styles; as well as our personalities.

When the authors of the chapters were asked to share their thoughts about their collaborative experiences the following descriptors came to mind: energizing, tapestry of ideas and experiences, mutual respect, synergistic, challenging, confusing, uneasy, informative, engaging, and rewarding.

Others shared these thoughts:

- Our collaboration and different experiences/responsibilities helped us move between theory, policy, and practical application.
- It really taught me a whole lot … and has strongly reinforced very important values and meaning related to the practice of partnership, collaboration, and relationship building.
- I felt the lead author respected and incorporated my input very well. I think she also appreciated my "2nd eyes" (aka Deaf eyes) to the editing part.
- Our writing experience was like a "patchwork quilt" that incorporates years of work and results in a serviceable, yet unique product with some "rough spots."
- This collaborative writing experience was the most challenging project of my career.

The preparation of this book was a true interdisciplinary and collaborative experience that proved to be both challenging and rewarding for us all. Interdisciplinary collaboration, whether on a writing team or an early intervention team, is not easy.

You will likely notice that we have paid special attention to terminology. This may at first seem strange or just different from the terminology you are accustomed to seeing in other literature. The terminology used was based on input from several individuals with different perspectives, all with an eye toward presenting an accurate and respectful view of being deaf or hard of hearing. Most notably, you will not see the term "hearing loss" used to describe newborns who are born deaf or hard of hearing. Newborns do not technically "lose" their hearing and, therefore, their hearing status is not about "loss." We have avoided terms such as "diagnosis" and "degree of hearing loss" and whenever possible we use "family" or "parents and other caregivers" to reflect the importance of the child's whole family. We do not use "D/HH," but instead we use "people who are deaf or hard of hearing" or "deaf or hard-of-hearing people." We determined that the shorthand D/HH, though taking up significantly less space, was less personal and respectful.

The book is organized into two parts. Part I addresses the foundational knowledge needed by early intervention providers. The first two chapters present the knowledge, skills, and dispositions early intervention specialists need, and how to develop and sustain exemplary practice. Chapter 3 emphasizes the diversity of families along many dimensions, including, but not limited, to linguistic and cultural perspectives. This chapter challenges readers to examine their own beliefs and biases and proposes suggestions for how to establish partnerships with families. Chapter 4 focuses on legislation, policies, and research providing readers with the information that frames the structure of early intervention programs and services and informs best practices. Chapter 5 discusses collaboration with deaf and hard-of-hearing communities, highlighting an essential component of early intervention programming that is often missing and undervalued.

Part II of the book focuses on the implementation of early intervention practices. Its first chapter, Chapter 6, about "getting started," addresses the early hearing screening and evaluation process as well as how to work with families and other professionals who are major players in the life of an infant who is deaf or hard of hearing. Chapter 7 includes important guidelines for the effective assessment of the abilities and needs of all infants and toddlers who are deaf or hard of hearing. Chapter 8 describes the heart of early intervention programming for these children and their families. It reviews what we know about early language acquisition and highlights two different approaches: an ASL/English Bilingual approach and a Listening and Spoken Language approach. Chapter 9 pulls together the work of the preceding chapters by describing the Individualized Family Service Plan (IFSP) process and the development of appropriate programming and services. The final chapter provides the reader with a perspective on early intervention from within "challenging national contexts." It encourages the reader to reflect on the assumptions that are made from the point of view of resource-wealthy countries that shape, and often bias, our understanding of early intervention practices.

Each chapter includes a vignette that helps the reader apply evidence-based information to real-life circumstances. Chapters include guiding questions for the reader, indicate which of the nine areas of core competencies from the *Knowledge and Skills of Early Intervention Providers* found in the appendix of the Supplement to the Joint Committee on Infant Hearing 2007 Position Statement (JCIH, 2013) are addressed, and provides suggested activities and recommended resources.

This book is written for all who are involved in the early hearing detection and intervention process. Those who will find this text most valuable will be early intervention specialists from different disciplinary backgrounds, program directors and other administrative staff, as well as those who are concerned with the implementation of best practices and effective programs for infants, toddlers, and their families.

Marilyn Sass-Lehrer

ACKNOWLEDGMENTS

This book is clearly the result of the knowledge, skills, and expertise of many very talented professionals in the field of early intervention for children who are deaf or hard of hearing and their families. Our work is built on the backs of many others who came before us. Their vision and commitment to early intervention are apparent on each of the pages of this book. One of these visionaries was Marion Downs whose extraordinary life has been an inspiration to many of us in this field. In addition to the outstanding authors of these chapters, for whom I have the utmost respect, many people "behind the scenes" have made this book possible.

I begin first with my family, who has buoyed my efforts at every turn. My mother used to say, "Nothing worth doing is ever easy." For whatever reason, I turned that into "Everything worth doing is worth overdoing," a phrase attributed to Mick Jagger. I seem to have a knack for finding the most difficult ways of achieving even the simplest of goals, and then overdoing it. Thankfully, my husband, Sande, has put up with me for many years, and has been my strongest supporter. I am so grateful to him, to my daughter, Carly, and to my other family members and friends who, despite my quirks, have stood by and cheered me on, whether running the New York City Marathon or writing books.

Professionally, I am most sincerely grateful to Dr. Kathryn P. Meadow-Orlans, who was my first mentor. Kay was the perfect mentor and role model to me as a researcher, writer, free and independent thinker, hard worker, and the best collaborator ever. Her support and encouragement have given me confidence throughout my professional career to do what I believe is right and to pursue professional dreams I would never have imagined. My heartfelt appreciation goes out to Kay.

My friend and colleague, Beth Benedict, has been another key mentor to me. We can only hope to find a few really good friends and colleagues in life (I think my mother told me that as well). Beth is surely one of them. She has contributed more to my professional development and career than she can imagine. My dear friend, Beth, who reminds us at every opportunity: "Individually we are one drop. Together, we are an ocean" (Ryunosuke Satoro).

I have been truly blessed to have had many wonderful students and graduate assistants throughout my career who have contributed significantly to many projects—not only through their dedication and hard work, but also through their thoughtfulness and generosity. One very special former student and now colleague, Nicole Hutchinson, has been the anchor and the keel for this project. She has righted the boat whenever a crisis emerged and has contributed to both the content and formatting of the book. She is now an expert on APA style and whatever grammatical challenges you can throw her way. She is also a stellar early intervention professional with an amazing future ahead. I am very fortunate to have Nicole in my life both professionally and personally.

Finally, my thanks to Oxford University Press who agreed that the time was right for a book on early intervention and interdisciplinary practice to join the ranks of their excellent series, *Professional Perspectives on Deafness*.

CONTRIBUTORS

Beth S. Benedict
Faculty Fellow, Undergraduate
  Admissions and Outreach
Deaf and Hard of Hearing
  Infants, Toddlers and Families
  Interdisciplinary Program
American Society for Deaf
  Children
Gallaudet University
Washington, DC

Jodee Crace
Early Education and Family
  Support Provider and
  Consultant
Westfield, IN
American Society for Deaf
  Children
Deaf and Hard of Hearing
  Infants, Toddlers and Families
  Interdisciplinary Program
Gallaudet University
Washington, DC

Rosemary Gallegos
New Mexico School for
   the Deaf, Superintendent
Santa Fe, NM

Maribel Gárate
Department of Education
Gallaudet University
Washington, DC

Kristi Halus
Early Intervention and
   Involvement Division
New Mexico School for
   the Deaf
Santa Fe, NM

Nicole Hutchinson
Early Intervention Deaf and
   Hard of Hearing
The River School
Washington, DC

Susan Lenihan
Department of Communication
   Disorders and Deaf Education
Fontbonne University
St. Louis, MO

Linda Lytle
Department of Counseling
Gallaudet University
Washington, DC

Mary Pat Moeller
Center for Childhood Deafness
   and Language Development
   Laboratory
Boys Town National Research
   Hospital
Omaha, NE

Mary Ellen Nevins
Department of Audiology and
   Speech Pathology
University of Arkansas for Medical
   Sciences
Little Rock, AR

Debra Nussbaum
Laurent Clerc National Deaf
   Education Center
Gallaudet University
Washington, DC

Stephanie Olson
Bill Daniels Center for Children's
   Hearing
Children's Hospital Colorado
Aurora, CO

Paula Pittman
SKI-HI Institute
Utah State University
Logan, UT
Utah Schools for the Deaf
   and Blind
Ogden, UT

Ann Porter
Aussie Deaf Kids
Brunswick Heads, New South
  Wales
Australia

Barbara Raimondo
Policy Consultant
Washington Grove, MD
Deaf and Hard of Hearing
  Infants, Toddlers and Families
  Interdisciplinary Program
Gallaudet University
Washington, DC

Marilyn Sass-Lehrer
Department of Education
Deaf and Hard of Hearing
  Infants, Toddlers and Families
  Interdisciplinary Program
Gallaudet University
Washington, DC

Angela Shoup
Department of Otolaryngology
Division of Communicative and
  Vestibular Disorders
University of Texas Southwestern
  Medical Center/Children's
  Health/Parkland Health and
  Hospital System
Dallas, TX

Rachel St. John
Family Focused Center for Deaf
  and Hard of Hearing Children
Department of Otolaryngology
Dallas Children's/University of
  Texas Southwestern Medical
  Center Dallas
Dallas, TX

Claudine Störbeck
Centre for Deaf Studies
HI HOPES
University of the Witwatersrand
Johannesburg, SA
Visiting Professor
University of Manchester
Manchester, UK

Arlene Stredler-Brown
Department of Speech, Language,
  and Hearing Sciences
University of Colorado
Boulder, CO
Visiting Lecturer
University of British Columbia
Vancouver, BC
Canada

Amy Szarkowski
Deaf and Hard of Hearing
   Program
Department of Otolaryngology
Boston Children's Hospital
Department of Psychiatry
Harvard Medical School
Boston, MA
Deaf and Hard of Hearing
   Infants, Toddlers and Families
   Interdisciplinary Program
Gallaudet University
Washington, DC

Cheryl L. Wu
Department of Counseling
Gallaudet University
Washington, DC

Christine Yoshinaga-Itano
Department of Speech, Language,
   and Hearing Sciences
Institute of Cognitive Science,
   Center for Neurosciences
University of Colorado
Boulder, CO

Alys Young
School of Nursing, Midwifery and
   Social Work
University of Manchester
Manchester, UK
Visiting Professor
Centre for Deaf Studies
University of Witwatersrand
Johannesburg, SA

PART I

Early Intervention Foundations

1 What Every Early Intervention Professional Should Know

Marilyn Sass-Lehrer, Mary Pat Moeller, and Arlene Stredler-Brown

Dr. Smith is the director of a statewide early intervention program and is responsible for ensuring the quality of services provided by the early interventionists in her state. She is also responsible for providing professional development to support these interventionists. She recognizes that these providers need specialized expertise, but she is uncertain about the specific needs of early intervention professionals who work with infants and toddlers who are deaf or hard of hearing and their families. Dr. Smith is searching for guidance about what to include in a professional development program. She asks, "What knowledge, skill sets, and dispositions are needed by providers to optimize the early development of infants and toddlers who are deaf or hard of hearing and to support their families?" She wonders how she will verify that the early intervention providers in her program have the requisite skills.

GUIDING QUESTIONS

1. What current best practice guidelines and recommended practices could serve as a guide to the implementation of quality early intervention services with families of infants and toddlers who are deaf or hard of hearing?
2. How are the recommendations for working with young children who are deaf or hard of hearing similar to, and yet different from, the practices recommended in the early childhood special education literature?
3. How might a core set of competencies based on best practice standards in early childhood special education, deaf education, and related disciplines be used to improve the quality of services delivered by early intervention specialists?

COMPETENCIES ADDRESSED IN THIS CHAPTER

This chapter describes the need for clear articulation of the knowledge, skill sets, and dispositions required by early intervention providers in their work with infants and toddlers who are deaf or hard of hearing and their families. It prepares readers to consider how *The Knowledge and Skills of Early Intervention Providers* [Joint Committee on Infant Hearing (JCIH), 2013] can be used in their programs to support these children and their families in attaining the best possible outcomes.

INTRODUCTION

Newborn hearing screening and early identification of hearing ability have become the standard of practice in the United States and many other countries. Infants and toddlers who are deaf or hard of hearing should be referred for early intervention services as soon as their hearing status has been confirmed (JCIH, 2007; Moeller, Carr, Seaver, Stredler-Brown, & Holzinger, 2013). For many infants this occurs during the first few weeks of life. These infants, as a group, are very diverse, with varied hearing and developmental abilities. Infants who are referred for early intervention services have hearing abilities that range from profoundly deaf bilaterally (in both ears) to hard of hearing with thresholds in the minimal/mild range bilaterally or unilaterally (in one ear). They may arrive as full term, strong healthy babies or medically fragile newborns. They may have a disability that impacts their physical development or cognitive ability, or they may be fully able in all developmental areas except for the ability to hear. Notably, it is estimated that 35–40% of all children who are deaf or hard of hearing have other conditions or disabilities (Gallaudet Research Institute, 2010; Yoshinaga-Itano, Sedey, Coulter, & Mehl, 1998).

Families with deaf or hard-of-hearing children, like all families, have a range of abilities, aspirations, resources, and experiences. The parents or caregivers may be deaf or hearing. They may be well educated or have limited schooling. They may have access to numerous family and community resources or have few formal and informal support systems. Many families communicate using a language other than spoken English; they may identify with cultural communities whose beliefs and values are unfamiliar to the professionals they meet. Being deaf or hard of hearing is not exclusive to any culture, geography, or human condition. Families with children who are deaf or hard of hearing have different perspectives and expectations of early intervention specialists, and the services they receive need to fit their distinct life situations (Dromi & Ingber, 1999; and Chapter 3, Families: Partnerships in Practice). Families benefit when professionals are open to learning and understanding each family's context, are willing to engage in reflective practices, and are able to adapt their interactions in ways that best fit the family (Hanson & Lynch, 2013).

Dr. Smith, like other statewide early intervention program directors, faces the challenge of ensuring that all professionals, regardless of their backgrounds and training, have the skills to meet the needs of infants and toddlers who are deaf or hard of hearing. Providers in her state come from varied professional disciplines (e.g., Speech-Language Pathology, Audiology, Deaf Education, Early Childhood Special Education). Each of these professionals brings expertise from his or her respective specialty fields. Training requirements are discipline specific so there is a high likelihood that professionals have unique gaps in the information, skills, or dispositions they need to work effectively with infants, toddlers, and their families (Arehart & Yoshinaga-Itano, 1999; Rice & Lenihan, 2005; Roush, Harrison, Palsha, & Davidson, 1992). This chapter focuses on the knowledge, skills, and dispositions all early interventionists need to provide high-quality services to young children who are deaf or hard of hearing and their families.

EDUCATIONAL BACKGROUND OF EARLY INTERVENTION SPECIALISTS

The quantity and quality of coursework and experience in early intervention preparation programs vary greatly among professions. Less than half of the early intervention providers of children who are deaf or hard of hearing have been trained as teachers of deaf children (Proctor, Niemeyer, & Compton, 2005; Stredler-Brown & Arehart, 2000). Teachers of deaf children have expertise regarding the effects of being deaf or hard of hearing on communication and know how to promote communication access. However, they may be lacking in the specialized knowledge and skills required to work with infants and toddlers and their families (Campbell, Chiarello, Wilcox, & Milbourne, 2009; Jones & Ewing, 2002; Meadow-Orlans, Mertens, & Sass-Lehrer, 2003; Rice & Lenihan, 2005; Roush et al., 1992; Roush, Bess, Gravel, Harrison, Lenihan, & Marvelli, 2004). Speech-language pathologists (SLPs) have very different preservice training than other early intervention service providers. SLPs will have had coursework related to communication and language development; they may not have received specialty training, however, related to the different approaches and modalities used to promote communication access for children who are deaf or hard of hearing. In contrast, early childhood educators may have training in family-centered practice and early developmental milestones, but lack specific training to manage hearing technology, understand deaf culture, or guide the family in ways to communicate with their deaf or hard-of-hearing child. Research from Proctor et al. (2005) suggests that early intervention providers lacked specialty training in auditory–verbal therapy and sign language, and that in-service on these specific topics was challenging to obtain (Proctor et al., 2005).

Given the current state of affairs in personnel preparation, it is not surprising that many early intervention specialists, regardless of their academic backgrounds, begin their work with children who are deaf or hard of hearing with limited experience (Roush et al., 2004). Clear articulation of the specialized competencies, dispositions, knowledge, and skills needed to serve deaf or hard-of-hearing infants and their families could lead to improved early intervention services and outcomes for children and their families.

EARLY CHILDHOOD EDUCATION LEGISLATION, POLICY, AND ACCOUNTABILITY

Legislation and Policy

The qualifications of personnel who provide services to infants and toddlers are established by federal law in the United States through the Individuals with Disabilities Education Improvement Act Part C [Individuals with Disabilities Education Improvement Act (IDEA), 2004]. See Box 1.1 for a summary of this legislation. Qualified providers, according to Part C of IDEA, include professionals from the education and health care fields. IDEA Part C regulations define qualified personnel as ". . . personnel who have met State approved or recognized certification, licensing, registration or other comparable requirements that apply to the areas in which the individuals are conducting evaluations or assessments or providing early intervention services" (IDEA, 2011: 34 CFR §303.31). Each state has a designated Part C coordinator responsible for ensuring that early intervention services are provided by personnel who meet these requirements (IDEA, 2004). Specialists working with deaf or hard-of-hearing infants, toddlers, and their families need knowledge and skill sets that extend beyond the minimal qualifications as described in the legislation.

The disciplines of early childhood education (ECE) and early childhood special education (ECSE) have collaborated to develop personnel standards guided by research, legislation, and policy initiatives. The National Association for the Education of Young Children (NAEYC) and the Division for Early Childhood (DEC), a subdivision of the

---

BOX 1.1 PART C OF IDEA: THE EARLY INTERVENTION PROGRAM FOR INFANTS
AND TODDLERS WITH DISABILITIES

- Established by Congress in 1986
- Federal grant to help states provide comprehensive statewide services
- Designed to improve/expand services to eligible infants from birth to 3 years old
- Focuses on building capacity of families to meet their child's needs
- Includes the following components:
  - Eligibility Requirements
  - Child Find and Referral
  - Evaluation and Assessments
  - Individualized Family Service Plan (IFSP)
  - Early Intervention Services
  - Personnel Development and Qualifications
  - Family Rights and Procedural Safeguards
  - Child and Family Outcomes Data
  - State Interagency Coordinating Council
  - Policies on Natural Environments
  - Transition from Part C (Early Intervention) to Part B (Special Education)

Council for Exceptional Children (CEC), have established personnel preparation standards and identified knowledge and skills for early childhood special educators and early interventionists (Chandler et al., 2012; Division for Early Childhood, 2014; National Association for the Education of Young Children, 2009; Winton, McCollum, & Catlett, 2008). These professional standards are based on several factors: (1) professional and family values and philosophical perspectives regarding early childhood; (2) recommended practices for teaching and supporting young children's development and establishing positive relationships with families; (3) evidence-based strategies and assessment practices; and (4) desired outcomes for young children and families (McCollum & Stayton, 1996).

Accountability

Dr. Smith is well aware of the federal initiative in the United States that now requires states to provide evidence of positive outcomes for young children and their families [see the Early Childhood Technical Assistance Center (ECTA) weblink under Recommended Resources for this chapter]. States must report the progress their programs are making to meet early learning standards, outcomes that are identified as part of the Individualized Family Service Plan (IFSP), or goals from the Individualized Education Plan (IEP). These measures of accountability have raised expectations for professionals who deliver services to very young children and their families, including children who are deaf and hard of hearing.

Professionals must have the appropriate knowledge, skills, and dispositions to make a positive difference in child and family outcomes (Bailey et al., 2006; Chandler et al., 2012). Bruder (2010) recommended that the field of early intervention adopt a "culture of accountability across all dimensions of service provision (p. 346)." This requires clear delineation of competencies and best practices of providers that link to positive child and family outcomes.

Competencies

Dr. Smith must ensure that her early intervention specialists are competent. This includes educators and therapists providing direct services as well as those working in consultative, advocacy, training, and other leadership roles. In 1990, Fenichel and Eggbeer described competence as

> . . . the ability to do the right thing at the right time for the right reasons. Competence involves the capacity to analyze a situation, consider alternative approaches, select and skillfully apply the best observation or intervention techniques, evaluate the outcome, and articulate the rationale for each step of the process. Competence generally requires a combination of knowledge, skills and experience. Competence for work with infants and families cannot be inferred from the completion of academic coursework alone; it must be demonstrated. (p. 9)

Ten years later, Bruder (2010) noted that there is a growing gap between what is known to be effective practices in early childhood intervention and the content of personnel preparation programs as well as the practices of professionals in the field. Thorp and McCullom (1994) have defined the following four competency areas for early intervention specialists regardless of the unique individual strengths and challenges of the child or the family:

1. Child-related competencies (knowledge of cognitive, social, and affective development; skills in developmental assessment; design of learning environments; strategies to promote engagement and interaction; skills in data collection and evaluation).
2. Family-related competencies (strategies for including family members as partners in planning and implementing intervention, strategies for promoting interaction between parent and child).
3. Team-related competencies (skills in integrating the knowledge and recommendations of multiple disciplines into the child's and family's daily routines).
4. Agency-related competencies (knowledge of community resources, developing blended service plans).

Professional competence implies the ability to collaborate with professionals who have different disciplinary backgrounds as part of an interdisciplinary team (Winton et al., 2008). Professionals must also have the skills to work with children and families with different abilities and needs and in different settings, such as the home, early childhood center, play group, or clinic. Although Part C of IDEA emphasizes the home as the preferred learning environment for young children between birth and 3 years old, professionals working with children who are deaf or hard of hearing consider additional environments in the community and early intervention program sites that may provide a wealth of learning opportunities for these children and their families (ASHA-CED Joint Committee, 2006).

Dispositions

Dr. Smith is aware that beyond content knowledge and skills, the early intervention professionals in her state must also possess personal qualities and dispositions to promote positive outcomes for children and their families. The National Council for Accreditation of Teacher Education (NCATE, 2015) describes professional dispositions as follows:

> Professional attitudes, values, and beliefs demonstrated through both verbal and non-verbal behaviors as educators interact with students, families, colleagues, and communities.

At the heart of the work of the early interventionist is the ability to develop positive, respectful, and collaborative relationships with families (Klein & Gilkerson, 2000). In addition to an understanding of family-centered principles (see Chapter 3, *Families: Partnerships in Practice*, for more information on family centeredness), professionals must possess strong communication skills including the ability to actively listen to families' stories and be able to communicate empathy and compassion. Families must be able to develop a trusting relationship with the professionals who work closely with them at a time that is often very emotional and personal for them. Professionals must demonstrate confidentiality and trustworthiness, and must show that they value and respect the family's priorities and concerns. Although professionals may have personal values and beliefs that do not align with those of the family with whom they are working, it is essential that professionals set aside their own views in order to support the family as the family moves from the unknown to a place in which they are able to make informed decisions on behalf of their child and their entire family.

NAEYC suggests that dispositions should be addressed intentionally and systematically and in the same manner as knowledge and skills when designing and implementing early childhood professional preparation programs. Although knowledge and skills can be acquired through academic experiences, many of the fundamental dispositions include personal qualities that are intuitive and may be challenging to acquire.

Program directors and administrators may want to keep this in mind when selecting professionals to work in their early intervention programs.

LEGISLATION AND POLICIES FOR EARLY INTERVENTION SPECIALISTS WORKING WITH CHILDREN WHO ARE DEAF OR HARD OF HEARING

Legislation and policy initiatives have set guidelines and standards that support the quality of services and the qualifications of personnel for *all* infants and toddlers who are eligible for early intervention. In addition, there are federal laws and policies that specifically apply to infants and toddlers who are deaf or hard of hearing.

Legislation

The Newborn and Infant Hearing Screening and Intervention Act, first passed in 1999, provided support and guidance to state personnel as they planned, developed, and implemented statewide newborn and infant hearing screening programs. This Act was reauthorized as the Early Hearing Detection and Intervention Act (2010) and expanded the focus on diagnostic and early intervention services. The more recent bill advocates for prompt evaluation and identification of children referred from newborn hearing screening programs and appropriate educational, audiological, and medical services for children identified as deaf or hard of hearing. The reauthorized legislation addresses the recruitment, retention, education, and training of qualified personnel. State agencies are encouraged to adopt models that effectively reduce loss to follow-up and ensure an adequate supply of qualified personnel to meet the screening, evaluation, and early intervention needs of children. The Early Hearing Detection and Intervention Act is described in more detail in Chapter 4.

Policies and Initiatives

As more infants and toddlers are identified through newborn hearing screening, there has been a growing interest in the quality of the providers serving these children and their families. Policy initiatives have arisen in an effort to ensure that well-trained early intervention specialists work with deaf or hard-of-hearing infants.

There is evidence that children who are deaf or hard of hearing receiving early intervention have better opportunities to achieve age-appropriate language and cognitive skills than children who are identified later (Calderon, 2000; Kennedy et al., 2006; Moeller, 2000; Wake, Hughes, Poulakis, Collins, & Rickards, 2004; Yoshinaga-Itano, 2003). Researchers have suggested that professionals with specialized knowledge, skills, and experience contribute to the positive outcomes experienced by infants and toddlers who have the benefit of early and comprehensive services (Calderon, 2000; Moeller et al., 2007; Nittrouer & Burton, 2001; Yoshinaga-Itano, 2003). Since the early years of the twenty-first century, initiatives have focused on the identification and dissemination of the requisite knowledge and skills of early intervention providers (Compton, Neimeyer, & Shroyer, 2001; JCIH, 2007, 2013; Marge & Marge, 2005; Nelson, Bougatsos, & Nygren, 2008).

Compton et al. (2001) identified a set of standards for professionals working with infants and toddlers who are deaf or hard of hearing. The standards were derived from an analysis of existing principles in deaf education and early intervention, synthesized by national experts, and reviewed by practicing professionals, family members, and training professionals. This process identified these focus areas: (1) major legislation; (2) relationships with families; (3) infant development; (4) communication; (5) teaming and service provision; (6) assessment; (7) technology; and (8) ethics/professionalism.

The Consensus Conference on Effective Educational and Health Care Interventions for Infants and Young Children with Hearing Loss was held in 2004. The meeting participants identified evidence-based research that contributed to high-quality early intervention for young children who are deaf or hard of hearing. A report from the Consensus Conference (Marge & Marge, 2005) included recommendations for effective programming, defined characteristics of qualified providers, and summarized implications for professional practice.

The Year 2007 Position Statement of the Joint Committee on Infant Hearing (JCIH) underscored the need for trained early intervention specialists and recommended that early intervention programs ensure professionals have the special skills needed to provide families with ". . . the highest quality of service specific to children with hearing loss" (p. 909). The JCIH Position Statement also stated that ". . . professionals should be highly qualified in their respective fields and should be skilled communicators who are knowledgeable and sensitive to the importance of enhancing families' strengths and supporting their priorities. . . ." (p. 909).

The 2013 *Supplement to the 2007 JCIH Position Statement: Principles and Guidelines for Early Intervention After Confirmation That a Child is Deaf or Hard of Hearing* (JCIH, 2013) focused exclusively on early intervention and outlined the best practices to facilitate optimal outcomes for children and their families. Goal 3 of this document proposes that "All children who are deaf or hard of hearing birth to three years of age and their families have early intervention providers who have the professional qualifications and core knowledge and skills to optimize the child's development and child/family well-being" (p. 1328). This document includes the following recommendations for state and territorial programs:

1. Adopt and implement guidelines that address the professional qualifications required for providing family-centered intervention to families and children who are deaf or hard of hearing from birth to age 3.
2. Ensure stakeholders' participation in the adoption and implementation of these guidelines.
3. Provide the resources needed for professionals to obtain the core knowledge and skills to serve children who are deaf and hard of hearing from birth to age 3 and their families. (See Chapter 4 for more information on the 2007 JCIH Position Statement and the JCIH Supplement to the 2007 Position Statement.)

In 2013, a panel of experts developed an international consensus statement identifying ten foundational principles underlying the provision of early intervention (Moeller et al., 2013). The panel included parents, deaf professionals, early intervention program leaders, early intervention specialists, and researchers from around the world. Panelists identified research evidence to support the 10 fundamental principles. Principle 7 addresses Qualified Providers and states:

> Providers are well trained and have specialized knowledge and skills related to working with children who are D/HH [deaf or hard of hearing] and their families. Providers possess the core competencies to support families in optimizing the child's development and child-family well-being. (p. 439)

The United States Preventive Services Task Force (USPSTF) released a statement recommending the practice of universal newborn hearing screening. The statement indicated there was good evidence that hearing screening is highly accurate and leads to earlier identification and intervention services as well as improved language outcomes (Nelson et al., 2008). Although more research is needed, the quality of intervention services is likely an important factor influencing child and family outcomes.

THE KNOWLEDGE AND SKILLS DOCUMENT

Research findings and policy documents suggest a link between the quality of the early intervention and child outcomes. This premise underscores the need to understand exactly what knowledge and which skills consistently lead to quality services for infants who are deaf or hard of hearing and their families.

The landscape of early intervention for infants, toddlers, and their families has changed markedly in recent years. Infants enter early intervention at ages younger than ever before (Dalzell et al., 2000; Halpin, Smith, Widen, & Chernoff, 2010; Holte et al., 2012), are often from culturally diverse families, and may have complex medical and educational needs. Hearing technologies have evolved presenting the need for increased specialized expertise. In response to these changes, professionals are called upon to transform their knowledge, skills, and practices. Providers need to be well versed in the tenets of culturally competent, family-centered practices. Providers need dispositions,

knowledge, and skills in developmental, communicative, and technological areas that are up to date and specific to working with this population of children.

Dr. Smith, and other state and regional program directors, often lack
guidance from their state, district, or territory regarding who is qualified
to work as an early intervention provider. The legislation, policies, and
research described above represent a critical first step in developing a
document that describes the knowledge, skills, and dispositions of highly
effective early intervention providers. The authors of this chapter built
upon the previous work to define competencies in the form of a knowledge and skills document. The goals were (1) to provide administrative
guidance; (2) to offer direction based on policies; and (3) to support professional development. The overall aim was to enhance the competence
of all professionals working with infants who are deaf or hard of hearing
and their families.

Development of the Knowledge and Skills Document

The authors engaged in a 3-year project to describe the core knowledge
and skills that are needed by professionals to maximize positive outcomes for very young deaf or hard-of-hearing infants and toddlers. The
process began with a needs assessment survey in 2007. The survey was
sent to national advocacy groups representing the interests of individuals who are deaf, member organizations of the Council on the Education
of the Deaf (CED), national organizations offering technical assistance
and support for early childhood initiatives, national training programs,
and a national organization representing special education in public education. Survey results strongly supported the need to identify the core
knowledge and skills to work effectively with infants and toddlers under
3 years of age who are deaf or hard of hearing. One respondent stated that
"there is too much at stake for children who are deaf or hard of hearing
and their families to be receiving services from an individual who has no
knowledge of the deaf or hard of hearing and the language issues they
face" (Sass-Lehrer, Stredler-Brown, & Moeller, 2008). The results of this
survey were presented at the Early Hearing Detection and Intervention
conference in 2008.

The authors then set out to examine sets of existing documents that specifically addressed the knowledge and skills needed by an early interventionist working with this population. Documents were included if they were developed through a collaborative effort that reflected the opinions of researchers, practitioners, and families. Eight documents met these criteria. These documents ranged from extensive coverage of the knowledge and skills to brief position statements. A list of the eight documents can be found in Appendix 1 of the JCIH Supplement to the 2007 Position Statement (JCIH, 2013).

The CENTe-R document (Compton et al., 2001) was one of the identified documents and was used as a starting point for our review. This document was most closely aligned with the overall goal of developing a comprehensive listing of knowledge and skills for early intervention specialists. The authors of this chapter reviewed the CENTe-R standards and agreed upon nine broad competency areas that are somewhat distinct from the original CENTe-R focus areas. Each author individually reviewed the standards in the CENTe-R document and placed each item in one of the nine newly established categories. Disagreements were resolved through consensus.

The authors developed descriptions of each of the nine competency areas. Two of the three authors reviewed each of the remaining seven documents independently. During this process, the authors identified relevant items about professional knowledge and skills from each of the remaining seven documents. Statements similar to those in the document of Compton et al. (2001) were noted. Additional statements related to knowledge and skills were placed in one of the respective nine categories. After all the documents were reviewed, the authors met to identify redundancies and potential gaps. A few items were not mentioned in any of the eight documents, for example: (1) understanding family systems; (2) skills to build partnerships; and (3) application of evidence-based practice. These items were added to the list of core competencies. At the end of the process, editorial revisions were made to enhance readability and consistency in language. The final document includes a total of 116 knowledge and skill statements.

The completed document was presented to the Joint Committee on Infant Hearing, and the document was incorporated as an appendix in the 2013 Supplement to the JCIH Position Statement.

Specialized Dispositions, Knowledge, and Skill Sets

The *Knowledge and Skills of Early Intervention Providers* (JCIH, 2013) reflects both general and specialized areas of competence. General areas of competence include professional knowledge and skills that specialists need to work with any young child who has a developmental or physical characteristic that typically results in a developmental delay in one or more areas. Specialized skills are those that are unique areas of competence for professionals who work with deaf or hard-of-hearing infants, toddlers, and their families. Table 1.1 describes these specialized knowledge, skills, and dispositions drawn from the *Knowledge and Skills* document described above (JCIH, 2013). Table 1.1 expands and extends each of the competency areas and provides examples of selected specialized skills essential to meet the unique needs of infants and toddlers who are deaf or hard of hearing and their families.

Potential Applications of the Knowledge and Skills Document

Program directors, such as Dr. Smith, can utilize the *Knowledge and Skills of Early Intervention Providers* (JCIH, 2013) and the expanded competencies in Table 1.1 in a variety of ways to ensure quality service provision by the early intervention specialists in her state. The knowledge and skill areas could be used (1) as a tool for the selection and hiring of early intervention providers; (2) as a self-assessment instrument allowing providers to identify their own strengths and professional development and learning needs; (3) as a guide for the development of professional learning activities; (4) as a method to identify and support research; and (5) as a guide to inform policy on effective practices (Sass-Lehrer, Stredler–Brown, Moeller, Clark, & Hutchinson, 2011).

Hiring Early Intervention Specialists

Finding and selecting early intervention specialists can be challenging because applicants have academic preparation in deaf education, early

Table 1.1 *Specialized Knowledge, Skill Sets, and Dispositions for Professionals Working with Infants Who Are Deaf or Hard of Hearing (DHH)*[a],b

Competency Area	Unique Knowledge or Skill Sets
Family-Centered Practice: Family–Professional Partnerships, Decision Making, and Family Support	Have the information and skills to support families as they navigate many complex decisions regarding language choice(s), communication approaches, technology, and services (often in the first few months of infants' lives) in the face of controversy, varied opinions, and limitations in evidence.
	Must be well versed in the ongoing process of informed choice, including providing information on benefits, risks, and uncertainties.
	Must understand the types of support that promote family adjustment, including family-to-family contacts and opportunities to interact with DHH individuals.
Socially, Culturally, and Linguistically Responsive Practices Including Deaf/Hard-of-Hearing Cultures and Communities: Sensitivity to and respect for an individual family's characteristics	Understand and appreciate deaf cultural perspectives.
	Are fluent in native Sign Language (e.g., American Sign Language or other native Sign Language) if working with deaf families in early intervention. This fluency promotes partnership and allows the early intervention (EI) specialist to build upon family strengths.
	Demonstrate respect for choices made by families and understand the unique cultural issues that may influence their decision making.
	Understand the complexity of being deaf in addition to other cultural or community affiliations and traditions.

(continued)

Table 1.1 *Continued*

Competency Area	Unique Knowledge or Skill Sets
Language Acquisition and Communication Development: Typical development and communication approaches available to children with hearing loss, and the impact of hearing loss on access to communication	Understand how the child's hearing abilities can influence language access.
	Work with the family to promote language accessibility, regardless of the communication approach taken.
	Understand the impact of technology on language access for individual children; foster maximal use of residual hearing in children developing spoken language.
	Understand the developmental stages of the native Sign Language when families and children are acquiring Sign Language.
	Are familiar with all approaches to communication development; if not conversant with an approach of interest to the family, are able to find appropriate models and resources.
	Provide models of infant-directed Sign Language use (including appropriate use of facial grammar, sign prosody, etc.).
	Provide models of infant-directed spoken language use (including appropriate variation in suprasegmental aspects of speech).
	Are able to monitor language development, regardless of the language or communication approach.
	Are able to promote responsive interactions and use of strategies known to enhance linguistic development in infants who are DHH.
	Help families understand the importance of language access and the need to provide full and consistent input to promote language growth.
	Support families in developing a language-rich environment regardless of the approaches used.
	Facilitate the development of fluent signing skills in families who elect to sign to promote child language access.

Factors Influencing Infant and Toddler Development	Recognize the key role of family-to-family support from others who have children who are DHH in promoting family well-being.
	Recognize that family-support organizations such as the A.G. Bell Association for the Deaf and Hard of Hearing, the American Society for Deaf Children, and Hands & Voices have special expertise to offer, and assist families in accessing them.
	Are able to differentiate the characteristics of typical and atypical development in infants who are DHH to support a differential diagnosis.
	Collaborate effectively with medical, therapeutic, and educational professionals to address the impact of additional disabilities in cognitive, vision, or motor development on DHH children's access to and/or expression of language.
	Know how to modify intervention approaches to address the needs of DHH infants who have additional cognitive or other developmental delays.
	Understand the synergistic effects on development when infants have multiple developmental challenges in addition to being DHH.

(continued)

Table 1.1 *Continued*

Competency Area	Unique Knowledge or Skill Sets
Screening, Evaluation, and Assessment: Interpretation of hearing screening and audiological diagnostic information; ongoing developmental assessment; and use of developmental assessment tools to monitor progress	Understand newborn hearing screening and audiological assessment procedures.
	Know how to provide affective and informational support following a referral from newborn hearing screening, and how the process may differ from the past (when screening was not available).
	Understand and interpret results of Otoacoustic Emissions and Auditory Brainstem Response testing and support the family in understanding the results.
	Understand and interpret behavioral audiological results and support the family in understanding the consequences for the child's development.
	Use a combination of authentic assessments, criterion referenced tools, and standardized instruments to measure and monitor progress and set goals.
	Know the strengths and limitations of these tools with infants who are DHH, and know how to adapt procedures appropriately as needed.
	Are knowledgeable and proficient in the assessment of language that is acquired through Sign Language.
	Are knowledgeable and proficient in the interpretation of spoken language assessments and the ways in which audibility may influence performance.
	Are knowledgeable and proficient in assessing infants who are DHH who have multiple disabilities.

Technology: Supporting development by using technology to access auditory, visual, and/or tactile information	Are highly familiar with auditory, visual, and tactile technologies used to promote development in young children who are DHH.
	Are able to troubleshoot technologies to ensure proper functioning; understand the need to regularly monitor technology.
	Support families in determining their needs and accessing needed technologies.
	Support families in consistently using, maintaining the proper functioning, and evaluating the effectiveness of technologies.
	Are well aware of current technologies used by deaf people that may have applications for hearing families raising deaf children.
	Are conversant with the current literature on expected rates of listening and spoken language development for children with cochlear implants and hearing aids.
Planning and Implementation of Services: Creating a lesson plan, conducting a home visit, developing the IFSP, and using appropriate curriculums, methods, and resources	Provide social and emotional support; understand common reactions in hearing families who are told that their infant is DHH.
	Incorporate knowledge of the ways in which hearing status influences communication development; incorporate this knowledge as a guide for planning work with families and their young children.
	Understand the components that make effective educational programs for children who are DHH, including continuing use of effective communication approaches; rely on this knowledge to support families of children who are DHH during the transition from early intervention to preschool services.

(continued)

Table 1.1 *Continued*

Competency Area	Unique Knowledge or Skill Sets
Collaboration and Interdisciplinary Models and Practices	Serve as members of an interdisciplinary team that may include, at a minimum, audiologists, ear-nose-and-throat physicians, primary care physicians, DHH professionals, cochlear implant team members, speech-language pathologists, teachers of the deaf, early childhood special education (ECSE) professionals, services coordinators, and other parents.
	Partner with service coordinators (SC) who may be unfamiliar with infants who are DHH; share information and support the service coordinators' roles.
	Ensure that information unique to children who are DHH and their families is consistently shared across team members.
	Consider information from the full team as the family works through decision-making processes related to selecting and using communication approaches and/or assistive technologies.
	Recognize the biases that can create barriers to practice with DHH infants; work to remove those barriers.
	Collaborate with professionals and agencies that can provide resources or expertise families need and/or request (e.g., DHH mentors, access to visual and auditory technologies, listening therapy to promote Cochlear Implant use, mental health specialists with knowledge about DHH).
Professional and Ethical Behavior: Foundations of early intervention practice, legislation, policies, and research	Routinely implement evidence-based practice; monitor current research findings with practice implications for children who are DHH.
	Work to recognize biases and demonstrate positive dispositions and transparency with families.
	Maintain appropriate professional boundaries with families and other professionals. For example, providers recognize when their skills (e.g., fluency in sign language or specific skills in auditory development) are insufficient to address what is needed and, in response, add team members to ensure that the child's and family's needs are met.

[a]Early intervention providers who work with infants who are deaf or hard of hearing and their families need to have the same set of knowledge and skills required of any EI professional. However, they *also* need specialized knowledge and skills that are specific to serving this group of children and their families. This table is not intended to be exhaustive; rather, it provides examples of some content, disposition, knowledge, or skill areas that are needed to serve families of deaf or hard-of-hearing infants.
[b]Adapted from JCIH (2013).

childhood special education, audiology, speech-language pathology, and other disciplines. The Knowledge and Skills document lists competency areas that early interventionists should possess regardless of professional training. Position announcements and interview questions can be gleaned from this document. For example, interview questions might include the following: "Describe the resources you might draw upon to provide support for families with deaf or hard-of-hearing infants or toddlers?" or "What strategies might you use to promote informed decision making related to communication modalities and language use?"

Self-Assessment Tool

Early intervention professionals could use this document to assess their own knowledge and skills. For example, in the area of Family-Centered Practices, professionals could rate each of the knowledge and skill statements according to the following: (1) How important is this skill area to your work? (2) How confident are you in this area? and (3) Rate your need for professional development of this competency. See Table 1.2 for an example. Professionals could then be asked to prioritize their top needs for professional development. Program directors, such as Dr. Smith, could use this information to identify topics for professional in-service trainings.

Professional Learning

Professional development and learning specialists can use the knowledge and skills document to design a program of studies for preservice or practicing professionals. University training programs, professional organizations, and entities offering certificate programs can use the knowledge and skill statements in this document to design their programs. The various strategies and approaches used in training would depend upon the community of learners. (See Chapter 2, *Developing and Sustaining Exemplary Practice Through Professional Learning*. See Table 1.3 for an example of how a student learning outcome, learning strategy, and an assessment of student learning could be developed based on one of the competency statements.)

Table 1.2 *Example of Using the Knowledge and Skills Document for Self-Assessment*

Competency Area Family-Centered Practice: Family–Professional Partnerships, Decision Making, and Family Support

Sample Competencies	Rate the Importance of This Competency to Your Work	Rate Your Confidence in This Competency	Rate Your Need for Professional Development in This Competency	Prioritize the Competencies to Set Goals for Your Current Professional Development (Check mark the appropriate competencies)
Recognize the expertise and major impact of families on children's growth and development	1 2 3 4 5	1 2 3 4 5	1 2 3 4 5	
Understand family systems and family dynamics	1 2 3 4 5	1 2 3 4 5	1 2 3 4 5	
Establish respectful reciprocal relationships with families	1 2 3 4 5	1 2 3 4 5	1 2 3 4 5	
Use appropriate and effective active listening with families and other professionals	1 2 3 4 5	1 2 3 4 5	1 2 3 4 5	
Facilitate families' identification of concerns, priorities, and resources	1 2 3 4 5	1 2 3 4 5	1 2 3 4 5	

Table 1.3 *Example of Using the Knowledge and Skills Document to Guide Professional Learning*

Competency Area: Family-Centered Practice: Family–Professional Partnerships, Decision Making, and Family Support

Sample Competency	Student Learning Outcome	Learning Strategies	Assessment of Student Learning Outcome
Understanding family systems and family dynamics	Describe family supports and resources using family systems theory	Presentation on family systems and family dynamics; family studies	Using an ecological systems framework describe your own family systems and illustrate the micro, meso, exo, and macro systems

Early Intervention Research

Program directors might use the document to identify and verify effective practices based on the competency areas. For example, early intervention program administrators may want to learn more about families' perceptions of their collaboration with professionals in the development and implementation of the IFSP. Selected areas from the document might be identified to investigate the effectiveness of different approaches used to maximize family collaboration and engagement.

Policy

IDEA Part C describes minimal qualifications for early intervention specialists in the United States, but does not address the knowledge and skills that are unique to providers working with infants and toddlers who are deaf or hard of hearing and their families. Certification requirements for these early interventionists vary from state to state and are rarely comprehensive. A survey of 45 states plus the District of Columbia in the United States revealed that the following competency areas were frequently missing from their lists of knowledge and skills essential for early intervention professionals who work with deaf and hard-of-hearing children in their states: (1) language acquisition, especially ASL and sign systems; (2) family-centered practices; (3) planning and implementing services; (4) collaboration and interdisciplinary practices; (5) professional behaviors and ethics; (6) technology: auditory, visual, and tactile; and (7) social, cultural, and linguistic diversity (Sass-Lehrer et al., 2010). The Knowledge and Skills document could provide a starting point for the development of a specialized credential for early intervention providers of deaf or hard-of-hearing children.

SUMMARY

Professionals working with infants who are deaf or hard of hearing need specialized knowledge and skills that go beyond those required of early childhood specialists who work with other special populations. In addition, most preservice professional programs and professional learning opportunities fall short of meeting the needs of these specialists. The gaps in knowledge and skills of early intervention professionals vary not only by the academic discipline in which the professional received training, but also by the quality of their field experiences.

State directors, such as Dr. Smith, who are responsible for the quality of services in their States, need to consider providing targeted support and training to ensure that their providers have the skills they need. The *Knowledge and Skills of Early Intervention Providers* (JCIH, 2013) lists competencies that were derived from eight position statements and technical reports and can be used as a guide for training. These competencies are supported by research and expert opinion and are endorsed by related professional organizations. Table 1.1 Specialized Knowledge, Skill Sets, and Dispositions for Professionals Working with Infants Who Are Deaf or Hard of Hearing elaborates on each of the nine competency areas and extends these to describe the unique expertise required of specialists who work with this population.

This text is organized based on the knowledge, skills, and dispositions discussed in this chapter. Each ensuing chapter identifies the broad competency areas addressed and provides evidence-based information to support the professional learning and development of early intervention specialists. Chapter 2 describes components of effective professional learning for professional development specialists and early intervention professionals. The design, implementation, and evaluation of professional learning are essential to the provision of the best possible services for deaf or hard-of-hearing infants and toddlers and their families. Subsequent chapters of this book provide the reader with in depth understanding of the expertise required of professionals to support optimal outcomes for all infants and toddlers who are deaf or hard of hearing and their families.

Acknowledgments: We would like to acknowledge Karen Clark, Nicole Hutchinson, and Kimberly (Tarasenko) Leong for their contributions to the development of The Knowledge and Skills of Early Intervention Providers (JCIH, 2013).

SUGGESTED ACTIVITIES

1. Refer to the *Knowledge and Skills of Early Intervention Providers*, in the Supplement to the 2007 JCIH Position Statement, Appendix 1 (2013). Go to http://pediatrics.aappublications.org/content/131/4/e1324.full. Select one of the nine competency areas and rate each of the statements under that area according to (1) the importance of this knowledge, skill, or disposition to your work; (2) your competence in this area; and (3) its value for your professional development. Then describe what this self-assessment tells you about your needs for professional learning.

2. Review the 10 principles from the *Best practices in family-centered early intervention for children who are deaf or hard of hearing: An international consensus statement* (Moeller et al., 2013). http://jdsde.oxfordjournals.org/content/18/4/429.full.pdf+html.
   In what areas do you think you could improve your expertise?

3. Select one of the nine competency areas in the *Knowledge and Skills of Early Intervention Providers* (JCIH, 2013). Do a web search to find good evidence (research, professional opinion, or family experience) that supports

three of the statements in this competency area. Summarize the evidence you found and present this to your colleagues.

4. Visit the websites from the following organizations: (1) Alexander Graham Bell Association for the Deaf and Hard of Hearing, (2) American Speech-Language and Hearing Association, (3) National Association of the Deaf, and (4) Conference of Educational Administrators of Schools and Programs for the Deaf. Identify commonalities and differences in their statements regarding the knowledge and skills of early intervention specialists.

RECOMMENDED RESOURCES

1. American Speech-Language and Hearing Association, Core Knowledge and Skills in Early Intervention Speech Language Pathology Practice (2008). http://www.asha.org/policy/KS2008-00292.htm.

   This document includes the knowledge and skills as well as roles and guiding principles for speech-language pathologists working with infants, toddlers, and their families.

2. American Speech-Language and Hearing Association and the Council on Education of the Deaf (2008), Service Provision to Children Who Are Deaf and Hard of Hearing, Birth to 36 Months. http://www.asha.org/policy/TR2008-00301/.

   This technical report was developed by the Joint Committee of ASHA and CED. The report addresses critical issues in the provision of quality services including newborn hearing screening, family involvement, and interdisciplinary collaboration.

3. Conference of Educational Administrators of Schools and Programs for the Deaf, Position on Early Intervention Programs for Children with Hearing Loss (2006). http://www.ceasd.org/acrobat/CEASD_EHDI.pdf.

   This organization of educational leaders has a position statement on early intervention programs that includes the organization's recommendations for early intervention programming and qualifications of providers.

4. Division for Early Childhood (DEC) Personnel Standards for Early Education and Early Intervention (Division for Early Childhood, 2014).

   DEC, a division of the Council for Exceptional Children, promotes policies and disseminates evidence-based knowledge to promote optimal outcomes for young children with special developmental and learning needs and their families. The DEC position statement includes key concepts guiding the preparation of early intervention specialists and recommendations for state licensure of these professionals. http://www.dec-sped.org/recommendedpractices.

5. Division for Early Childhood Code of Ethics (2009). www.dec-sped.org/papers.

DEC's Code of Ethics includes principles and practices to guide early intervention programs and providers. The statement addresses professional conduct, professionals' dilemmas in research and practice, and a commitment to ethical and evidence-based practice.

6. Early Childhood Technical Assistance Center (ECTA). http://www.ectacenter.org/eco/.

The Early Childhood Technical Assistance Center, is funded by the Office of Special Education in the United States. ECTA assists states in the implementation of systems for the evaluation of child and family outcomes in early intervention and early childhood programs.

7. National Association for the Education of Young Children (NAEYC), Position Statements. www.naeyc.org/positionstatements.

NAEYC has position statements on topics including early childhood practice, policy, and professional development. NAEYC standards and guidelines address anti-discrimination, code of ethical conduct, developmentally appropriate practice, early childhood program standards, and standards for professional preparation.

8. National Association of the Deaf (NAD), Position Statement on Early Hearing Detection and Intervention. http://www.nad.org/issues/early-intervention/position-statement-early-hearing-detection-and-intervention.

NAD is an organization in the United States by and for individuals who are deaf or hard or hearing. The position statement of the NAD endorses a positive attitude toward individuals who are deaf or hard of hearing and emphasizes the importance of providing services that include all language and communication opportunities and appropriate cultural and linguistic support for the child's development.

REFERENCES

American Speech-Language-Hearing Association (ASHA) and the Council on Education of the Deaf (CED) Joint Committee. (2006). *Fact sheet: Natural environments for infants and toddlers who are deaf or hard of hearing and their families.* Retrieved from http://www.asha.org/aud/Natural-Environments-for-Infants-and-Toddlers/.

Arehart, K. H., & Yoshinaga-Itano, C. (1999). The role of educators of the deaf in the early identification of hearing loss. *American Annals of the Deaf, 144*(1), 19–23.

Bailey, D. B., Bruder, M. B., Hebbeler, K., Carta, J., Defosset, M., Greenwood, C., . . . & Barton, L. (2006). Recommended outcomes for families of young children with disabilities. *Journal of Early Intervention, 28*(4), 227–251.

Bruder, M. B. (2010). Early childhood intervention: A promise to the future of children and families. *Exceptional Children, 76*(3), 339–355.

Calderon, R. (2000). Parental involvement in deaf children's educational programs as a predictor of child's language, early reading, and social-emotional development. *Journal of Deaf Studies and Deaf Education, 5*(2), 140–155.

Campbell, P. H., Chiarello, L., Wilcox, M. J., & Milbourne, S. (2009). Preparing therapists as effective practitioners in early intervention. *Infants & Young Children, 22*(1), 21–31.

Chandler, L. K., Cochran, D. C., Christensen, K. A., Dinnebeil, L. A., Gallagher, P. A., Lifter, L., . . . Spino, M. (2012). The alignment of CEC/DEC and NAEYC personnel preparation standards. *Topics in Early Childhood Special Education, 32*(1), 52–63.

Compton, M. V., Niemeyer, J. A., & Shroyer, E. (2001). *CENTe-R: Collaborative early intervention national training e-resource needs assessment.* Unpublished manuscript. Greensboro, NC: University of North Carolina.

Dalzell, L., Orlando, M., MacDonald, M., Berg, A., Bradley, M., Cacace, A., . . . Prieve, B. (2000). The New York State universal newborn hearing screening demonstration project: Ages of hearing loss identification, hearing aid fitting, and enrollment in early intervention. *Ear and Hearing, 21*(2), 118–130.

Division for Early Childhood. (2014). DEC Recommended Practices in early intervention and early childhood special education 2014. Retrieved from http://www.dec-sped.org/recommendedpractices.

Dromi, E., & Ingber, S. (1999). Israeli mothers' expectations from early intervention with their preschool deaf children. *Journal of Deaf Studies and Deaf Education, 4*(1), 50–68.

Early Hearing Detection and Intervention Act, House Resolution 1246 § 3199 (2010).

Fenichel, E. S., & Eggbeer, L. (1990). *Preparing practitioners to work with infants, toddlers and their families. Issues and recommendations for professions.* Arlington, VA: National Center for Clinical Infant Programs.

Gallaudet Research Institute. (2010). *Regional and national summary report from the 2007–2008 annual survey of deaf and hard of hearing children and youth.* Retrieved from http://research.gallaudet.edu/Demographics/2008_National_Summary.pdf.

Halpin, K. S., Smith, K. Y., Widen, J. E., & Chertoff, M. E. (2010). Effects of universal newborn hearing screening on an early intervention program for children with hearing loss, birth to 3 year of age. *Journal of the American Academy of Audiology, 21,* 169–175. doi:10.3766/jaaa.21.3.5.

Hanson, M., & Lynch, E. (2013). *Understanding families: Supportive approaches to diversity, disability, and risk* (2nd ed.). Baltimore, MD: Brookes Publishing Co.

Holte, L., Walker, E., Oleson, J. J., Spratford, M., Moeller, M. P., Rousch, P., . . . Tomblin, J. B. (2012). Factors influencing follow-up to newboarn hearing screening for infants who are hard of hearing. *American Journal of Audiology, 21*(2), 163–174. doi:10.1044/1059-0889(2012/12-0016).

Individuals With Disabilities Education Improvement Act of 2004, 20 U.S.C. 33 § 1400 et seq. (2004). Reauthorization of the Individuals with Disabilities Education Act of 1990.

Joint Committee on Infant Hearing. (2007). Year 2007 position statement: Principles and guidelines for early hearing detection and intervention programs. *Pediatrics, 120,* 898–921. doi:10.1542/peds.2007-2333.

Joint Committee on Infant Hearing. (2013). Supplement to the JCIH 2007 position statement: Principles and guidelines for intervention after confirmation that a child is deaf or hard of hearing. *Pediatrics,131*(4), e1324–1349. doi:10.1542/peds.2013-0008.

Jones, T., & Ewing, K. (2002). An analysis of teacher preparation in deaf education programs approved by the Council on Education of the Deaf. *American Annals of the Deaf, 147*(5), 71–78.

Kennedy, C. R., McCann, D. C., Campbell, M. J., Law, C. M., Mullee, M., Petrou, S., . . . Stevenson, J. (2006). Language ability after early detection of permanent childhood hearing impairment. *New England Journal of Medicine, 18*(354), 2131–2141.

Klein, R., & Gilkerson, L. (2000). Personnel preparation for early childhood intervention programmes. In J. P. Shonkoff & S. J. Meisels (Eds.), *Handbook of early childhood intervention* (2nd ed., pp. 454–483). Cambridge, England: Cambridge University Press.

Marge, D. K., & Marge, M. (2005). *Beyond newborn hearing screening: Meeting the educational and heath care needs of infants and young children with hearing loss in America.* Report of the National Consensus Conference on Effective Educational and Health Care Interventions for Infants and Young Children with Hearing Loss, September 10–12, 2004. Syracuse, NY: Department of Physical Medicine and Rehabilitation, SUNY Upstate Medical University.

McCollum, J. A., & Stayton, V. D. (1996). Preparing early childhood special educators. In D. Bricker & A. Widerstrom (Eds.), *Preparing personnel to work with infants and young children* (pp. 67–90). Baltimore, MD: Brookes Publishing Co.

Meadow-Orlans, K. P., Mertens, D. M., & Sass-Lehrer, M. A. (2003). *Parents and their deaf children: The early years*. Washington, DC: Gallaudet University Press.

Moeller, M. P. (2000). Early intervention and language development in children who are deaf and hard of hearing. *Pediatrics, 106*(3), e43–51.

Moeller, M. P., Carr, G., Seaver, L., Stredler-Brown, A., & Holzinger, D. (2013). Best practices in family-centered early intervention for children who are deaf or hard of hearing: An international consensus statement. *Journal of Deaf Studies and Deaf Education, 18*(4), 429–445. doi:10.1093/deafed/ent034.

Moeller, M. P., Hoover, B., Putman, C., Arbataitis, K., Bohnenkamp, G., Peterson, B., . . . Stelmachowicz, P. G. (2007). Vocalizations of infants with hearing loss compared with infants with normal hearing: Part II—Transition to words. *Ear and Hearing, 28*, 628–642.

National Association for the Education of Young Children. (2009). *NAEYC Standards for early childhood professional preparation programs*. Washington, DC: NAEYC.

National Council for Accreditation of Teacher Education. (2015). *NCATE glossary*. Retrieved from http://www.ncate.org/Standards/NCATEUnitStandards/NCATEGlossary/tabid/477/Default.aspx.

Nelson, H. D., Bougatsos, C., & Nygren, P. (2008). Universal newborn hearing screening: Systematic review to update the 2001 US preventative services task force recommendation. *Pediatrics, 122*(1), e266–276. doi:10.1542/peds.2007-1422.

Nittrouer, S., & Burton, L. (2001). The role of early language experience in the development of speech perception and language processing abilities in children with hearing loss. *The Volta Review, 103*, 5–37.

Proctor, R., Niemeyer, J. A., & Compton, M. V. (2005). Training needs of early intervention personnel working with infants and toddlers who are deaf or hard of hearing. *Volta Review, 105*(2), 113–128.

Rice, G. B., & Lenihan, S. (2005). Early intervention in auditory/oral deaf education: Parent and professional perspectives. *The Volta Review, 105*(1), 73–96.

Roush, J., Bess, F., Gravel, J., Harrison, M., Lenihan, S., & Marvelli, A. (2004). Preparation of Personnel to Serve Children with Hearing Loss and their Families: Current Status and Future Needs. *Proceedings of the Summit on*

Deafness: Spoken Language in the 21st Century, Predicting Future Trends in Deafness. Washington, DC.

Roush, J., Harrison, M., Palsha, S., & Davidson, D. (1992). A national survey of educational preparation programs for early intervention specialists. *American Annals of the Deaf, 137*(5), 425.

Sass-Lehrer, M., Stredler-Brown, A., Hutchinson, N., Tarasenko, K., Moeller, M. P., Clark, K. (2010, March). *Knowledge and skills of early intervention specialists: Where are the gaps?* Paper presented at the Early Hearing Detection and Intervention Conference, Chicago, IL.

Sass-Lehrer, M., Stredler-Brown, A., & Moeller, M. P. (2008, February). *Focusing on the "I" in EHDI.* Paper presented at the Early Hearing Detection and Intervention Conference, New Orleans, LA.

Sass-Lehrer, M., Stredler-Brown, A., Moeller, M. P, Clark, K., & Hutchinson, N. (2011, February). *Defining core competencies: A three year investigation.* Paper presented at the Early Hearing Detection and Intervention Conference, Atlanta, GA.

Stredler-Brown, A., & Arehart, K. (2000). Universal newborn hearing screening: Impact on early intervention services. *The Volta Review, 100*(5), 85–117.

Thorp, E. K., & McCollum, J. A. (1994). Defining the infancy specialization in early childhood special education. In L. J. Johnson, R. J. Gallagher, M. J. LaMontagne, J. B. Jordan, J. J. Gallagher, P. L. Hutinger, & M. B. Karnes (Eds.), *Meeting early intervention challenges: Issues from birth to three* (pp. 167–183). Baltimore, MD: Brookes Publishing Co.

Wake, M., Hughes, E. K., Poulakis, Z., Collins, C., & Rickards, F. W. (2004). Outcomes of children with mild-profound congenital hearing loss at 7 to 8 years: A population study. *Ear Hear 25*(1), 1–8.

Winton, P., McCollum, J. A., & Catlett, C. (2008). *Practical approaches to early childhood professional development: Evidence, strategies, and resources.* Washington, DC: Zero to Three.

Yoshinaga-Itano, C. (2003). From screening to early identification and intervention: Discovering predictors to successful outcomes for children with significant hearing loss. *Journal of Deaf Studies and Deaf Education, 8*(1), 11–30.

Yoshinaga-Itano, C., Sedey, A. L., Coulter, D. K., & Mehl, A. L. (1998). The language of early- and later-identified children with hearing loss. *Pediatrics, 102,* 1161–1171.

2 Developing and Sustaining Exemplary Practice through Professional Learning

Mary Ellen Nevins and Marilyn Sass-Lehrer

Davin is an 8-year alumna of a teacher education program that prepares professionals to work with children who are deaf or hard of hearing. Her K-12 certification supported her in her first position, teaching kindergarten in a countywide program for children who are deaf or hard of hearing. While employed there, Davin attended school-sponsored inservice workshops for topics such as behavior management, autism spectrum disorder, assessments, and, most recently, the new districtwide math curriculum. In addition, she attended her state's biannual conference for teachers of children who are deaf or hard of hearing.

After a recent move to another state with her family, Davin applied for a position as an early intervention specialist in the infant program in her county. She was the only professional with a background in working with children who are deaf or hard of hearing and was awarded the position despite her inexperience in working with families of very young children. Given an urgent need to get "up to speed" to do her best in that position, Davin wondered about the options for managing her personal learning journey so that she might work effectively with infants and toddlers and their families. Once she enhances her dispositions, skills, and knowledge for working with very young children, how might she sustain her new practice?

GUIDING QUESTIONS

1. What is exemplary practice for early interventionists working with infants and toddlers who are deaf of hard of hearing and how does an interventionist become a competent provider?
2. How do professionals develop a "learner first" posture to develop and sustain their career journey?
3. How can professionals leverage digital tools to acquire the twenty-first-century skills of communication, collaboration, creativity, and critical thinking, in an effort to develop these same skills in the children with whom they will work?
4. What is the role of the mentor/coach, either expert or peer, in guiding professionals to exemplary practice?

COMPETENCIES ADDRESSED IN THIS CHAPTER

1. Collaboration and Interdisciplinary Models and Practices
2. Professional and Ethical Behavior: Fundamentals of early intervention practice, legislation, policies, and research

---

INTRODUCTION

This chapter will define exemplary practice for all early intervention professionals and provide a description of the stages of developing competence. It will furnish an overview of professional learning and types of professional learning opportunities available today. Implications of adult learning and research on brain-compatible strategies will be considered in a review of face-to-face, online, and blended/hybrid models of professional learning. The chapter will also offer a discussion of the digital tools that support twenty-first century professional learning and close with a discussion of essential features of mentoring and coaching as part of a continuum of professional learning experiences.

Professional learning is a shared responsibility involving individual professionals, school and district leaders, education agencies, higher education, federal government, and educational organizations (Killion, 2012). This chapter has value not only for professionals engaged in developing and sustaining exemplary practice, but also for the supervisors and administrators responsible for providing and overseeing their continuing education. Individuals who lead professional learning experiences whether in a college classroom or online course, or serving as a mentor in an in-person or remote capacity, are encouraged to examine their own practices in light of the exemplary practices described in this chapter. With careful attention to the principles suggested here, professionals providing these learning experiences can determine whether they are implementing practices that best meet the needs of today's aspiring learners.

For professional practice in early intervention for infants and toddlers who are deaf or hard of hearing and their families to be deemed exemplary, two important components must be present. The first component entails the general dispositions, skill sets, and knowledge base of *all* competent early intervention providers:

- infant and toddler development and assessment
- family-centered practice
- cultural knowledge and sensitivity
- interdisciplinary collaboration
- effective communication
- legislation, policies, and procedures
- professional and ethical behaviors

Regardless of the unique needs of the child and family, these essential elements undergird a breadth of dispositions, skills, and knowledge that transcend individual accommodations for a child and family. The second aspect of exemplary practice for professionals working with families of children who are deaf or hard of hearing acknowledges the dispositions, skills, and knowledge associated with working with this specialty, infants and toddlers who are deaf or hard of hearing:

- identification and assessment of hearing levels and implications for programming and services
- assistive technology(ies) for people who are deaf or hard of hearing, auditory and visual
- support and resources for families with deaf or hard-of-hearing children and professionals
- legislation, policies, and best practice recommendations for children who are deaf or hard of hearing
- Deaf Communities and Deaf Culture[a]
- deaf and hard-of-hearing Listening and Spoken Language communities
- language and communication expertise in the language(s) and modalities used by people who are deaf or hard of hearing
- child–family communication effectiveness
- developmental assessment for infants and toddlers who are deaf or hard of hearing
- programming and services for infants and toddlers who are deaf or hard of hearing and those with disabilities and their families

Chapter 1, *What Every Early Intervention Professional Should Know,* lists the general competency areas needed to work with infants, toddlers, and their families as well as the specialty skills needed to work with infants and toddlers who are deaf or hard of hearing. Table 1.1 in Chapter 1 provides specific examples of dispositions, knowledge, and skills relevant to each competency area and how the competency area is applied when working with families and young deaf or hard-of-hearing children.

In addition to these two essential sets of competencies for early intervention practice, professionals should also be mindful of the fact that today's infants and toddlers are tomorrow's school-aged children. As such, professionals are charged with developing the twenty-first century

---

[a]Deaf used with an upper case "D" refers to people who consider themselves culturally Deaf or who identify with the Deaf Community.

skills that will be required for success in home and school, postsecond-ary education, college, and careers. These skills include communication, critical thinking, creativity, and collaboration. It is incumbent upon the early intervention professional to envision what lies ahead for each infant and toddler who is deaf or hard of hearing as the journey begins. With this long-term perspective, professionals can assist families in jump start-ing children's acquisition of the valuable skills they need for their future learning and later in the workplace.

DEVELOPING AND SUSTAINING EXEMPLARY PRACTICE

Given the components of exemplary practice for professionals working with families of children who are deaf or hard of hearing, it is vital that all professionals engage in honest self-assessment of their dispositions, skills, and knowledge as they begin their professional career and then periodi-cally throughout their career journey. Although Davin may have expert competence with regard to teaching primary-aged children who are deaf or hard of hearing, she will need to learn more about infants and toddlers and working with families before she can effectively provide quality ser-vice. She must ask herself the questions: what do I need to know and what do I need to be able to do? As recommended in Chapter 1, Davin might first assess her current dispositions, skills, and knowledge as driven by the document published in Appendix 1 to the Supplement to the 2007 Position Statement: Principles and Guidelines for Early Intervention after Confirmation That a Child Is Deaf or Hard of Hearing [Joint Committee on Infant Hearing (JCIH), 2013]. The *Knowledge and Skills of Early Intervention Providers for Children Who Are Deaf or Hard of Hearing and Their Families* document includes the general competency areas provid-ers should have to deliver comprehensive early developmental services. Table 1.2 in Chapter 1 provides an example of how these competencies can be used as a self-assessment tool. Armed with that self-analysis, Davin can identify her learning needs; once identified, she can plan a professional learning agenda that fits her own personal learning style, leverages today's digital tools, and creates a path toward competence and

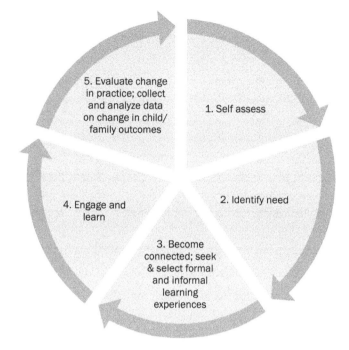

Figure 2.1 Personal Learning Agenda Planning Process.

exemplary practice in working with infants and toddlers and their families. Figure 2.1, Personal Learning Agenda Planning Process, may assist in conceptualizing the process for Davin's professional learning.

In following this process, Davin identifies infant and toddler development and coaching families as areas for immediate learning. With this goal in mind, she begins to prepare for her new position before she is even assigned her first family.

DEVELOPING A PERSONAL LEARNING AGENDA

Luckily, for Davin, there has never been a more exciting time than today to engage in professional learning. The growing intersection of technology and collaboration has given rise to a movement of "Connected Learning Communities" (Nussbaum-Beach & Hall, 2012). This new direction advocates a learner first attitude and a three-pronged approach to continuous professional learning. A learner first attitude suggests that professionals take responsibility for their own learning and become less dependent on others to create opportunities for them to develop professionally. This can be accomplished, in part, by the active engagement in Connected Learning Communities. These comprise Professional Learning Communities (PLCs), Personal Learning Networks (PLNs), and Communities of Practice (CoPs). These offer the kind of experiences that contribute to developing (and sustaining) the exemplary practice suggested above.

Professional Learning Communities (PLCs)

In the model of Nussbaum-Beach and Hall (2012), Professional Learning Communities are often the face-to-face colleagues at a workplace who collaborate for the purpose of realizing better outcomes for their constituencies. Each individual member of the PLC is self-empowered but, at the same time, is committed to the common goals of the community. According to the authors

> Professional learning communities are about continuous improvement, shared leadership and [school] reform. High functioning professional learning communities engage in collective and continuous inquiry, participate in thoughtful conversations about their professional learning, devise strategies to improve instruction, act on what they have created and reflect together. (p. 29)

Thus, Davin's new colleagues at her agency make up the members of *her* professional learning community in the same way that schools are referenced above. The excerpt above is empowering and at the same time suggests a personal responsibility in pursuit of excellence within the PLC. In many cases, the PLC will be interdisciplinary; educators, speech-language pathologists, audiologists, physical and occupational therapists, social workers, counselors, and others will be part of a vibrant, face-to-face (F2F) learning group. In some circumstances, early intervention service providers have no F2F community. Their professional interdisciplinary community must be virtual. The increasing connectivity of the workforce is supported by increasingly powerful digital tools (detailed in a subsequent section of this chapter) and makes it possible to develop deep and collegial relationships that build community even when there is no physical interaction.

Personal Learning Networks (PLNs)

A second prong of the Connected Educator model details the creation of PLNs, "which ... are about individuals gathering information and sharing resources (offered by other professionals who become part of one's network) that enhance their personal and professional learning" (Nussbaum-Beach & Hall, 2012, p. 31). PLNs may include professionals coming together to discuss a particular issue at a workshop or other forum, or connecting virtually, online. The authors caution that in order to do this effectively, an individual must have sufficient knowledge of the digital tools available and, at the same time, have access to trustworthy resources. For the early interventionist, the beauty of the PLN is that although it includes professionals traditionally considered part of the interdisciplinary team, it may reach well beyond the field of working with children who are deaf or hard of hearing and their families. Any individual's PLN is customized to areas of interest and scope of practice and, for early interventionists, may include resources and experts in fields such as health literacy, behavior change, and systems administration, to name just a few. The development of a Personal Learning Network takes time and a commitment to the judicious exploitation of the virtual opportunities to connect with others that abound on the web; the promise of its power makes it a compelling undertaking for any professional interested in both personal and professional growth in this twenty-first century.

Communities of Practice (CoPs)

Communities of Practice, the third component of the Connected Learning Communities model, form for the purpose of enabling professionals within the community to become increasingly more effective at their craft. In addition, CoPs may focus on a particular area of interest; for early interventionists this may mean a focus on the delivery of services through telepractice, learning about early brain development, or the effects of "toxic stress" on development. Like Personal Learning

Networks, CoPs, are likely to have more of a virtual than physical presence and seek to elicit the collective wisdom of its members for solving real problems of practice. CoPs operate on the belief that assembling group knowledge leads to developing individual knowledge employing a "none of us is as good as all of us mentality" (Nussbaum-Beach & Hall, 2012, p. 33). Becoming a good citizen of a CoP requires active engagement and contribution, with the tacit understanding that whatever is learned is shared with your Professional Learning Community and the Personal Learning Network as well.

Dynamic participation in these three types of connected learning experiences will no doubt contribute to growing competence in any one of a number of skill sets in a host of domains. But how will Davin build these networks and know that she is improving her competence as an early intervention professional? Davin might find it helpful to consider the stages of developing competence as she journeys from novice to expert in a specific knowledge area and skill set. The discussion of competence that follows describes the general, outward signs of competence, but also provides context for application to the early intervention professional.

Exploring Competence

As a performance-based phenomena, competence is a situationally influenced manifestation of one's craft (Howell, 1982). Thus, having identified a substantial number of competencies required of an early intervention specialist for infants and toddlers who are deaf or hard of hearing and their families in Chapter 1, *What Every Early Intervention Professional Should Know*, we create a link between competencies and becoming a competent professional. In an attempt to define the word competence, Daniel Goleman (1981) has indicated that competencies should not be delineated as aspects of a given job, but as special characteristics of those who do the job best. This suggests perhaps that in contrast to widespread practice, the descriptor "minimal" as in "minimal competencies" should never be applied to the delineation of competence or competencies in employment requirements for early interventionists. Furthermore, it must be acknowledged that in the development of competencies, each family that the early interventionist meets creates a unique opportunity to learn anew, to co-learn with families, and to develop family-specific skills as dictated by a distinct presenting profile. According to Hanft, Rush, and Shelden (2004) there is always something new to learn in supporting families "in ordinary and extraordinary life situations" (p. XII). These experiences are added to the ever-growing skill set and further expand the competencies of the practicing professional.

There are recognized levels of competence in every field of endeavor. A general understanding of these established levels may inform an individual's journey from novice to expert, especially with regard to an early intervention specialist. Professionals should note that levels of competence at a given time in the career journey will vary; as innovative practices are identified, the process of new learning, skill acquisition, and experience accrual begins once again. The identification of points of personal competence across a range of competencies is the outcome of the self-assessment referenced earlier.

Unconscious Incompetence (Howell, 1982)

At the level of Unconscious Incompetence, an individual may be objectively judged as executing tasks poorly but, unfortunately, is unaware of inept performance. This blissful condition of the unconsciously incompetent worker is the source of grave concern to co-workers and supervisors for there is no motivation for the individual to make improvements or seek continuing education for building knowledge and skills. Without a disposition to enhance a professional career journey through continuing education, service providers at this level may actually do more harm than good. This has serious implications for professionals working with young deaf or hard-of-hearing infants and toddlers and their families at a time of critical importance for quality support. General early interventionists or developmental therapists who are unaware of the unique communication needs of children who are deaf or hard of hearing and their families may be representative of a segment of this level of (in)competence.

Conscious Incompetence

Along the continuum of competence, Howell's second level, Conscious Incompetence, represents the point at which "ignorant bliss" withers and you become aware that actions are not achieving the desired results. Recognition of this disconnect is an important career journey milestone for many; it often creates the dissonance from which action to make improvements will follow. In essence, once incompetence is acknowledged, the quest to dispel its negative effect on the psyche is compelling. Most workers, regardless of their specialty field, cannot help but seek the professional education that will make their work more effective. With regard to her own knowledge and skills, Davin's self-assessment helped identify her Conscious Incompetence in the areas of infant and toddler development as well as in a coaching model of intervention with families. By identifying these two areas of incompetence Davin acknowledged an immediate need to address these limitations to assist her movement to the next level of competence.

Conscious Competence

At the level of Conscious Competence, an individual executes tasks with real understanding. An analytic perspective frames the work and "in the moment" assessment of actions and results is possible. Flexibility and judicious decision making develop as a result of increasing experience and allow for more effective ways of providing services. Planning and simulation (e.g., rehearsal, practice, or role playing) ensure smooth implementation of the tasks of any work. Conscious competence represents a solid performance of craft; the service provider is capable, knowledgeable, and skilled. The early intervention professional who is Consciously Competent actively plans and rehearses in order to have quality exchanges with families and young children and meaningful and collaborative conversations with colleagues. When Davin reaches this level of competence, her intervention sessions will run smoothly because she will have thoughtfully planned for and practiced the activities she plans to share with the family. Davin will prepare for her family session by first meeting with a colleague who has agreed to work with her. In preparation for the meeting with her colleague, Davin will identify the key messages she would like to communicate to the family. Roleplaying her family coaching conversations with her colleague will help to ensure that the messages she hopes to communicate will be clear.

Unconscious Competence

Whereas Conscious Competence requires mental effort and vigilance to maintain quality performance, Unconscious Competence, on the other hand, represents a level of operation that is virtually "automatic." A vast store of experiences enhances the skills and knowledge of the practitioner such that a "big picture" view surrounds every exchange by an expert provider. With an experience-rich perspective, attention is freed to be responsive to the unique details of any given situation; data are interpreted without conscious deliberation. Unconsciously competent providers are expert practitioners in their respective domains, yet they are easily able to revert to more conscious and analytic performance as required by novel situations and demands for new content learning or procedural innovation. This is especially apparent when an early intervention expert takes a learner first posture to embed newly adopted standards or advanced technological tools into "state of the art" service delivery for the families and children with whom he or she works.

Conscious Unconscious Competence

Not every expert practitioner functioning at the level of Unconscious Competence aspires to or reaches the level of Conscious Unconscious Competence (Pike, 2003). The individual operating at this masterful level of competence dissects his or her own expertise, taking the now automatic and reflexive dispositions, skills, and knowledge to analyze and distill into their essence. In so doing, the master is able to guide and, importantly, take the learner perspective of an individual currently operating at a lower level of competence. Overcoming "the curse of knowledge" barrier (Heath & Heath, 2007), individuals at the level of Conscious Unconscious Competence can, despite its difficulty, call to mind what it is like to lack that knowledge, skill, or disposition. These individuals, then, become the most effective instructors or coaches because of the reflective analysis of their own craft and the power to identify and narrate the steps to achieving high levels of competence. Early intervention professionals who function at this level of competence model the behaviors of exemplary practice and push its limits to new frontiers. Davin will look for someone at this level to be her mentor/coach.

Movement along a continuum of competence within any given aspect of practice is the result of the development and refinement of core dispositions, the ongoing acquisition of necessary skills, the constant expansion of a pertinent knowledge base, and the never-ending accrual of a store of varied and relevant experiences. In embracing a learner-first posture to seek competence, a vibrant career journey is fueled by powerful professional learning experiences.

PROFESSIONAL LEARNING

The purpose of all professional learning activities in early intervention is the ultimate improvement in infant or toddler and family outcomes. Thus, continuing education is not an end in and of itself, but only a means to an end. As stated earlier, contemporary professional learning experiences reinforce a "connected learner approach" that recognizes that although some knowledge *for* practice is necessary, knowledge *in* practice and knowledge *of* practice provide the most comprehensive opportunity to learn deeply (Cochran-Smith & Lytle, 1999). Although some of Davin's learning journey will include independent knowledge building, she will want to take full advantage of her learning networks and communities that will allow her to reflect, share with others, and obtain feedback on both her new learning and practice.

Activities or experiences that may be considered professional learning include both formal and informal opportunities. Informal opportunities are defined as being more learner driven (e.g., participating in a web chat, perusing resources suggested by someone in a Personal Learning Network) and are contrasted with those formal experiences that are more traditional and structured (e.g., attending a workshop, or taking an online course). Depending upon your learning goal and strategy for participating each can be a productive professional learning experience.

Online Learning

The number of online learning opportunities is increasing rapidly. Universities, professional organizations, and state-wide early intervention collaboratives have initiated online degree and certificate programs as well as individual course offerings and learning modules. In addition, there is an abundance of information and resources available through professional organizations and networks that provide online learning opportunities. (See Recommended Resources at the end of this chapter for examples of the types of online learning opportunities of interest to early intervention professionals.)

Anxious to begin the process, Davin might choose to initiate her learning journey by pursuing some informal opportunities that are immediately available to her rather than wait for a regional conference on infant–toddler development that is still 6 months away. Because she identified infant–toddler development as one of her urgent knowledge needs, she starts with an online search on national standards for early learning and explores a number of websites for organizations dedicated to the birth to 3 years age group. Davin's first effort brings her to the website of Zero to Three (see Recommended Resources) where she spends a great deal of time following links within the Behavior and Development tab. On a return visit to the website the following day, she learns that although there are no national standards for infant and toddler development, a document entitled Early Learning Guidelines for Infants and Toddlers: Recommendations for States is available for her review. This document, in turn, provides links to those states that have developed standards; she finds that her state has a comprehensive document for providers and follows the link. Thus, Davin's knowledge building commences.

Personal Knowledge Management (PKM)

Recognition of the staggering figures regarding the pace of knowledge development [e.g., it has been suggested that medical knowledge is doubling every 8 years (Carroll, 2011)] begs the question, "How can one keep pace with all that there is to know in any field?" One potential approach to this daunting task calls for the development of a system of Personal Knowledge Management or PKM (Jarche, 2013). According to Jarche, "Personal knowledge management is a set of processes, individually constructed, to help each of us make sense of our world and work more effectively" (p. 2). In Jarche's *Seek-Sense-Share* construct, individuals *seek* out the information they need to inform their work. Bits of information are accumulated from trusted sources, and individuals capture this knowledge for consumption. Jarche then advises purposeful reflection, or the *sense* component of this model. Here knowledge is put into practice for application; "experimentation" with the new knowledge encourages deeper learning. The final phase of this three-part model is the critical *share* element. As part of the process, collaborating with colleagues for the purpose of exchanging ideas helps to strengthen the ownership of the knowledge. It is in this retelling that the social implications of knowledge building become obvious; shared ideas can be expanded, challenged, or improved upon in conversations between and among colleagues. Davin might consider exploring the utility of a PKM approach within her new professional learning community to support her career journey. She might, for example, come across a study that explores natural learning environments in early intervention practice (Dunst, Bruder, Trivette, & Hamby, 2006). After reading the article, she begins to think about her own understanding of the role of everyday activities and the natural environment. Davin decides that she needs to refine her understanding of the practices in place at her agency; she forwards information about the study to her colleagues. By the time of the next staffing, the topic has found its way onto the agenda and a deep conversation about practices ensues. In exemplifying a PKM approach to new learning, Davin not only acquires new personal knowledge, but also benefits from the discussion with colleagues from different disciplinary backgrounds that adds to the diversity of ideas surrounding the team's practice. As a byproduct, the early intervention program where Davin works takes the opportunity to codify its practices for developing intervention plans; session outcomes for families improve overall as professionals operationalize their natural learning environment practices. How does this scenario become the rule, rather than the exception? And what about an early interventionist who functions as an independent contractor with limited face-to-face interaction with colleagues? Solutions lie in the creation of a digital footprint that allows access to a new kind of professional learning.

DIGITAL TOOLS THAT SUPPORT PROFESSIONAL LEARNING

Without a doubt, failure to harness available digital tools to improve practices in the workplace through continuous professional learning is short sighted in this twenty-first century. From the use of tools to assist with archiving learning artifacts, to document-sharing tools for cloud-based collaboration, to social media sites that facilitate connecting with colleagues, technology has radically changed the landscape of professional education. The sheer number of choices for internet-enabled opportunities might suggest that there is something for everybody, even for those professionals who have yet to consider the possibilities. All that is needed is a firm resolve to commit time to explore, select, and then implement those tools that will enhance a professional learning routine.

In the same manner that professional learning is a means to improving child and family outcomes and not an end in itself, so too are digital tools a means to professional learning, not ends in themselves (Nussbaum-Beach & Hall, 2012). Professionals are cautioned to be well aware of the ephemeral nature of digital tools and consider that today's preferred tool might be obsolete tomorrow given the lightning pace of innovation in this arena. One practical way to stay abreast of the most useful digital tools is to refer to an annual poll of the top 100 Tools for Learning as offered each year for the past 7 years (Hart, 2014). Twitter remains at the top of Hart's list for 2014 as a social networking and microblogging service; it currently wields great potential for professional learning. Whether used to "follow" individuals or a topical group through the use of a hashtag, Twitter can broaden the professional learning network from the desktop computer or mobile phone. Davin's first use of Twitter was for social and consumer-related purposes. She has recently begun to follow Ellen Galinsky (@ellengalinsky), noted author of *Mind in the Making*, @toosmalltofail, a partnership between the Bill, Hillary, and Chelsea Clinton Foundation and Next Generation, to improve the health and well-being of children ages birth to 5 years. She also follows @AGBellAssoc, a group that addresses listening and spoken language opportunities for deaf and hard-of-hearing children, and @VL2Science, the Visual Language and Visual Learning Center at Gallaudet University. She finds that starting each morning with a quick look at her Twitter account (as organized by TweetDeck) will often lead her to a resource that she can then share with the families with whom she works and with other professionals in her growing network. She is by no means an expert user of this tool, but has made a personal commitment to continue to increase the number of professionals that she is following as well as growing her own participation beyond simply being a lurking consumer.

Another highly rated tool in Hart's Top 100 list (number 2 for 2014) is the use of Google Drive/Google Docs. Google Docs will automatically save to the cloud any changes to a document as they occur. This has very real practical implications for any collaborative work shared across many contributors, be it a new set of procedures for early intervention sessions, an updated agency contact list, or a group presentation for an upcoming conference.

Face-to-Face (F2F) and In Person Learning

As a practical matter, Davin will continue her learner first posture when attending formal, in person, conferences and workshops. Luckily, compelling research about adult learning (Knowles, 1990) and brain-compatible learning strategies (Jensen, 2007; Tate, 2004) has reshaped standards for effective professional learning that is offered in face-to-face as well as online formats. Of particular note for the contemporary adult learner are the 12 Principles of Adult Learning outlined by Vella (2002) that are still relevant today. Heeding recommendations for (1) participation, the learner identifies what is to be learned; (2) safety, the learner is willing to take risks in new learning; (3) immediacy, the learning meets an imminent need of the learner; (4) engagement, the learner is actively involved in creating new meaning; and (5) accountability, the learner reflects and assesses new learning, today's learning leaders design experiences that embrace these principles. However, learners must balance knowledge acquisition with skill development to avoid the inadvertent creation of a "Knowing-Doing Gap" (Pfeffer & Sutton, 2000). This phenomenon is by no means exclusively an education or early intervention one. In fact, the term "knowing-doing gap" was coined by authors writing for the *Harvard Business School Press*. The thrust of their book is an emphasis on the manner in which successful companies turn knowledge into action; so too must professional learning experiences in early intervention provide opportunities to connect knowledge to practice and mind its own knowing-doing gap.

Beyond attention to adult learning models, recent research in neuroscience of the brain has given rise to the study of how the brain learns best. Brain-compatible learning strategies and techniques can be applied to both children and adults; implications for the design of professional learning experiences suggest attention to the procedural components of learning such as attention span limits, input limitations, and set-aside time for learning. Additionally, considerations for content and process issues mandate attention to the identification of key principles, holistic thinking, and an orientation to cooperative learning (Jensen, 2007).

Regardless of the design of a presentation and the skill set of its presenter(s) there is always much to learn when professionals gather. One blogger created a tip sheet for professionals headed to a recent symposium. She reminded her followers that attending a face-to-face learning experience should be more than earning continuing education units (CEUs) or a chance to get away (W. DeMoss, personal communication, September 21, 2013). According to DeMoss, it is a short-term opportunity to "up-level" or improve practice and connect with others. Davin might consider these suggestions as she prepares to attend a regional conference on early learning. See Table 2.1, Tips for Getting the Most Out of the Symposium Experience.

Today's face-to-face professional learning should be practical, relevant, and goal oriented. Effective professional learning facilitators will

Table 2.1 *Tips for Getting the Most Out of the Symposium Experience*

1. Choose to attend a session on a familiar topic	Listen for new ideas and ways to approach the subject. What has changed since you last read about the topic? What opportunity do you have to connect with this presenter in order to continue a dialogue virtually after the conference? Who do you know who would love to get this information?
2. Choose to attend a session on a topic that is new or a challenge for you	How do you compare the new information to what you already know? What is your take away from the session? What is the one idea that you have to apply this to your practice when you are home? Who are the thought leaders in this area? How could you connect with them to continue a dialogue virtually after the conference?
3. Walk through the exhibit hall with a new set of eyes	Focus on what's new. Often exhibitors have demonstrations of new products. Watch and listen. Even if a product does not directly apply to your practice, can you identify a colleague who would appreciate the new resource or contact information? Visit the vendors that represent technologies beneficial for infants or toddlers who are deaf or hard of hearing or their families. What do you need to know that would assist you in guiding and coaching families to use or maintain this equipment? Learn more about the vendor's website, customer service, or troubleshooting guide. If you do not know, ask who your regional representative is so you can make a virtual connection when you get home.
4. Exchange contact information with seatmates in each session	If you attend 10 sessions, that would be up to 20 new professional contacts to connect with virtually. Discover if they are on Facebook, LinkedIn, or Twitter.
5. Attend the general sessions and other sponsored events	This is a great way to meet new professionals, learn from thought leaders, and get more involved.

value the experiences that the adult learner brings and will allow for some self-direction in navigating content and acquiring skills. More importantly, quality professional learning experiences respect the participant and create a climate of partnership in learning within any community gathered for the purpose of improving family and child outcomes.

COURSEWORK

Formal coursework as offered by a college or university in a "bricks and mortar" location can no longer be the standard route to a degree or a certificate in early intervention for infants and toddlers who are deaf or hard of hearing and their families. Practically speaking, the ease with which a national (or international) cohort can be formed virtually for the purpose of enhancing dispositions, skills, and knowledge in this specialty field makes it an attractive alternative to full-time or even part-time study on site. A number of online programs also require a F2F component, resulting in a blended or hybrid model. But not all coursework is taken for an advanced degree, certificate, or license. Any number of discipline-specific or discipline-related, credit-bearing classes from a recognized institution of higher learning can add value to an individual's professional competencies without matriculation for a degree. Given the broad spectrum of competencies identified for early interventionists working with infants and toddlers who are deaf or hard of hearing and their families, it is plausible that some knowledge acquisition can be supported by coursework in the general domain. In fact, Davin recently decided to look online to explore opportunities for professional learning that she can access from home. She was disappointed that she could not find a free Massive Open Online Course (MOOC) on sites such as Coursera, Udacity, and edX regarding infants and toddlers, but did learn of an Infant Specialist Certificate program at Erikson Institute in Chicago. After reviewing information from Erikson as well as a number of other institutions, Davin is considering taking her first online course, Infant/Toddler Screening and Assessment. She will use her new position as a lens through which she can learn more about the needs of this age group with whom she has only begun to work.

COACHING AND MENTORING

One of the richest professional learning experiences is the participation in an effective mentor–mentee relationship. Mentoring is designed to facilitate the transfer of knowledge, skills, attitudes, beliefs, and values between an experienced and less experienced practitioner (Gallacher, 1995). Mentoring entails an interpersonal relationship in which the mentee receives both professional and personal benefits. On the other hand, a coaching relationship is often instituted to support a learner who asks for assistance, wants to acquire a new skill, desires help in solving a problem, needs encouragement, or wants a new challenge (Hanft et al., 2004). The process of providing coaching assistance mirrors the guiding relationship between early interventionists and families; in the case of mentoring, the relationship is professional–professional in nature. With a focus on asking, not telling, and a disposition of trust in developing competence, a coaching relationship can be equally effective with novice professionals or those on a path from "good to great." As a newcomer to early intervention, Davin is open to establishing a relationship with one of the more experienced providers in her agency. She is sure that her inclination for direct teaching will need some transformation in order to fully reflect family-centered intervention practices. But before approaching a prospective mentor or coach, Davin wants to be sure that she is clear about the expectations for participating in such a partnership.

Characteristics and Attributes of Mentees and Learners

To receive full benefit from the mentor or coach experience, Davin must call upon her disposition to assume personal responsibility for her own growth and development. Once again, her authentic learner-first posture will facilitate the creation of a coaching process that allows for

> . . . non-judgemental interaction between the coaching partners, reflection, and observation paired with feedback to prompt a learner's self discovery and acquire or refine new skills. (Hanft et al., 2004, p. 18)

In addition, there are also personal qualities of a learner that enhance the development of an effective coaching relationship; these include flexibility, enthusiasm, a positive attitude, and a willingness to take risks (Gallacher, 1995). Davin believes she possesses these qualities but wants to strengthen her ability to reflect, listen deeply, and participate in the collaborative conversations that help change practice. She approaches one of her colleagues who agrees to serve as her coach, but before agreeing to beginning this relationship, the prospective coach wants an assurance from Davin that she will agree to videotape her sessions to enable them to view sessions together. The coaching professional wants to be sure that Davin will have the opportunity to observe and reflect on her own practice, rather than limiting her learning to what is seen through the perspective of her coach's eyes.

Coaching Coaches

The key elements of the professional coaching process, observation, action, and reflection, are the very same as those required of the learner when serving as a coach working with families and their infant or toddler who is deaf or hard of hearing. After the process is initiated and ground rules are set, the observation phase begins. This may take any one of a number of forms. The coach may observe the learner; the learner may observe the coach demonstrating a particular skill or action; the learner may engage in a self-observation; and/or the learner and coach together may observe the child and family interacting (Hanft et al., 2004). This observation phase generates the data that then drive the coaching conversations. The purpose of coaching conversations is to offer meaningful feedback; serendipitously, it offers the learner an opportunity to be on the other end of the coaching conversation, obtaining a perspective of how families might feel on that side of the exchange.

The action phase of the coaching process refers to the events of a session, or a simulation or role play of a session, that have been targeted for the application of some particular act, behavior, or skill. Modeling by a coach or actual practice of a new strategy by a learner are two possible elements of this phase of the process. These, too, are supported by the coaching conversations that precede and/or follow the action.

When the learner and coach analyze the action components through reflective conversations, a particular episode of the coaching process is completed. The conversational dance played out here begins with self-analysis on the part of the learner as driven by probing questions asked by the coach. Again, according to Hanft et al. (2004), feedback

> . . . should always follow reflection by the learner as the coach's intent is to learn what the coaching partner's insights, ideas, and reflections are before the coach provides his or her own. (p. 48)

Providing meaningful feedback to a learner is a skill set all its own. Most professionals will agree that negative feedback that is direct and communicates what is wrong ends up alienating the learner, rather than encouraging the learner to develop better practices. On the other hand, conciliatory feedback (Perkins, 2003) offers positive but vague commentary. Although it avoids conflict and values the relationship over the message, it may be perceived as superficial and evasive by its recipients. A third type of feedback, communicative feedback (Perkins, 2003), employs a three-step process for its authentic use. First, the coach asks clarifying questions for understanding, for example, "Which of the two strategies did you see the families respond to more enthusiastically?" The second step calls for the expression of a specific value statement, for example, "Your thoughtful design of the dressing routine experience added value to the session today." The third and final step offers a reflective question or statement and invites a thoughtful response from the learner, for example, "What do you think might have happened if dad were in the session with mom today?" Thus, communicative feedback allows for a true conversation between coach and learner. It might be suggested that the ability to become your own coach can be encouraged through a gradual release of responsibility of framing the prompts from the coach to the learner. The ultimate goal of the process is to empower the interventionist to be a self-reflective practitioner, capable of observing and refining the dispositions and skill set that contribute to exemplary practice.

Peer Mentoring or Coaching

There is always value in collaborating with a colleague to improve practice. When professionals team for the purpose of embedding knowledge and skills into practice, collaborative coaching relationships can emerge. In much the same way that a Professional Learning Community forms to advance practice, peer coaching extends the clear focus of learning to the development of observable skills. Critical ingredients for successful peer coaching initiatives include voluntary participation, mutual respect, and nonjudgmental support (Hanft et al., 2004). Peer coaching requires administrative support, time, and flexibility of staff to yield positive results. Peer coaching should be considered a high impact professional learning experience for early interventionists as they develop and sustain exemplary practice.

LOOKING BACK AND PLANNING AHEAD

After 1 year in her new position, Davin reflects on her learning journey. She now has a better understanding of infant and toddler development, and often refers to the developmental checklists she found online. Her attendance at a regional conference on early development yielded some professional contacts, both experts and peers. She now follows two of the presenters on Twitter and Skypes regularly with another early interventionist from the western part of the state who also works with infants and toddlers who are deaf or hard of hearing. She also discovered a new text, *Nurturing language and learning: Development of deaf and hard-of-hearing infants and toddlers* by Spencer and Koester (2015) that will be a great resource for her. Slowly but surely Davin is gaining greater confidence in her ability to coach families; she is thankful that she has a coach who has been able to find time to observe some of her sessions and spends time in providing feedback that assists her in developing competence. As she looks forward to a second year with the agency, Davin has selected some new goals for her personal learning agenda. The online course on Infant/Toddler Assessment is a top priority for her; she makes a note to check on the application deadline.

She sees that it is almost time to leave for her next session; she reviews her plans and prepares to meet the next family and is looking forward to learning with them this week. Her mentor sees her as she heads out and reminds her to think about her use of open-ended questions. Davin has become a connected learner.

SUMMARY

Continuous learning is expected of all individuals in the professional workforce today. Technological advances that support professional learning have created a new landscape for developing and sustaining the skills and knowledge that are required for virtually any field imaginable. This, in turn, has created a tremendous opportunity for families of infants and toddlers who are deaf or hard of hearing to have access to a well-qualified and competent service provider despite their geographic location. New learning opportunities continue to develop and gain greater acceptance as the belief that high impact professional education is an essential path to improved practice. Early interventionists must pair their passion for what they do with a pursuit of excellence in how they do it by adopting a learner first attitude for professional growth. With this essential disposition they will be positioned to improve outcomes for the families and the infants and toddlers with whom they work.

Acknowledgments: We would like to acknowledge Wendy DeMoss and Beth S. Benedict for their careful reading and suggestions for this chapter. Their input was instrumental in crafting the content and structure of this final product.

SUGGESTED ACTIVITIES

1. Read more about Twenty-First Century Skills: watch YouTube video https://www.youtube.com/watch?v=GegtmlJPdrM. Identify three areas of knowledge and skills that you would like to enhance over the next year. Explain why these knowledge and skill areas are important for your work with infants and toddlers who are deaf or hard of hearing and their families.

2. Learn more about how to use Twitter by requesting a free copy of the Twitter Handbook for teachers at the following link: http://plpnetwork. com/2012/06/08/free-13-page-twitter-guide-teachers/. Sign up for a Twitter account and find five professional contacts/organizations to follow. Create a routine that supports regular review of your Twitter feed; retweet posts of interest to your own followers.

3. Contact your state early hearing detection and intervention (EHDI) program and/or the National Center for Hearing Assessment Management (NCHAM) (http://infanthearing.org) to discover professional development trainings and other resources available. Identify one professional learning opportunity that meets your needs and interests and make it happen.

4. Select one of the nine competency areas in the Knowledge and Skills of Early Intervention Providers (JCIH, 2013). Assess your stage of competence (Howell, 1982, as described in this chapter) for each of the knowledge and skill statements in this section. Identify three competencies that you believe are below the "Conscious Competent" stage. Describe a learning strategy described in the chapter that you believe can enhance your developing competence in those selected areas.

RECOMMENDED RESOURCES

1. The Alexander Graham Bell Association for the Deaf and Hard of Hearing
   Information and resources, calendar of educational programs for professionals including certificate programs, symposia, conferences, and seminars. See http://listeningandspokenlanguage.org/Document. aspx?id=1802.

2. Division for Early Childhood
   A Division of the Council for Exceptional Children hosts an annual conference and publishes recommended practices and policy documents to promote best practices for young children with special needs and their families. See http://www.dec-sped.org/.

3. Gallaudet University, Graduate School and Center for Continuing Studies
   Degree and certificate programs on campus and online focused on early intervention and early childhood. See http://www.gallaudet.edu/academics_and_research/graduate_programs.html; http://www.gallaudet.edu/ccs.html.

4. The Laurent Clerc National Deaf Education Center

The Clerc Center, at Gallaudet University in Washington, DC, provides information and resources, training and technical assistance, webinars, products, and publications for professionals. See http://www.gallaudet.edu/clerc_center.html.

5. LSLogic

   LSLogic is online portal to a wide range of learning opportunities. LSLogic offers modules and courses, hosts Connected Learning Communities, provides access to video observations, and matches mentors/coaches to learners interested in upleveling skills in listening and spoken language practice. See www.lslogic.org.

6. The National Center for Hearing Assessment Management (NCHAM)

   A national resource center for families and professionals supporting newborn hearing screening, early identification, and intervention programs. NCHAM hosts an annual meeting, conferences, and workshops. See http://infanthearing.org/.

7. The National Center for Hearing Assessment Management E-Book: A Resource guide for early hearing detection and intervention (EHDI).

   This online resource includes chapters on a range of topics from newborn hearing screening, hearing evaluation, and delivering early intervention services for deaf and hard-of-hearing children and their families. The E-Book is updated annually. See http://www.infanthearing.org/ehdi-ebook/.

8. Victorian Deaf Education Institute

   The Victorian Deaf Education Institute offers innovative professional learning in partnership with schools, universities, and professional organizations. Instructors include high caliber speakers who range from leading global experts and academics to practicing teaching and allied health professionals. See http://www.deafeducation.vic.edu.au/Pages/home.aspx.

REFERENCES

Carroll, J. (2011). *Education.* Retrieved from http://www.jimcarroll.com/category/trends/education-trends/#.UukiyxBdWSp.

Cochran-Smith, M., & Lytle, S. L. (1999). Relationships of knowledge and practice: Teacher learning in communities. *Review of Research in Education, 24,* 249–305.

Dunst, C. J., Bruder, M. B., Trivette, C. M., & Hamby, D. W. (2006). Everyday activity settings, natural learning environments, and early intervention practices. *Journal of Policy and Practice in Intellectual Disabilities, 3,* 3–10.

Gallacher, K. (1995). *Coaching partnerships: Refining early intervention practices.* Missoula, MT: Montana University Affiliated Rural Institute on Disabilities.

Goleman, D. (1981). The New Competency Test: Matching the right people to the right jobs. *Psychology Today, 15,* 35–46.

Hanft, B. E., Rush, D. D., & Sheldon, M. L. (2004). *Coaching families and colleagues in early childhood.* Baltimore, MD: Brookes Publishing Co.

Hart, J. (2014). *Top 100 tools for learning 2014.* Retrieved from http://www.slideshare.net/janehart/top-100-tools-for-learning-2014.

Heath, C., & Heath, D. (2007). *Made to stick.* New York, NY: Broadway Books.

Howell, W. S. (1982). *The empathic communicator.* Prospect Heights, IL: Waveland Press.

Jarche, H. (2013). PKM Personal Knowledge Management. Retrieved from http://www.jarche.com/wp-content/uploads/2013/03/PKM-2013.pdf.

Jensen, E. (2007). *Introduction to brain compatible learning* (2nd ed.). Thousand Oaks, CA: Corwin Press.

Joint Committee on Infant Hearing. (2013). Supplement to the JCIH 2007 position statement: Principles and guidelines for intervention after confirmation that a child is deaf or hard of hearing. *Pediatrics, 131*(4), e1324–1349. doi:10.1542/peds.2013-0008.

Killion, J. (2012). *Meet the promise of content standards: Professional learning required.* Oxford, OH: Leaning Forward.

Knowles, M. S. (1990). *The adult learner: A neglected species.* Houston, TX: Gulf Press.

Nussbaum-Beach, S., & Hall, L. R. (2012). *The connected educator: Learning and leading in a digital age.* Bloomington, IN: Solution Tree Press.

Perkins, D. (2003). *King Arthur's round table: How collaborative conversations create smart organizations.* Hoboken, NJ: Wiley.

Pfeffer, J., & Sutton, R. I. (2000). *The knowing-doing gap: How smart companies turn knowledge into action.* Boston, MA: Harvard Business School Publishing.

Pike, R. W. (2003). *Creative training techniques handbook* (3rd ed). Amherst, MA: HRD Press, Inc.

Spencer, P. E., & Koester, L. S. (2015). *Nurturing language and learning: Development of deaf and hard-of-hearing infants and toddlers.* New York, NY: Oxford University Press.

Tate, M. (2004). *"Sit and get" won't grow dendrites: 20 professional learning strategies that engage the adult brain.* Thousand Oaks, CA: Corwin Press.

Vella, J. (2002). *Learning to listen, learning to teach. The power of dialogue in educating adults.* San Francisco, CA: Jossey-Bass.

3 Families: Partnerships in Practice

Marilyn Sass-Lehrer, Ann Porter, and Cheryl L. Wu

Sally Ann, a speech and language pathologist, has just met with a couple, Li and Sunny, who recently learned that their infant son is deaf. Li and Sunny moved to the United States from China for better job opportunities. They have lived in the United States for only a few months and have already secured satisfactory employment. They both understand and speak English at a conversational level, however, they are more comfortable using their native language of Mandarin Chinese. They want what is best for their son, Kevin, and are struggling to come to terms with what being deaf means and how this might impact their family. Both Li and Sunny are consumed by thoughts of what caused Kevin to be deaf and what they might be able to do to "fix" or "correct" his condition. They are worried about the stigmas surrounding disability in the Chinese community and are concerned that their families will encourage them to come home so that they can assist in taking care of Kevin.

When Sally Ann, the early intervention service coordinator, contacted Li and Sunny, they were surprised to learn that there were programs and services available to them. Sally Ann hopes to develop a good relationship with Sunny and Li and is aware that she knows very little about their cultural heritage and how they will respond to having a deaf child. She wants to help them understand Kevin's special qualities and develop the confidence they need to make the right decisions for Kevin, but frankly she doesn't know where to begin.

GUIDING QUESTIONS

1. How can early intervention specialists establish effective culturally responsive relationships with families? How might this differ from family to family?
2. How can early intervention specialists be culturally responsive in their interactions with families with different experiences, beliefs, and values?
3. What practices might the interdisciplinary team employ to support meaningful family involvement and informed decision making?
4. How might specialists collaborate to support families and promote their abilities to advocate for their children?

COMPETENCIES ADDRESSED IN THIS CHAPTER

1. Family-Centered Practices: Family–Professional Partnerships, Decision Making, and Family Support
2. Socially, Culturally, and Linguistically Responsive Practices including Deaf and Hard-of-Hearing Cultures and Communities; Sensitivity to and Respect for an Individual Family's Characteristics

---

INTRODUCTION

The work of the early intervention specialist begins with the family. Li and Sunny, the parents in the vignette for this chapter, are like other parents and caregivers of young deaf or hard-of-hearing children. They share the same hopes, dreams, and concerns that all families have: Will my child be safe, healthy, and happy? Will my child have friends? What kind of education will my child receive? Will my child find good employment and be able to take care of a family? Families with children who are deaf or hard of hearing, especially those who have no previous experience with what it means to be deaf have even more questions: How will we communicate with our child? What programs and services are available for our family? Would assistive technologies benefit our child? How will we know what is best for our child's future? Who will help us?

This chapter opens with a summary of the family's impact on early child development and family well-being. A discussion of the role of families in early intervention is followed by family involvement, the principles of family-centered practices, and family and professional partnerships. Next is an overview of family support and guidelines for informed family decision making. Families' cultural beliefs influence their perspectives on many issues from child rearing to participation in early intervention and, therefore, the importance of professionals' cultural competence is integrated throughout the chapter. The chapter concludes with advice for professionals.

FAMILIES' IMPACT DURING THE EARLY YEARS

Families and the Home Environment

Families are a powerful influence on their children's early development. Scientists regularly present new evidence on the importance of the earliest months and years of life and the capability of the infant brain (Schiller, 2010). Compelling scientific discoveries on early brain development emphasize the significance of the family and the home environment as the primary source for nurturing an infant's development. Early intervention programs focus on the family because they know that the quality of the home environment makes a significant difference in a child's development (Bodner-Johnson, 1986; Dickinson & Tabors, 2001; Hart & Risley, 1995; Meece, 2002).

Urie Bronfenbrenner (1979, 1986) developed a framework that provides professionals with insight into development through an understanding of the child's environment. Bronfenbrenner's ecological systems model describes the contexts that influence development and the transactional relationships among the people, the social and economic conditions, and the institutions in our environment. The family, a central component of Bronfenbrenner's ecological systems framework, has unique characteristics, structures, and relationships. Understanding familial relationships, cultural beliefs, and interactions with others in their communities, places of work, and other key settings provides professionals with insight into the child's environment and appreciation of the family's perspective.

Early intervention professionals need to be aware that each child is a part of a larger family system that may include extended family members and others who play significant roles in the life of the child. Lynch and Hanson (2011) remind professionals that "family" is not limited to the child's biological parents and may encompass an extended kinship network that is involved in the child's life in different ways and has varying roles related to child rearing, decision making, and the child's daily activities. Professionals need to ask families who they consider to be part of their extended family system and establish effective relationships with all of those who play an important role in the life of the child.

Changes that affect an individual or any part of the family system have an impact on all family members. For example, the birth of a baby, though typically a very welcome life event, can temporarily disrupt the family system and compel the family to reorganize as they accommodate this new family member. When the baby who is born shares the characteristics of other family members and the family's community, the newborn is assumed to fit into the existing family structure. Family members generally expect that changes needed to meet the demands of caring for a new baby will be manageable. When families discover that their baby is different from what they expected or has special needs, families need to make adaptations that impact everyone in the family.

Family reactions to the birth of a baby who is deaf or hard of hearing vary from disappointment to joy, sadness to relief, and denial to acceptance.

Professionals who have the skills to support families emotionally and are knowledgeable about children who are deaf or hard of hearing can go a long way toward minimizing family concerns and stress by optimizing the family's abilities to adapt to meet their child's developmental needs (Hintermair, 2006; Pipp-Siegel, Sedey, & Yoshinaga-Itano, 2002; Young & Tattersall, 2007; and Chapter 6, *Getting Started: Hearing Screening, Evaluation, and Next Steps*).

Building Relationships with Families

Having a new baby in a family can be overwhelming both physically and emotionally. The fact that Sunny and Li's son is deaf has practical implications that may strain their family's resources. For example, they must find time for appointments with specialists such as the audiologist and Ear, Nose, and Throat doctor and may need to figure out how to pay for hearing aids. The childcare plans they arranged prior to Kevin's birth may no longer be appropriate, and they may need to consider other arrangements that are further from home or more costly. In addition, Li and Sunny need information about what it means to be deaf or hard of hearing, about communication and available technologies, and about programs and services. Prior to Kevin's birth, they did not know anyone who was deaf other than Sunny's great uncle who gradually lost his hearing as an elderly man. Families often discover that family interactions, family resources, and parenting and support services change as they accommodate to the needs of a newborn who is deaf or hard of hearing (Jackson & Turnbull, 2004). Li and Sunny discovered that adapting to meet Kevin's needs had an effect on their work, budget, and family time together.

Getting to know the family and developing a trusting and mutually respectful relationship are the first steps for the early intervention team (Meadow-Orlans, Mertens, & Sass-Lehrer, 2003). The number of young children who are deaf or hard of hearing with diverse cultural, racial, ethnic, and socioeconomic characteristics is increasing whereas the number of professionals who are deaf or hard of hearing or have multicultural backgrounds remains low (Wu & Grant, 2013). Professionals with limited knowledge of families whose life experiences differ from their own may face challenges developing positive relationships with these families.

Having a deaf or hard-of-hearing child takes on different meanings for families. Whereas some families will readily accept that their child is deaf, others may believe that being deaf is a temporary situation that will go away over time, or that a cochlear implant or other medical treatment will "fix" the problem. Some families struggle with the belief that they hold some responsibility for their child's condition, or that their community will shun them or their child. Professionals must have the dispositions, knowledge, and skill sets to convey sensitivity and provide support that reflects an understanding of each family's unique experience.

To develop a mutually respectful relationship with Li and Sunny, Sally Ann must not only seek to understand their perspectives and the realities of their lives, but also examine her own beliefs and biases. Sally Ann has her own ideas about what would be best for Kevin and will need to acknowledge her biases and manage them appropriately. She and the other professionals on the team might discuss their perspectives about Li and Sunny's situation and how their biases might impact their relationship with the family. Families' values and beliefs stem from their life experiences and their culture, language, and communities. An intentional focus on Li and Sunny's values and beliefs and their vision for Kevin's future will enable the team to develop a positive relationship with the family and provide appropriate support in the areas that are most important to the family.

A Social Justice Framework adapted by Wu and Grant (2013) suggests a six-part model for working with culturally diverse families. Part I of this approach addresses cultural encounters and reflections. Table 3.1 illustrates a Social Justice Framework applied to the chapter vignette. The table describes both the content and process aspects of communication and interaction involved in a dynamic relationship. Content refers to "what" an individual wants to convey, that is, the information or guidance to be shared. Process refers to "the way" in which that information is conveyed. Developing a process of interaction that is compassionate, curious, and respectful of each others' values and roles helps build a strong relationship and supports the effectiveness of giving and receiving

Table 3.1 *Social Justice Framework Applied to Chapter Vignette[a]*

Stage Defined	Process	Content
Stage I Cultural Encounters and Reflections	What do I/my team bring to the relationship? Values, Perceptions, Goals, Knowledge, Lack of Knowledge, Cultural Resources What do we think/feel when we look at this family? What do we "think" are the family's Values, Perceptions, Goals, Knowledge, Lack of Knowledge, Cultural Resources What do we think the family thinks/feels when they look at us?	American and Chinese Perspectives Parenting Family Relationships Community Helping Professionals Education Disability Deaf/Hard of Hearing Communication Assistive Technology
Stage II Dialogue Among the Team with the Family	What cultural and language resources do I/my team and the family need? What are my/my team's goals, roles, and understanding of how our program works? What are the family's goals, roles, and their understanding of how their family functions? How does the family/team understand each other's goals?	Cultural and Language Resources Language Interpreters Cultural Mediators Chinese cultural agency, health or social services, church/spiritual home Chinese parents of deaf children Chinese deaf adults
Stage III Conceptualization	Clarify my/my team's understanding of the family's whole situation; goals, roles, family functioning, and their understanding of being deaf	

continued

Table 3.1 *Continued*

Stage Defined	Process	Content
Stage IV Action Planning for Social Justice	Engage in a dialogue with my team and the family to reach mutual agreement regarding the following: Decision making, coordination, communication regarding the plan Desired outcomes and goals Action plan and timelines Resources and supports desired (ensure equity and accessibility)	Capacity of all players and equity regarding power/control
Stage V Implementation, Experimentation, and Evaluation	Team and family follow the plan and adapt/modify it as needed Experiment with available resources Together identify accountability measures to ensure social justice and equity Evaluate it from all perspectives, i.e., child, family, team	What worked? What did not work? How do we know? What needs to be done differently?
Stage VI Recursive Process	Engage in dialogue with team and with family Reflect about what is different now compared with when we began to work together Go through previous steps to ensure continued understanding and clarify misunderstandings Consider how the partnership is developing and how it might improve	

[a]Adapted from Wu, C. L., & Grant, N. C. (2013). Multicultural deaf children and their hearing families: Working with a constellation of diversities. In C. C. Lee (Ed.), *Multicultural issues in counseling: New approaches to diversity* (4th ed., pp. 235–257) Alexandria, VA: American Counseling Association.

information (content), being able to work together, identifying issues and resources, and decision making.

Family Well-Being

The quality of an infant's early experiences is dependent in large measure upon the emotional and physical availability and responsiveness of the infant's primary caregivers (Pressman, Pipp-Siegel, Yoshinaga-Itano, Kubicek, & Emde, 2000). Caregiver and child attachment is crucial to early learning and development (Bowlby, 1988). Supportive and loving relationships between infants and their caregivers foster early brain development and establish a foundation of trust and security (Shore, 2003). Infants who feel safe, secure, and protected are more likely to feel confident enough to explore and interact with their environment than infants who do not feel secure.

Many factors can affect healthy socio-emotional attachment including individual child characteristics and caregiver and child communication proficiency (Traci & Koester, 2011). Attachment may be compromised if parents or caregivers are overwhelmed, depressed, or emotionally distracted and less responsive to the needs of their infants than if they were not. Although hearing parents and caregivers of deaf infants may at first find it challenging to interpret and respond appropriately to their deaf infants' behaviors, support from professionals, other families, and deaf adults can help them become more sensitive and responsive. For more information on responsive parenting with children who are deaf or hard of hearing, see Meadow-Orlans, Spencer, and Koester (2004). Families are resilient and with the help of other families, adults who are deaf, and professionals with specialized training are just as likely to form positive attachments with their children as hearing families with hearing children (Meadow-Orlans et al., 2004; Spencer & Koester, 2015).

Li and Sunny's overall sense of well-being will determine the extent to which they are able to provide a secure and nurturing home environment for Kevin to flourish. Family Quality of Life is defined by the Beach Center on Disability at the University of Kansas as ". . . the extent to which families' needs are met, family members enjoy their time together, and family members have a chance to do the things that are important to them" (Beach Center on Disability, 2014).

Making adaptations in everyday life brought about by having a child who is deaf or hard of hearing is a complex process for hearing families. Families need multiple layers of support that envelop them on their path to success. Although the meaning of success varies from family to family, the ability of each family to reach its goals will depend upon the capacity of the family to adapt to the unique needs of their child and family. A respectful and collaborative approach from all stakeholders in the system and an understanding of the important role that each one plays contribute to the well-being of the family and their confidence in their ability to raise a child who is deaf or hard of hearing [Global Coalition of Parents of Children Who Are Deaf and Hard of Hearing (GPOD), 2010b].

ROLE OF THE FAMILY AND POLICIES IN EARLY INTERVENTION

Prior to the full implementation of newborn hearing screening programs in many developed countries, it was usually the family who first realized that their child was unable to hear. A lack of knowledgeable professionals and resources frequently left the family without support or guidance. In many countries throughout the world in which newborn hearing programs are not yet established, it is still families who first discover their child is deaf, and the responsibility to find resources rests with them. (See Chapter 10, *Early Intervention in Challenging National Contexts*.)

Families have long been recognized as essential to the development of children who have developmental, communicative, or educational needs (Bailey, Raspa, & Fox, 2012; Bronfenbrenner, 1979; Dunst, Trivette, & Deal, 1988). In the United States, legislative policies and programs have institutionalized family participation and their rightful positions as advocates, decision makers, and partners with professionals (Turnbull, Turnbull, Erwin, Soodak, & Shogren, 2011). The 2004 amendments to the Individuals with Disabilities Education Improvement Act (IDEA) in the United States emphasized family participation in all aspects of early intervention programming. The legislation cites decades of research and experience demonstrating the positive effects on child outcomes through strengthening the family role and responsibility. IDEA provides supportive services for families that include for example, family training, managing assistive technologies, counseling, home visits, transportation, social work, sign language instruction, and providing families with information, skills, and other support [Individuals with Disabilities Education Improvement Act (IDEA), 2004]. (See Chapter 4, *Legislation, Policies, and Role of Research in Shaping Early Intervention* for more information about IDEA.) The Individualized Family Service Plan (IFSP), a requirement of IDEA, provides a process for family participation by including families as partners in the initial and ongoing assessment of their child, the identification of their child's needs and their family's priorities, and the selection of resources and services.

FAMILY INVOLVEMENT

Sally Ann's primary goal is to support and encourage Li and Sunny's involvement, and she questions where she should begin. Sally Ann might first expand her knowledge of family involvement and consider how her own values and beliefs influence the expectations she has for Li and Sunny. She might then explore Li and Sunny's perspective on family involvement including how they envision their involvement and how the interdisciplinary team can provide support to optimize their participation.

Family involvement is a partnership between families and the professionals with whom they work. It includes a range of behaviors that supports a child's development. A family's own educational experiences as well as their culture strongly influence the family's perception of the meaning of involvement and the manner in which they prefer to be involved. Consequently, a family's approach to engaging their child may be different, though equally nurturing and supportive, than the interactional practices suggested by a professional who has been influenced by a western, Euro-American cultural perspective. For example, some families are not comfortable playing with their children or play with their children in ways that are not familiar to professionals with cultural experiences different from a family's traditions. Trusting relationships with families require an understanding and appreciation of the social and cultural capital of families and their communities and avoiding assumptions about families based on their cultural heritage (Cohrssen, Church, & Tayler, 2009).

Family involvement has traditionally been understood from the perspective of teachers and schools. Families who were considered to be highly involved were those who volunteered in the classroom, chaperoned field trips, helped their children complete their homework, or were actively involved in the school's parent–teacher association. This limited view of family involvement continues in some communities today, but is no longer possible or relevant with increasing numbers of mothers in the workforce and growing social, cultural, and economic diversity. Extensive research on family involvement indicates that there are myriad ways in which families can make a difference in their child's early development and education.

Children whose families are highly involved in their development tend to have the best outcomes. Carter (2002) examined 70 studies of family involvement and identified several themes that reinforce the importance of family involvement throughout a child's school years. Many of the studies linked family involvement to improvements in achievement scores. An additional finding frequently noted in these studies was that despite the achievement differences that exist among children with diverse cultural, ethnic, and socioeconomic backgrounds, family involvement helped to close the achievement "gap." Henderson and Berla (1994) noted that rather than social status or income levels, the best indicators of achievement are the following:

- Parents who create a home environment that encourages learning
- Parents' expression of high educational expectations
- Parents' interest in and willingness to participate in their children's education, both at school and in the community

Professionals are charged to engage families in many different ways. Family–professional partnerships are crucial to ensure that strategies for family involvement reflect the diversity of families and the special characteristics of their children (Halgunseth, Peterson, Stark, & Moodie, 2009). Families that are highly involved in their children's early intervention program, in general, are better able to communicate with their children and contribute more to their children's progress than those who are not as actively involved (Calderon, 2000; Moeller, 2000).

Families with children who are deaf or hard of hearing are involved from the first day they learn of their child's hearing status. In addition to responsibilities associated with caring for a newborn, families must also arrange for appointments with specialists and obtain new information and skills that will maximize their interactions with their infants. This may be especially complicated when a family needs to consider things such as care for other children or family members, work schedules, or transportation. Families such as Li and Sunny discover that making appointments or following up with recommendations from specialists is even more difficult when information is not presented in their native language or in a culturally meaningful way (Sass-Lehrer, 2004).

As Sally Ann reflects on her views and understandings about family involvement, she must consider Li and Sunny's cultural context, life circumstances, resources, and competencies. Sally Ann should work with Li and Sunny to ensure that appointments are made at times that fit their schedules so that they can participate as much as possible. If transportation is a challenge, she could work with the social worker on her team to find community resources that are available. Because Li and Sunny are more comfortable with Mandarin than English, Sally Ann would need to work with them to explore appropriate language interpreters and translators and be sure all information is accessible to them. Li and Sunny are recent immigrants whose families live far away and are not available to provide support on a regular basis. She and others on the interdisciplinary team need to extend support that will enable them to develop the confidence and competence they need to be involved to the maximum extent possible.

Sarimski, Hintermair, and Lang (2012) examined the relationships among several variables including parental stress and satisfaction with early intervention services. The results of their investigation suggested that caregivers with stronger perceptions of their parenting competence reported lower levels of parent–child and family-related stress. These families also reported greater satisfaction with the professional support they received from their early intervention program. The researchers concluded that parental competence was associated with the ability of professionals to successfully involve families in early intervention and promote their sense of empowerment.

High levels of family involvement, along with the provision of timely and quality early intervention services, tend to be the strongest predictors of language outcomes for young deaf children (Moeller, 2000; Calderon, 2000). Professionals must be sensitive to each family's priorities and life-style, recognizing that family satisfaction and well-being are nourished by the family's ability to engage in the activities they love, and they should be encouraged to pursue their goals for themselves and their children (Moeller, Carr, Seaver, Stredler-Brown, & Holzinger, 2013).

FAMILY-CENTERED PRACTICE

Family-centered principles are a cornerstone of best practices in early intervention. Implementation of these principles requires recognition of the centrality of the family and support for family well-being as essential to the overall development of the child. In contrast to a more traditional approach that focuses on the child alone, a family-centered perspective focuses on the child within the context of the family (Lynch & Hanson, 2011). Family-centered practice is a philosophy or framework for working with families that includes a core set of beliefs and attitudes about families and implications for how early interventionists interact with families.

Family-centered tenets are reflected in the best practices of professionals in different disciplines including audiology, speech-language pathology, education, early childhood special education, counseling, social work, and many health-related fields. Allen and Petr (1996) identify three common elements as central to family-centered practice among these disciplines: (1) view the family as a unit of attention; (2) guide services through family choice and empowerment in decision making; and (3) focus on building strengths and capabilities of families.

Every stage of early intervention from newborn hearing screening and assessment to the implementation and monitoring of child and family outcomes reflects the central principles of family-centered practice. The quality of early intervention is largely dependent upon the professional's ability to put these principles into practice. Sally Ann may find the transition from a child-centered perspective to one that focuses on the child within the family unit to be a challenge. She accepts the principles of family-centered practice as summarized in Table 3.2; however, she is unsure how or if she can implement these while working with Li and Sunny. For example, it is very difficult for Sally Ann to accept that Li and Sunny, new parents with no knowledge of raising a deaf child, could possibly be considered "experts on their child." How will they know what is best for Kevin? She considers herself an expert on deaf children and believes strongly that young children must have early and consistent amplification. Suppose Li and Sunny decide that they do not want Kevin to wear his hearing aids in public and want to wait until Kevin is older. How could she respect their decision and how would she respond?

A deeper understanding of Li and Sunny's values and traditions would inform Sally Ann's response to issues such as wearing hearing aids in public or using sign language with Kevin. Many families, and especially more traditional Chinese families, are concerned about the stigma associated with having a child with a disability and may believe that hearing aids and sign language draw attention to their child being deaf and thus cause the family embarrassment. This kind of cultural information can shape how Sally Ann and the other members of the team discuss these issues with Li and Sunny.

Effectively implementing a family-centered approach requires both administrators and professionals to go beyond cultural sensitivity to being culturally responsive. Culturally responsive behaviors are demonstrated through both attitudes and actions (Tervalon & Murray-Garcia, 1998). Cultural competence implies the ability to "... think, feel and act in ways that acknowledge, respect, and build on ethnic-socio-cultural and linguistic ability" (Lynch & Hanson, 1993, p. 50). Becoming culturally competent is a process that requires ongoing learning from the families and others we work with as well as the courage and humility to recognize

Table 3.2 *Family-Centered Services: Guiding Principles and Practices*
for Delivery of Family-Centered Services[a]

Principle 1	The overriding purpose of providing family-centered help is family empowerment, which in turn benefits the well-being and development of the child.
Principle 2	Mutual trust, respect, honesty, and open communication characterize the family–provider relationship.
Principle 3	Families are active participants in all aspects of decision making. They are the ultimate decision makers in the amount, type of assistance, and the support they seek to use.
Principle 4	The ongoing work between families and providers is about identifying family concerns (priorities, hopes, needs, goals, or wishes), finding family strengths, and the services and supports that will provide necessary resources to meet those needs.
Principle 5	Efforts are made to build upon and use families' informal community support systems before relying solely on professional, formal services.
Principle 6	Providers across all disciplines collaborate with families to provide resources that best match what the family needs.
Principle 7	Support and resources need to be flexible, individualized, and responsive to the changing needs of families.
Principle 8	Providers are cognizant and respectful of families' culture, beliefs, and attitudes as they plan and carry out all interventions.

[a]Adapted from Iowa's Early ACCESS and Iowa SCRIPT (2004).

what we do not know and need to learn. Making mistakes, or responding in ways that we later recognize as insensitive or misguided, is part of
the learning process. Being culturally responsive implies the ability to
improve our behaviors when our words or actions are awkward or inappropriate. See Lynch and Hanson (2011) and the National Center for
Cultural Competence in the resources section at the end of this chapter.

   Implementing a family-centered approach can be challenging and
requires program administrators and professionals to examine their
beliefs and practices as they commit to ensuring program practices

that reflect these principles. In the scenario presented above, Sally Ann does not need to relinquish her professional role or avoid sharing the knowledge she has as an expert in the area of deaf education with Li and Sunny. She does, however, need to convey her respect for their views and understanding of their family situation as she works with them as equal partners to determine what will be best for Kevin and their family. Early intervention professionals who understand the family's cultural and linguistic context can better identify family strengths, needs, and preferred goals and adapt their help-giving strategies to fit the individual family (Lynch & Hanson, 2011).

Hintermair (2004, 2006) proposed a "resource oriented" approach that encourages professionals to identify and reinforce families' and children's resources and strengths. Strategies that build on families' strengths include ensuring that families have strong support networks available to them including other families with deaf children and adults who are deaf (Global Coalition of Parents of Children Who Are Deaf and Hard of Hearing, 2010b; Hintermair, 2000, 2006; Meadow-Orlans et al., 2003; Moeller et al., 2013).

Early intervention programs for children who are deaf or hard of hearing and their families in the United States, Australia, the United Kingdom, and many other countries embrace a family-centered perspective, although the implementation of these practices varies (Moeller et al., 2013). For example, although open communication between professionals and families is a tenet of family-centered practices, sharing information about topics such as immigration status, religious beliefs, marital status, or health issues could jeopardize access to services in some countries or geopolitical contexts.

Beginning and maintaining a family-centered approach can be challenging for both programs and professionals (Cohrssen et al., 2009). A study by Roush, Harrison, and Palsha (1991) in the United States found that professionals providing early intervention services to deaf or hard-of-hearing children and their families have struggled to implement a family-centered approach. The researchers proposed that although professionals believed in the philosophical underpinnings of family-centered practice the lack of specialized training and experiences working with families might have explained why professionals had difficulty putting them into practice. Their findings are supported by more recent studies of early intervention providers who support a family-centered philosophy, but in practice have difficulty involving families in specific aspects of the early intervention process (Ingber & Dromi, 2010) or are more child oriented than family focused (Dunst, Boyd, Trivette, & Hamby, 2002; Fleming, Sawyer, & Campbell, 2011; Peterson, Luze, Eshbaugh, Jeon, & Kantz, 2007).

The knowledge and skills for promoting family-centered practice, family–professional partnerships, decision making, and family support by professionals working with infants and toddlers who are deaf or hard of hearing and their families are listed in Appendix 1 of the Joint Committee on Infant Hearing (JCIH) Supplement (2013). (Also see Table 1.1 in Chapter 1, *What Every Early Intervention Professional Should Know,* for a listing of the knowledge and skills that are unique to professionals working with this population.)

Family–Professional Partnerships

Establishing effective family–professional partnerships is fundamental to implementing family-centered practice. Partnerships with families begin with developing positive relationships built on mutual respect and understanding (Kelly & Barnard, 1999). Sally Ann needs to consider not only how she will establish a trusting relationship with Li and Sunny, but also how her colleagues with expertise in other specialty areas will work with the family. She is optimistic that every member of the interdisciplinary team appreciates the value of partnering with families and will include Li and Sunny as equal partners on the team.

Collaboration among professionals on the team is essential to providing a cohesive and supportive professional network for the family (National Deaf Children's Society, 2002). Parents participating in early intervention programs in Israel responded to a questionnaire designed to assess their attitudes and beliefs about family-centered programming (Ingber & Dromi, 2010). The parents in this study emphasized their desire for more collaboration and support by a team that works together and with parents. Collaboration with professionals on the team may help Li and Sunny adjust to their son being deaf and what this means for their family situation (Shonkoff, Hauser-Cram, Krauss, & Upshur, 1992). Partnerships with professionals on the team may boost their family's ability to maximize Kevin's development in emotional, social, cognitive, communicative, and linguistic areas (Meadow-Orlans et al., 2003).

Turnbull et al. (2011) define partnership this way:

> Partnership refers to a relationship in which families (not just parents) and professionals agree to build on each others' expertise and resources as appropriate for the purpose of making and implementing decisions that will directly benefit students and indirectly benefit other members and professionals. (p. 137)

Turnbull et al. (2011) identified seven principles of family professional partnerships. These include (1) communication; (2) professional competence; (3) respect; (4) trust; (5) commitment; (6) equality; and (7) advocacy.

Families differ in the ways they choose to collaborate with the early intervention team. Although many families are eager to participate as partners, others are less comfortable taking on roles that they believe should be assumed by professionals. Previous experience with professionals and bureaucracies, as well as beliefs about the role of professionals, may influence a family's perceptions of authority and their relationship with professionals.

Family participation may also vary depending upon their situation and capabilities as well as their knowledge or perceived importance of an issue in relation to their priorities and goals. Li and Sunny may be highly engaged with the team to gather information about appropriate childcare arrangements, transportation, and costs so that Li can return to work as soon as possible. They may be highly involved for several weeks at a time and then feel a need to be less engaged for a while. Professionals must be sensitive to family priorities and other issues that may change how they interact with the team, or limit the time they devote to their child's early intervention programming. Respect for families varying levels and patterns of engagement supports family–professional partnerships.

Sally Ann should aim to establish a partnership with Li and Sunny that reflects sharing power *with* the family. Professionals who see themselves as experts may demonstrate behaviors that reflect *power over* the family. This approach may inadvertently discourage families from contributing their expertise and may diminish families' influence as partners. Although the balance of power in a partnership may shift in the direction of the professional or the family from time to time, the team should promote families' skills to build power *within* the family and ultimately develop every family's sense of empowerment (Creighton & Kivel, 2011).

Sally Ann might help Li and Sunny understand the potential benefit of hearing aids or sign language for Kevin while building power within the family. For example, rather than telling Li and Sunny that they must keep Kevin's hearing aids on 24/7 (exerting power over the family), she might instead discuss with Li and Sunny the possibility of identifying some times and places they would feel comfortable with Kevin wearing his aids. Initially, Kevin might wear his hearing aids only at meal times at home or when they are sharing stories with Kevin. Over time, Li and Sunny might begin to feel more comfortable and decide on their own to increase Kevin's hearing aid wearing time and expand the settings in which he is using his hearing aids. Sally Ann might also encourage Li and Sunny to attend a family play group with other Chinese families. Meeting other families who may also be concerned about using listening technology or sign language and have considered their potential benefits may help Li and Sunny make their own decisions about whether hearing aids and sign language might be helpful for Kevin. Partnerships are flexible in nature and with guidance and support families will gradually develop the confidence to make decisions that are in the best interest of their child and family.

Fathers and other significant male caregivers have traditionally been less directly involved in early intervention programming than mothers, and Sally Ann, along with her colleagues, will need to work closely with the family to ensure that every effort is made to encourage and support both parents' participation. A study by Calderon and Low (1998) found that deaf or hard-of-hearing children whose fathers were present during early intervention sessions demonstrated better outcomes, especially in language and prereading skills. Flexibility in programming that allows for scheduling of sessions at times that are convenient for the family is one way that early intervention providers can support participation by all members of the family (National Deaf Children's Society, 2006). If only one member of the family is able to be present during a home visit or a center-based program activity, Sally Ann, in partnership with the other family members, might consider the most effective ways of sharing the information and events that transpired. Sally Ann and others could video Kevin's interactions, and discuss how the family might include opportunities for Kevin to engage in similar activities as part of his daily routine at home or with his childcare providers. Video technology such as Skype or Face Time, photographs, and notes can help keep all family members informed and support their engagement.

Family Support

Parents and caregivers discover early that many of their natural parenting strategies for interacting with their infant or toddler rely on the ability to hear and often do not elicit the responses from their baby they expected. The inability of families to connect with their infants in very fundamental ways can challenge a caregivers' sense of confidence and competence. Families who feel competent and make accommodations that support and nurture their child's early communication are likely to witness successful communication interactions with their children. Pressman et al. (2000) found a relationship between maternal sensitivity and child language development in their study. Pipp-Siegel and Biringen (2000) suggest that professionals with high levels of expertise not only in areas related to communication and language, but also in the provision of social–emotional support, are likely to be able to provide families with the information and support they need to be emotionally available to their infants.

Although professionals often focus on the quantity of verbal exchanges in sign or spoken language between families and their deaf or hard-of-hearing children, it is essential not to lose sight of the importance of the quality of the relationship between family members, other caregivers, and their children. Professionals should avoid the tendency to assess the effectiveness of family–child interaction in terms of number of words or complexity of grammatical exchanges. The quality of interactions between families and their little ones is even more important than the quantity of words or signs that the baby hears or sees (Turgeon, 2013).

Families' competence and confidence in guiding their children's development are enhanced when professionals are able to provide families with appropriate and timely support (Dromi & Ingber, 1999; Hintermair, 2000, 2006; Meadow-Orlans et al., 2003; Young & Tattersall, 2007). Support comes in a variety of forms and early intervention professionals can work closely with families to determine the kinds of support that would be most helpful to them. Professionals as well as spouses, extended family members, other families with deaf children, and adults who are deaf or hard of hearing have been identified as significant sources of support for families (Hintermair, 2000; Meadow-Orlans et al., 2003). Professionals should be sensitive to the fact that some families may feel more comfortable turning to family members, friends, or others in their community for support than to professionals.

Family-to-Family Support

The Global Coalition of Parents of Children Who Are Deaf or Hard of Hearing (GPOD) conducted a worldwide online survey of families raising deaf or hard-of-hearing children. The purpose of the survey was to understand the support needs of families around the world. Responses from families indicated that both professionals and families who have "walked the road before them" play a valuable role in providing support and information to families (Global Coalition of Parents of Children Who Are Deaf and Hard of Hearing, 2010a). Meeting other families who have children who are deaf or hard of hearing, especially those who share similar cultural beliefs and experiences, may be especially helpful. Families value the emotional support and information provided by experienced family members and many families like to connect with these families soon after they have learned that their child is deaf.

Family support programs for families with deaf or hard-of-hearing children have been developed in several states in the United States as well as elsewhere around the world. One example of this type of program is the Hands & Voices *Guide-By-Your-Side Program*. The *Guide-By-Your-Side Program* ". . . is an innovative program designed to provide emotional support and specialized knowledge from trained families of children who are deaf or hard of hearing." Although many early intervention programs around the world provide family-to-family support or mentoring programs, they are often informal. (See the Recommended Resources at the end of this chapter.)

Support from Deaf and Hard-of-Hearing Adults

Families also benefit from support from adults who are deaf or hard of hearing who can help them understand the experiences of being deaf, provide families with resources in the community, encourage families to set high expectations for their children, and help them acquire communication skills using the native signed or spoken language of their country. Getting to know adults who are deaf or hard of hearing encourages families to see their children's strengths and focus on their abilities and possibilities rather than their needs or limitations. Hintermair (2000) found that families who had many contacts with other families with deaf or hard-of-hearing children and adults who are deaf experienced less isolation, stronger emotional connections with their child, and better acceptance of their child. Other researchers have found that families experience improved interactions with their child as a result of having meaningful interactions with deaf or hard-of-hearing adults (Watkins, Pittman, & Walden, 1998). Professionals who themselves are deaf are valuable members of the early intervention interdisciplinary team (Benedict & Sass-Lehrer, 2007). (See Chapter 5, *Collaboration with Deaf and Hard-of-Hearing Communities*.)

Families benefit by learning from deaf adults how to maximize access to visual information and incorporate visual strategies used by deaf adults with their deaf children to develop effective communication strategies and positive connections with their children (Mohay, 2000; Spencer, 2003). For example, research focused on deaf parents raising children who are deaf or hard of hearing provides an abundance of information on how parents who are deaf intuitively adapt their communicative interactions to match their young child's visual access to language (Koester, Papoušek, & Smith-Grey, 2000; Meadow-Orlans et al., 2004). Examination of the strategies used by deaf parents reveals that deaf parents use visual language, that is, the family's native signed language or non-verbal communication such as facial expressions, body language, and gestures, all of which serve to attract and hold their baby's attention. Their communication techniques emphasize the importance of attending to visual and auditory turn taking and managing divided attention. Meeting deaf adults with Chinese backgrounds might help Li and Sunny better understand the experience of being deaf in the context of their cultural beliefs and traditions. (See Chapter 8, *Collaboration for Communication, Language, and Cognitive Development*.)

INFORMED DECISION MAKING

Families are faced with numerous decisions soon after they learn that their child is deaf or hard of hearing. The first decision typically involves the use of listening technology. Will the child be fitted with hearing aids? What kind? One or two? And in places in which there is no financial support for hearing technologies, families wonder how they will be able to pay for this equipment. The audiologist working with the child and the family typically provides advice regarding the selection of listening technologies and may discuss the possibility of cochlear implants for children who appear to be good candidates for this technology. These initial choices lead to the next set of decisions that involve the communication modality(ies) and language(s) the family will use with their child. These decisions then inform the family's selection of early intervention services (Wainscott, Sass-Lehrer, & Croyle, 2008).

Families without prior knowledge of what it means to be deaf or hard of hearing often find making decisions on behalf of their children stressful (Meadow-Orlans et al., 2003). Professionals may inadvertently add to this stress by pressuring families to make decisions quickly without providing them with enough time to process information about the various opportunities and to determine what is best for their child.

Individual family situations such as the family's primary language, cultural beliefs, geographic location, access to information (e.g., internet), or the availability of specialized services (e.g., sign language) can make the decision-making process complicated. Family members who are deaf and communicate primarily in a native sign language may face challenges obtaining full information about the opportunities available for their children from professionals who lack the signing skills to communicate effectively with them or who make assumptions about what these families want for their children (Meadow-Orlans et al., 2003). Access to information also affects families whose spoken language is not the same as the majority language of their country and families who are unable to read available materials. Professionals need to consider how to provide information to families in a form that is easily understood.

Decision making, like many other processes, is highly influenced by cultural beliefs and values and may be different family to family. The more culturally competent and knowledgeable the professional team, the more insightful and skilled they will be in engaging families in an effective decision-making process. Professionals may assume that families lack the skills to make decisions that are appropriate for their families, when in fact, the processes they use and the decisions they make differ from those of the professionals. For example, some families' decisions about their children are a communal process that involves the extended family or members of the family's community rather than only the primary caregivers. Professionals must also be aware of their personal biases not only when providing information to families, but in their expectations for how families react to the information they receive, seek other opinions, or respond to professional guidance. Developing relationships with families and becoming acquainted with how they make decisions will aid professionals in providing meaningful support to families and help families understand the complexity of the issues surrounding technology, language, and communication opportunities. Families need information about all the possibilities and guidance on how to realize the futures they envision for their child and family.

Experienced professionals and evidence-based practice documents support informed decision making in the achievement of successful outcomes [Joint Committee on Infant Hearing (JCIH), 2007; Moeller et al., 2013; Young et al., 2006]. Informed decision making is a process that guides families as they fully consider the opportunities available for their children, supports their active participation in the process, and results in families believing that they have made good decisions on behalf of their children (Dunst et al., 1988; Moeller & Condon, 1994; Young et al., 2006). The professionals' role is to provide families with comprehensive, balanced, and accurate information, assist them in understanding the information, and help families make decisions that are appropriate for their children. (See documents in the Recommended Resources from the National Deaf Children's Society, University of Manchester, in the United Kingdom, *Early Support: Helping Every Child Succeed. Informed Choice, Families and Deaf Children: Professional Handbook.*)

Many families use the internet, including websites and blogs, to share information and find support (Porter & Edirippulige, 2007; Zaidman-Zait & Jamieson, 2004). Professionals can encourage families to seek a variety of reputable sources of information and help them weigh the relative benefits and limitations of the range of opportunities. Professionals can also facilitate contacts with other families with deaf or hard-of-hearing children and adults who are deaf or hard of hearing.

The GPOD survey found that families in developing countries placed a higher level of importance on professionals' opinions than other families in developed countries. Across the world, over one-third of families reported that they did not feel in control of the decisions made regarding communication and education, and one-third of all families have a difficult time letting professionals know if they disagree with their recommendations (Global Coalition of Parents of Children Who Are Deaf and Hard of Hearing, 2010a). Whereas professionals may be tempted to hurry families along and tell them what they believe is best for their child, this ultimately is not in the child's or the family's best interest. Families will be faced with many decisions through the early and later years of their child's development, and the skills they acquire early on will help them become effective decision makers and advocates for their children and families.

Professionals may think they know what is best for a child and family, and may inadvertently filter information provided or attempt to influence their decisions. Instead, families should have access to all information and have time to digest and evaluate the opportunities available. There is no "one size fits all," and each family needs to find the way that will best suit their child and family. A family-centered approach that respects and honors the family's knowledge and expertise will empower the family and build their capacity to make informed decisions throughout their child's early years.

GUIDELINES FOR WORKING WITH FAMILIES

Advice for Professionals and Program Administrators

The advice to professionals from families who participated in the National Parent Project (Meadow-Orlans et al., 2003) conducted in the United States aligns with other interviews and surveys of families with very young children who are deaf or hard of hearing (e.g., Global Coalition of Parents of Children Who Are Deaf and Hard of Hearing, 2010a; Ingber & Dromi, 2010; Jackson, 2011; Zaidman-Zait, 2007). The National Parent Project conducted a national survey of families with children between 6 and 7 years of age, including additional telephone, TTY,[a] or face-to-face interviews and focus groups. These families shared their experiences during the first few years of their child's life, and their recommendations for other families and professionals. The advice they offered to professionals is summarized in Table 3.3.

SUMMARY

Professionals have the responsibility of demonstrating that the early intervention services provided make a positive difference for children and their families. Programs and services should be aimed toward building family competence and helping families acquire the knowledge and

---

[a]A TTY is a text telephone that is used by many deaf and hard-of-hearing people. Video phones, Skype, and Face Time have replaced TTYs in many places around the world.

Table 3.3 *The National Parent Project Recommendations for Professionals*[a]

Listen to Us	Families emphasized time and again the importance of active listening skills. Families want professionals to "hear" them and acknowledge their issues and concerns.
Respect Our Opinions	Professionals may not always agree with a family's perspective, but families believe they are the experts when it comes to what they want and need for their family.
Respect Our Feelings	Families differ in their reactions and feelings about having a deaf child. Professionals sometimes have preconceived ideas about what families should feel and this may ultimately damage the relationship between the family and the professional.
Be Knowledgeable	Families expect professionals to have accurate and current information to share with them. If the professional does not know the answer to a question, families appreciate it when they acknowledge that they do not know. Families expect, however, the professional to obtain the information or help the family find the resources and information they want.
Be Honest	Although not all news is good news, families want professionals to tell them the truth as they know it at the time.
Tell Us Everything	Families do not want professionals to control the information they receive. They expect professionals to provide comprehensive information regardless of their own professional opinions. Families do not want professionals to decide when the family is "ready" to receive specific information. Professionals should ask families, rather than make assumptions, about what families want or need to know and when they need it.
Treat Us with Respect	Families do not like it when professionals seem to "talk down" to them. Families expect to be treated as the adults they are with years of experience to offer.

(continued)

Table 3.3 (*Continued*)

Provide Resources for Support	Families want professionals to connect them with other families with deaf children and to provide them with resources to extend their understanding and obtain additional support.
Be Patient with Us	Families want professionals to show patience with them. Understanding and adjusting to having a child who is deaf or hard of hearing are processes that take more time for some families than others. Families also change their minds as they acquire more information and learn more about their child. Learning everything they need to know and developing the skills to promote their child's early language (i.e., learning to sign or learning to support their child's listening skills) take time. Families want professionals to be patient with them along this journey.
Communicate Clearly (sign or spoken language, or through interpreters)	Families appreciate professionals who are good communicators, and who can explain information to them in ways they can understand. Families want professionals to be sensitive to their ability to process new information. Families would like information shared in a way that is most meaningful and accessible to them.

[a]Meadow-Orlans, K., Mertens, D., & Sass-Lehrer, M. (2003). *Parents and their deaf children: The early years*. Washington, DC: Gallaudet University Press.

skills they need to help their child develop and learn. Sally Ann recognized that to be an effective provider there are many sets of skills that she needs. Underlying her effectiveness is her ability to establish a trusting and mutually respectful relationship with Li and Sunny. This requires her commitment to developing cross-cultural competence not only as it relates to cultural, linguistic, educational, and economic diversity, but also regarding the many ways in which people embrace being deaf (Leigh, 2009). She will need to examine her beliefs and attitudes continuously, and be mindful of generalizations or judgments that affect her perceptions about what is best for every infant or toddler who is deaf or hard of hearing and their family.

Working in partnership with families is an interactive learning process that involves getting to know one another and developing a mutually caring relationship. Just as Li and Sunny will depend upon the early intervention team for critical information, resources, and guidance, the team of professionals will also rely on Li and Sunny to help them understand their unique experiences and how the team of professionals can help them realize their hopes and dreams.

A family strength-based focus will permeate all aspects of Kevin's early intervention programming from the initial screening through transition to preschool. The team will recognize Li and Sunny as the constant in their son's life, and Sally Ann and the others on the team as transitory. Li and Sunny will gradually acquire the information they need to understand Kevin's abilities and needs and how they can best support his development. Sally Ann will provide Li and Sunny with information and resources to help them understand what it means to be deaf. She will pay particular attention to Li and Sunny's needs for support and will connect them with other families who have deaf or hard-of-hearing children. She will also ensure that they have ample opportunities to develop meaningful relationships with adults who are deaf, including those with Chinese backgrounds. She will need to monitor how well they are doing as a family and how services might be improved to better meet their changing needs.

Sally Ann is in a privileged position as she embarks on this journey with Li, Sunny, and Kevin. As partners along on this journey, they will encounter many interesting and exciting experiences, some bumps in the road, and maybe even some detours. Ultimately, with the guidance and support of the whole team, Li and Sunny will acquire the confidence and competence they need to support Kevin's overall development and become strong advocates for him through his growing years.

SUGGESTED ACTIVITIES

1. View the TED talk by Author Andrew Solomon on his best selling book, *Far from the Tree* http://www.ted.com/talks/andrew_solomon_love_no_matter_what.html. Select three quotes that have special meaning to you and

your work with families with deaf or hard-of-hearing infants and toddlers. Identify sections from this chapter that relate to Dr. Solomon's research.

2. What does family involvement mean to you? Think about how your family was involved in your education, or if you have children, how you are involved with their education. How does your experience compare with the research findings and recommendations in this chapter?

3. Research a family support program that focuses on families with young children who are deaf or hard of hearing. Consider the feasibility of offering this type of program in your community. How would you determine family interest? What resources would you need? How would you determine their effectiveness?

   A Guide-by-Your-Side

   http://www.handsandvoices.org/services/guide.htm.

   Shared Reading Program

   http://www.gallaudet.edu/clerc_center/information_and_resources/info_to_go/language_and_literacy/literacy_at_the_clerc_center/welcome_to_shared_reading_project.html.

   Integrated Reading Program

   http://www.csdb.org/intergrated-reading-project/.

   Family Sign Language Program

   http://www.necc.mass.edu/gallaudet/programs/family-sign-language-program/.

4. Complete the "Circles of my Multicultural Self"

   Go to http://www.edchange.org/multicultural/activities/circlesofself_handout.html and complete the questions on this page. Then go to "Circles of my Multicultural Self" activity www.edchange.org/multicultural/activities/circlesofself.html.

   Complete activities 1–3. Next consider how stereotypes of various aspects of your identity have influenced you and your perceptions of others who share or have identities different from you.

RECOMMENDED RESOURCES

1. Alexander Graham Bell Association for the Deaf and Hard of Hearing

   This association supports the development of listening and spoken language. The AGBell website has an entire section devoted to families. http://www.agbell.org.

2. American Society for Deaf Children

   This association advocates for families with children who are deaf or hard of hearing and supports all language and communication opportunities. http://www.deafchildren.org.

3. Aussie Deaf Kids

   This association, based in Australia, provides information, resources, and support for families with children who are deaf or hard of hearing. http://www.aussiedeafkids.org.au.

4. Boystown Press

   Boystown Press disseminates books, DVDs, and other materials for families of children who are deaf, hearing, or hard of hearing. *The Home Team: Early Intervention Illustrated* DVD focuses on best practices for family involvement and family-centered early intervention. http://www.boystownpress.org/index.php/deaf-hard-of-hearing/early-intervention.html.

5. BANDTEC: A Network for Diversity Training

   BANDTEC's mission is to promote the creation of an equitable society for children and their families by providing a continuum of professional development and leadership in diversity issues among early education and care providers.

   Contact BANDTEC at bandtec@earthlink.net.

6. Fédération Européenne des Parents d'Enfants Déficients Auditifs

   FEPEDA is a nongovernmental umbrella organization that represents associations of parents and friends of deaf and hard-of-hearing children in Europe. Members include national and regional organizations as well as individuals and small groups from all over the European Union, Central and Oriental Europe, and the Community of Independent States.

   http://www.fepeda.net/.

7. Lynch, E. W., & Hanson, M. (2011). *Developing cross-cultural competence: A guide for working with children and their families* (3rd ed.). Baltimore, MD: Brookes Publishing Co. and Hanson, M., & Lynch, E. (2013). *Understanding families: Supportive approaches to diversity, disability, and risk* (2nd ed.). Baltimore, MD: Brookes Publishing Co.

   These two books address the knowledge, skill sets, and dispositions necessary to enhance early intervention professionals' abilities to provide culturally competent services to families with diverse backgrounds and challenging home or environmental conditions.

8. Hands & Voices

    Hands & Voices is a parent-driven organization with chapters in many states around the United States and around the world. For a description of the program *A Guide-by-Your-Side*, Go to http://www.handsandvoices.org/services/guide.htm.

9. National Center for Cultural Competence (NCCC)

    The mission of NCCC is to support the design, implementation, and evaluation of culturally and linguistically competent services. The Center provides information for programs and professionals including assessments, training, and resources. http://nccc.georgetown.edu/.

10. National Deaf Children's Society: *Informed choice, families and deaf children: Professional handbook.* London, England: University of Manchester. This document explores the concept of informed choice related to the decisions families make on behalf of their children and the role of professionals. http://dera.ioe.ac.uk/1929/1/informed%20choice%20families%20and%20deaf%20children%20-%20professional%20handbook.pdf.

11. National Deaf Children's Society: *Helping you choose: Making informed choices for you and your child.* London, England: University of Manchester. http://www.ihs.manchester.ac.uk/events/pastworkshops/2012/CHRN200312/handbook.pdf. This document explores the concept of informed choice from a family perspective.

REFERENCES

Allen, R. I., & Petr, C. G. (1996). Toward developing standards and measurements for family centered practice in family support programs. In G. H. S. Singer, L. E. Powers, & A. L. Olson (Eds.), *Redefining family support* (pp. 57–86). Baltimore, MD: Brookes Publishing Co.

Bailey, D., Raspa, M., & Fox, L. (2012). What is the future of family outcomes and family-centered services? *Topics in Early Childhood Special Education, 31*(4), 216–223. doi:10.1177/0271121411427077

Beach Center on Disability. (2014). *Family quality of life.* Retrieved from http://www.beachcenter.org

Benedict, B. S., & Sass-Lehrer, M. (2007). Deaf and hearing partnerships: Ethical and communication considerations. *American Annals of the Deaf, 152*(3), 275–282.

Bodner-Johnson, B. (1986). The family environment and achievement of deaf students: A discriminant analysis. *Exceptional Children, 52,* 443–449.

Bowlby, J. (1988). *A secure base.* London, England: Tavistock/Routledge.

Bronfenbrenner, U. (1979). *The ecology of human development.* Cambridge, MA: Harvard University Press.

Bronfenbrenner, U. (1986). Ecology of the family as a context for human development research perspectives. *Developmental Psychology, 22,* 723–742.

Calderon, R. (2000). Parental involvement in deaf children's education programs as a predictor of child's language, early reading, and social-emotional development. *Journal of Deaf Studies and Deaf Education, 5*(2), 140–155. doi:10.1093/deafed/5.2.140.

Calderon, R., & Low, S. (1998). Early social-emotional, language, and academic development in children with hearing loss. *American Annals of the Deaf, 143*(3), 225–234.

Carter, S. (2002). *The impact of parent/family involvement on student outcomes: An annotated bibliography of research from the past decade.* Eugene, OR: Consortium for Appropriate Dispute Resolution in Special Education.

Cohrssen, C., Church, A., & Tayler, C. (2009). *Victorian early years learning and development framework: Evidence paper.* Melbourne, Australia: University of Melbourne Department of Education and Early Childhood Development. Retrieved from https://www.eduweb.vic.gov.au/edulibrary/public/earlylearning/evi-familycentred.pdf.

Creighton, A., & Kivel, P. (2011). *Helping teens stop violence, build community and stand for justice* (2nd ed.). Alameda, CA: Hunter House.

Dickinson, D. K., & Tabors, P.O. (Eds.). (2001). *Beginning literacy with language: Young children learning at home and school.* Baltimore, MD: Brookes Publishing Co.

Dromi, E., & Ingber, S. (1999). Israeli mothers' expectations from early intervention with their preschool deaf children. *Journal of Deaf Studies and Deaf Education, 4*(1), 50–68. doi:10.1093/deafed/4.1.50.

Dunst, C. J., Boyd, K., Trivette, C. M., & Hamby, D. W. (2002). Family-oriented program models and professional helpgiving practices. *Family Relations, 51*(3), 221–229.

Dunst, C. J., Trivette, C., & Deal, A. (1988). *Enabling and empowering families: Principles and guidelines for practice.* Cambridge, MA: Brookline.

Fleming, J. L., Sawyer, L. B., & Campbell, P. H. (2011). Early intervention providers' perspectives about implementing participation-based practices. *Topics in Early Childhood Special Education, 30*(4), 233–244. doi:10.1177/0271121410371986.

Global Coalition of Parents of Children Who Are Deaf and Hard of Hearing (GPOD). (2010a, June). *Support needs of families: Results of a worldwide survey of parents of deaf and hard of hearing children.* Poster session presented at the Newborn Hearing Symposium, Como, Italy.

Global Coalition of Parents of Children Who Are Deaf and Hard of Hearing (GPOD). (2010b). *Position statement and recommendations for family support in the development of newborn hearing screening systems (NHS)/early hearing detection and intervention systems (EHDI) worldwide.* Retrieved from https://sites.google.com/site/gpodhh/Home/position_statement.

Halgunseth, L.C., Peterson, A., Stark, D.R., & Moodie, S. (2009). *Family engagement, diverse families, and early childhood education programs: An integrated review of the literature.* Washington, DC: National Association for the Education of Young Children.

Hart, B., & Risley, T. R. (1995). *Meaningful differences in the everyday experience of young American children.* Baltimore, MD: Brookes Publishing Co.

Henderson, A. T., & Berla, N. (1994). *A new generation of evidence: The family is critical to student achievement.* Washington, DC: Center for Law and Education.

Hintermair, M. (2000). Hearing impairment, social networks, and coping: The need for families with hearing-impaired children to relate to other parents and to hearing-impaired adults. *American Annals of the Deaf, 145*(1), 41–53.

Hintermair, M. (2004). Sense of coherence: A relevant resource in the coping process of mothers of deaf and hard-of-hearing children? *Journal of Deaf Studies and Deaf Education, 9*(1), 15–26. doi:10.1093/deafed/enh005.

Hintermair, M. (2006). Parental resources, parental stress, and socioemotional development of deaf and hard of hearing children. *Journal of Deaf Studies and Deaf Education, 11*(4), 493–513. doi:10.1093/deafed/enl005.

Individuals With Disabilities Education Improvement Act of 2004, 20 U.S.C. 33 § 1400 et seq. (2004). Reauthorization of the Individuals with Disabilities Education Act of 1990.

Ingber, S., & Dromi, E. (2010). Actual versus desired family-centered practice in early intervention for children with hearing loss. *Journal of Deaf Studies and Deaf Education, 15*(1), 59–71. doi:10.1093/deafed/enp025.

Iowa Early Access and Iowa Script. (2004). *Family-centered services: Guiding principles and practices for delivering family-centered services.* Retrieved from https://www.educateiowa.gov/sites/files/ed/documents/Family%20Centered%20Services.pdf.

Jackson, C. W. (2011). Family supports and resources for parents of children who are deaf or hard of hearing. *American Annals of the Deaf, 156*(4), 343–362.

Jackson, C. W., & Turnbull, A. P. (2004). Impact of deafness on family life: A review of the literature. *Topics in Early Childhood Special Education*, 24(1), 15–29. doi:10.1177/1525740108314865.

Joint Committee on Infant Hearing. (2007). Year 2007 position statement: Principles and guidelines for early hearing detection and intervention programs. *Pediatrics, 120,* 898–921. doi:10.1542/peds.2007-2333.

Joint Committee on Infant Hearing. (2013). Supplement to the JCIH 2007 position statement: Principles and guidelines for intervention after confirmation that a child is deaf or hard of hearing. *Pediatrics,131*(4), e1324–1349. doi:10.1542/peds.2013-0008.

Kelly, J., & Barnard, K. (1999). Parent education within a relationship focused model. *Topics in Early Childhood Special Education, 19*(9), 151–157.

Koester, L.S. Papoušek, H., & Smith-Gray, S. (2000). Intuitive parenting, communication, and interaction with deaf infants. In P. E. Spencer, C. J. Erting, & M. Marschark (Eds.), *The deaf child in the family and at school: Essays in honor of Kathryn P. Meadow-Orlans* (pp. 55–71). Mahwah, NJ: Lawrence Erlbaum Associates.

Leigh, I. W. (2009). *A lens on deaf identities.* New York, NY: Oxford University Press.

Lynch, E. W., & Hanson, M. J. (1993). Changing demographics: Implications for training in early intervention. *Infants and Young Children, 6*(1), 50–55.

Lynch, E. W., & Hanson, M. (2011). *Developing cross-cultural competence: A guide for working with children and their families* (3rd ed.). Baltimore, MD: Brookes Publishing Co.

Meadow-Orlans, K., Mertens, D., & Sass-Lehrer, M. (2003). *Parents and their deaf children: The early years.* Washington, DC: Gallaudet University Press.

Meadow-Orlans, K. P., Spencer, P. E., & Koester, L. S. (2004). *The world of deaf infants: A longitudinal study.* New York, NY: Oxford University Press.

Meece, J. L. (2002). *Child and adolescent development for educators* (2nd ed.). New York, NY: McGraw-Hill.

Moeller, M. P. (2000). Early intervention and language development in children who are deaf and hard of hearing. *Pediatrics, 106*(3), e43. doi:10.1542/peds.106.3.e43.

Moeller, M. P., Carr, G., Seaver, L., Stredler-Brown, A., & Holzinger, D. (2013). Best practices in family-centered early intervention for children who are deaf or hard of hearing: An international consensus statement. *Journal of Deaf Studies and Deaf Education, 18*(4), 429–445. doi:10.1093/deafed/ent034.

Moeller, M. P., & Condon, M. (1994). D.E.I.P.: A collaborative problem solving-approach to early intervention. In J. Roush & N. Matkin (Eds.),

Infants and toddlers with hearing loss: Family centered assessment and intervention (pp. 163–192). Baltimore, MD: York Press.

Mohay, H. (2000). Language in sight: Mothers' strategies for making language visually available to deaf children. In P. E. Spencer, C. J. Erting, & M. Marschark (Eds.), *The deaf child in the family and at school: Essays in honor of Kathryn P. Meadow-Orlans* (pp. 151–166). Mahwah, NJ: Erlbaum Associates.

National Deaf Children's Society. (2002). *Quality standards in the early years: Guidelines on working with deaf children under two years old and their families.* London, England.

National Deaf Children's Society. (2006). *Has any thought to include me? Fathers' perceptions of having a deaf child and the services that support them.* London, England.

Peterson, C. A., Luze, G. J., Eshbaugh, E. M., Jeon, H., & Kantz, K. R. (2007). Enhancing parent-child interactions through home visiting: Promising practice or unfulfilled promise? *Journal of Early Intervention, 29*(2), 119–140. doi:10.1177/105381510702900205.

Pipp-Siegel, S., & Biringen, Z. (2000). Assessing the quality of relationships between parents and children: The emotional availability scales. *Volta Review, 100*(5), 237–249.

Pipp-Siegel, S., Sedey, A. L., & Yoshinaga-Itano, C. (2002). Predictors of parental stress in mothers of young children with hearing loss. *Journal of Deaf Studies and Deaf Education, 7*(1), 1–17. doi:10.1093/deafed/7.1.1.

Porter, A., & Edirippulige, S. (2007). Parents of deaf children seeking hearing loss-related information on the internet: The Australian experience. *Journal of Deaf Studies and Deaf Education, 12*(4), 518–529. doi:10.1093/deafed/enm009.

Pressman, L., Pipp-Siegel, S., Yoshinago-Itano, C., Kubicek, L., & Emde, R. (2000). Comparison of the links between emotional availability and language gain in young children with and without hearing loss. In C. Yoshinaga-Itano & A. Sedey (Eds.), *Language, speech and social-emotional development of children who are deaf or hard of hearing: The early years* (pp. 251–277). Washington, DC: The Volta Review.

Roush, J., Harrison, M., & Palsha, S. (1991). Family-centered early intervention: The perceptions of professionals. *American Annals of the Deaf, 136*(4), 360–366.

Sarimski, K., Hintermair, M., & Lang, M. (2012). Parental self-efficacy in family-centered early intervention. [Zutrauen in die eigene Kompetenz als bedeutsames Merkmal familienorientierter Fruhforderung.] *Praxis Der Kinderpsychologie und Kinderpsychiatrie, 61*(3), 183–197.

Sass-Lehrer, M. (2004). Early detection of hearing loss: Maintaining a family-centered perspective. *Seminars in Hearing, 25*(4), 295–307.

Schiller, P. (2010, November/December). Brain development research review and update. *Exchange, 196,* 26–30.

Shonkoff, J. P., Hauser-Cram, P., Krauss, M. W., & Upshur, C. C. (1992). Development of infants with disabilities and their children. *Monographs of the Society for Research in Child Development, 57*(6), serial no. 30.

Shore, R. (2003). *Rethinking the brain: New insights into early development.* Chicago, IL: Families and Work Institute.

Spencer, P. E. (2003). Parent-child interactions: Implications for intervention and development. In B. Bodner-Johnson & M. Sass-Lehrer (Eds.), *The young deaf or hard of hearing child: A family-centered approach to early education* (pp. 333–368). Baltimore, MD: Brookes Publishing Co.

Spencer, P. E., & Koester, L. S. (2015). *Nurturing language and learning: Development of deaf and hard-of-hearing infants and toddlers.* New York, NY: Oxford University Press.

Tervalon, M., & Murray-Garcia, J. (1998). Cultural humility versus cultural competence: A critical distinction in defining physician training outcomes in multicultural education. *Journal of Health Care for the Poor and Underserved, 9*(2), 117–125.

Traci, M., & Koester, L. S. (2011). Parent-infant interactions: A transactional approach to understanding the development of deaf infants. In P. Nathan, M. Marschark, & P. E. Spencer (Eds.), *The Oxford handbook of deaf studies, language and education, Volume 1* (2nd ed., pp. 200–213). New York, NY: Oxford University Press.

Turgeon, H., (2013). *The science of talking to your baby (and what no one tells you).* Retrieved from http://www.babble.com/baby/the-science-of-talking-to-your-baby/.

Turnbull, A. P., Turnbull, R., Erwin, E., Soodak, L., & Shogren, K. (2011). *Families, professionals and exceptionality: Positive outcomes through partnership and trust* (6th ed.). Boston, MA: Pearson.

Wainscott, S., Sass-Lehrer, M., & Croyle, C. (2008, March). *Decision making process of EHDI families.* Paper presented at the Early Hearing Detection and Intervention Conference, New Orleans, LA.

Watkins, S., Pittman, P., & Walden, B. (1998). The deaf mentor experimental project for young children who are deaf and their families. *American Annals of the Deaf, 143*(1), 29–34.

Wu, C. L., & Grant, N. C. (2013). Multicultural deaf children and the hearing families: Working with a constellation of diversities. In C. C. Lee (Ed.),

Multicultural issues in counseling: New approaches to diversity (4th ed., pp. 235–257). Alexandria, VA: American Counseling Association.

Young, A., Carr, G., Hunt, R., McCracken, W., Skipp, A., & Tattersall, H. (2006). Informed choice and deaf children: Underpinning concepts and enduring challenges. *Journal of Deaf Studies and Deaf Education, 11*(3), 322–336. doi:10.1093/deafed/enj041.

Young, A., & Tattersall, H. (2007). Universal newborn hearing screening and early identification of deafness: Parents' responses to knowing early and their expectations of child communication development. *Journal of Deaf Studies and Deaf Education, 12*(2), 209–220. doi:10.1093/deafed/enl033.

Zaidman-Zait, A. (2007). Parenting a child with a cochlear implant: A critical incident study. *Journal of Deaf Studies and Deaf Education, 12*(2), 221–241. doi:10.1093/deafed/enl032.

Zaidman-Zait, A., & Jamieson, J. R. (2004). Searching for cochlear implant information on the internet maze: Implications for parents and professionals. *Journal of Deaf Studies and Deaf Education, 9*(4), 413–426. doi:10.1093/deafed/enh046.

4 Legislation, Policies, and Role of Research in Shaping Early Intervention

Barbara Raimondo and Christine Yoshinaga-Itano

Mr. and Mrs. Zilmer, who live in the eastern part of the United States, would like both speech-language therapy services for their 12-month-old child, Amanda, and American Sign Language[a] (ASL) instruction for Amanda and the whole family. They have heard that there are benefits to having children learn both spoken language and ASL, and they don't want to limit Amanda's language access or development. The Zilmers are unaware of their rights, legislative requirements, or research on this topic and ask their service coordinator, Lou Ann, if this makes sense to her and if it is allowable. Lou Ann is not an expert in listening and spoken language development or ASL, and this is the first family with a deaf child with which she has worked. She wants to do whatever she can to facilitate Amanda's development and support the Zilmers, but is not sure of the resources available.

---

[a]American Sign Language is the visual–gestural language of the Deaf Community in the United States and parts of Canada. Each country has one or more signed languages. Signed languages, like spoken languages, have linguistic structure and grammatical rules.

GUIDING QUESTIONS

1. What services does the law require to be provided to deaf and hard-of-hearing children and their families in the United States? In what ways can law and policy be enhanced?
2. What does the evidence say regarding the use of different language and communication modalities with deaf and hard-of-hearing children?
3. What constitutes "best practice" in early intervention for deaf and hard-of-hearing children and their families?

COMPETENCIES ADDRESSED IN THIS CHAPTER

1. Professional and Ethical Behavior: Fundamentals of early intervention practice, legislation, policies, and research
2. Language Acquisition and Communication Development: Typical Development, Communication Approaches Available to Children with Hearing Loss, and Impact of Hearing Loss on Access to Communication

INTRODUCTION

Mr. and Mrs. Zilmer's request for early intervention services that will promote Amanda's development and support the family strikes at the main purpose of early intervention. The Zilmers were fortunate that Amanda's hearing levels were identified early, giving them ample opportunity to learn what is known about early intervention programs, explore the language and communication opportunities available, and understand their rights to services. This chapter summarizes the landscape of laws and policies related to early intervention programs and services for infants and toddlers who are deaf or hard of hearing in the United States. Evidence-based practices are presented along with implications for early intervention providers and program leaders. The chapter addresses special issues that impact the quality of programming and the rights of children and families regarding language and communication development.

EARLY HEARING DETECTION AND INTERVENTION (EHDI) LEGISLATION IN THE UNITED STATES

EHDI systems were established to prevent language and other developmental delays that result when a deaf or hard-of-hearing child is identified late and does not receive appropriate early intervention from specialized providers. Families such as the Zilmers, with very young deaf children, have a different experience today than most families 15 or 20 years ago. Prior to the establishment of EHDI systems, the average age of identification of a deaf child was 2½ years old. Hard-of-hearing children were often identified later. Each state in the United States has established an EHDI system based on the principles of 1-3-6: screening by age 1 month, identification by 3 months, and early intervention by 6 months [Joint Committee on Infant Hearing (JCIH), 2007]. The establishment of EHDI systems grew out of research that demonstrated that children who were identified by 6 months and received appropriate early intervention specific to their needs as a deaf or hard-of-hearing child from a qualified provider attained language outcomes within the normal range of development. These outcomes were significantly better than for those children who did not have similar benefits (Yoshinaga-Itano, Sedey, Coulter, & Mehl, 1998).

Funding in the United States for these programs is provided, in part, through the Early Detection, Diagnosis, and Treatment Regarding Hearing Loss in Newborns and Infants Act (42 U.S.C. § 280g-1) first passed in 1999 and reauthorized in 2010.[1] This Act is commonly referred to as the Early Hearing Detection and Intervention (EHDI) Act. For states to receive funds through this law their practices and policies must conform to the Act's requirements. The Act envisions a collaborative effort around supporting families and children. For example, the Act defines "early intervention" in two ways:

1. "Early intervention includes referral to and delivery of information and services by schools and agencies, including community,

consumer, and parent-based agencies and organizations and other programs mandated by [P]art C of the Individuals with Disabilities Education Act [20 U.S.C. §1431 *et seq.*], which offer programs specifically designed to meet the *unique language and communication needs* [emphasis added] of deaf and hard-of-hearing newborns, infants, toddlers, and children."

2. "The term 'early intervention' refers to providing appropriate services for the child with hearing loss … and ensuring that families of the child are provided comprehensive, consumer-oriented information about *the full range of family support, training, information services, and language and communication options and are given the opportunity to consider and obtain the full range of such appropriate services, educational and program placements*, [emphasis added] and other options for their child from highly qualified providers" [42 U.S.C. § 280g-1(e)(3)].

The United States EHDI law requires relevant federal agencies, including the Centers for Disease Control and Prevention (CDC) and the National Institutes of Health (NIH), to coordinate and collaborate with a range of stakeholders in the development of policy and the implementation of this law. Stakeholders include "consumer groups of and that serve individuals who are deaf and hard-of-hearing and their families; … persons who are deaf and hard-of-hearing and their families; other qualified professional personnel who are proficient in deaf and hard-of-hearing children's language and who possess the specialized knowledge, skills, and attributes needed to serve deaf and hard-of-hearing newborns, infants, toddlers, children, and their families …" [42 U.S.C. § 280g-1 (c)(1)].

The EHDI legislation envisions systems at the local, state, and national levels that support collaboration with diverse groups of people with different areas of expertise and experiences who can provide guidance and advice. The reason for this is to ensure that the systems are sensitive to the needs of families and children and are as effective as they can be. However, the law does not provide outcome measures or guidelines for monitoring these requirements, so it is not possible to know how effectively these mandates are being carried out. Only anecdotal evidence is available to gauge how well agencies carry out these collaboration mandates.

At the state level, state advisory panels, committees, or councils provide recommendations to their respective state's EHDI systems. Because each member of the advisory committee brings a particular perspective, it is important that members of the advisory committee represent all stakeholder groups. Some states mandate the composition of membership of the state advisory panel. For example, the state of Maryland EHDI law requires its advisory council include a representative of the school for the deaf and a representative from the state association of the deaf, as well as two parents of deaf or hard-of-hearing children, and others (Maryland Health-Gen Code § 13-603).

Most states do not include such a requirement. In some states there is an informal practice of including at least one deaf or hard-of-hearing person on the advisory panel. Although this is a step in the right direction, all EHDI state systems should strive to be responsive to the life experiences of people who are deaf or hard of hearing by ensuring their participation on state advisory panels. In keeping with the intent of the United States federal EHDI law, all states should take steps to ensure that their panels are inclusive of deaf and hard-of-hearing community members. Without the participation of deaf or hard-of-hearing individuals, state advisory panels miss out on important information and perspectives that can help them better serve families such as the Zilmers.

EARLY INTERVENTION LEGISLATION

"Part C" is the early intervention section of the United States Individuals with Disabilities Education Act (IDEA). IDEA governs the education of eligible children with disabilities and authorizes services in every state to serve deaf and hard-of-hearing infants and toddlers and their families. The intent of Part C is to identify the desired outcomes for children and families and to make available the services and supports they need to achieve those outcomes. It is worth noting that some states recognized the need for early intervention programs for deaf babies in the early 1970s, well before the passage of Part C in 1986 (Bruce & Illinois State University, 1986).

Eligibility

For families such as the Zilmer family to be eligible for early intervention services under Part C of IDEA, their infant or toddler must have a developmental delay or diagnosed condition, such as a "sensory impairment," that has a "high probability of resulting in developmental delay" (34 C.F.R. § 303.21). There is wide state-to-state variability (Uhler, Thomson, Cyr, Gabbard, & Yoshinaga-Itano, 2014) regarding the eligibility of children with hearing in the mild range and with unilateral hearing predominantly due to states' interpretation regarding the amount of developmental delay needed to qualify for services. However, this may not be the best approach. A committee convened by the IDEA Infant and Toddler Coordinators Association and the National Center for Hearing Assessment and Management (2011) notes "There is abundant evidence that permanent hearing loss of any degree and configuration results in developmental delays if appropriate early intervention is not provided" (p. 2). They state, "Ideally, Part C eligibility guidelines would encompass all infants with permanent hearing loss of any degree for either ear" (p. 3). Amanda's hearing levels are in the severe to profound range, making her eligible for services in her state.

Individualized Family Service Plan

When the Zilmers were referred to early intervention, an Individualized Family Service Plan (IFSP) for Amanda and the family was developed. The IFSP is a written plan that outlines the services families and children will receive. It is based on information about the child and family and is written by a multidisciplinary team that includes professionals with at least two different disciplinary areas of expertise that relate to the child's needs and the priorities and concerns of the family. The IFSP is evaluated once a year and is reviewed every 6 months, or more if needed or if the family requests. Before the IFSP was developed, the Zilmers participated in the following:

1. A multidisciplinary assessment of Amanda and identification of services appropriate to meet her needs. Appropriate qualified personnel

working with the team assessed her cognitive development, physical development, including vision and hearing, communication, social–emotional development, and adaptive development.

2. A family-directed assessment of the resources, priorities, and concerns of the Zilmers. This was based on discussions with the family. At their discretion the Zilmers shared with the multidisciplinary team the resources they have to support Amanda's development, for example, the family's skills, support from extended family, and access to information. The Zilmers expressed their priorities for Amanda, such as developing age-appropriate language in spoken language and sign language, and meeting other developmental milestones.

   The Zilmer family explicitly requested spoken language and ASL services. As equal members of the IFSP team their priorities needed to be considered. The family also shared concerns. For example, they were worried about locating quality childcare providers who would be skilled in communicating with deaf or hard-of-hearing toddlers.

3. Identification of the supports and services necessary to help the Zilmers meet the needs of their child.

Services offered under IDEA (Part C) include (1) family training, counseling, and home visits; (2) special instruction; (3) speech-language pathology and audiology; (4) sign language and cued language services[b]; (5) vision services; (6) assistive technology devices (such as hearing aids) and assistive technology services; and (7) other services (34 C.F.R. § 303.13).

The IFSP also must include the "name of the service coordinator from the profession most relevant to the child's or family's needs" [34 C.F.R. § 303.344(g)(1)]. In this case, Lou Ann is not from a deaf education background and thus does not meet this criterion. When service coordinators are not familiar with the language and communication development

---

[b] Cued Speech or Cued Language is a phonemically based visual communication system that uses hand shapes and hand positions with spoken English or other spoken languages as a supplement to speechreading

of deaf and hard-of-hearing infants and toddlers it becomes more difficult to for them to identify and help obtain the necessary services. (See Chapter 9, *Individualized Family Service Plans and Programming*, for more information.)

Natural Environments

According to Part C, services must be provided in the "natural environment" to the "maximum extent appropriate" and provided in other settings only when "early intervention services cannot be achieved satisfactorily in a natural environment" (34 C.F.R § 303.126). If services are not provided in the natural environment, a "justification" must be written [34 C.F.R. § 300.344(d)(1)(II)(A)]. Natural environments are "settings that are natural or typical for a same-aged infant or toddler without a disability," and "may include the home or community settings" (34 C.F.R. § 303.26). Lou Ann was aware of a specialized program for deaf and hard-of-hearing infants and toddlers in the area but was concerned that it did not meet the legal definition of natural environment. The program provided a "play group" twice a week for deaf and hard-of-hearing children run by teachers of the deaf, speech-language pathology services, audiology services, and family classes, including sign language classes. It also provided services in the home. She believed this program met the needs of Amanda and her family.

In 2006, the Joint Committee of the American Speech-Language-Hearing Association (ASHA) and the Council on Education of the Deaf (CED) provided clarification and recommendations on selecting natural environments for families and their young deaf or hard-of-hearing children. The Committee stated, in part:

> Natural environments for deaf or hard-of-hearing infants and toddlers are environments that include family members and caregivers, are developmentally appropriate, and provide direct communication with adults and peers through one or more fully accessible natural languages (e.g., American Sign Language,

spoken English, or Spanish). Natural signed and spoken languages are languages that originate and develop over time through ongoing social interaction among members of a cultural community. Natural environments include the home, childcare center, school, or other settings where the child's language(s) and communication modality (or modalities) are used by fluent adult users and where peers are using and/or acquiring the same languages through similar modalities. Natural environments should be easily accessible to families and provide opportunities for families to meet with professionals who are knowledgeable about language and communication development in children who are deaf or hard of hearing and to interact with other families who have similarly developing children, whether hearing, deaf or hard of hearing. Natural environments for infants and toddlers who are deaf or hard of hearing and their families should be places where all have full access to language and communication through visual, auditory, and/or tactile communication systems specific to that child and family. [American Speech-Language-Hearing Association (ASHA) and the Council on Education of the Deaf (CED) Joint Committee, 2006.]

Evidence-Based Practices in Early Intervention

Lou Ann, the Zilmer's service coordinator, in collaboration with specialists whose expertise is in working with infants and toddlers who are deaf or hard of hearing and their families, has the responsibility of understanding, sharing, and implementing recommendations for best practice in early intervention. An important question for families is how they will be able to determine whether an early intervention program is providing services that follow best practices. Buysse, Wesley, Snyder, and Winton (2006) offer the following definition for evidence-based practice for the early childhood profession field: "Evidence-based practice is a decision-making process that integrates the best available research evidence with family and professional wisdom and values" (p. 12). They recommend using the best available research evidence, professional expertise, defined as one's craft knowledge and experience, and family and consumer values that take into account their beliefs and expectations in making decisions.

In a 2010 publication *Evidence-Based Practice in Educating Deaf and Hard-of-Hearing Students*, Spencer and Marschark (2010) address the challenge of applying evidence-based practices in the field of deaf education. They suggest that because of the inherent limitations and gaps in the research available, consensus across findings from divergently conducted studies with diverse populations might be used to develop conclusions on issues related to early intervention as well as other issues in the education of deaf children (Spencer & Marschark, 2010). In fact, two consensus documents on best practices in early intervention published in 2013 developed a set of goals and recommendations for early intervention programming from the existing evidence with teams of experts that included family members, professionals, and people who are deaf. These documents are discussed below.

Child Outcomes and Quality of Early Intervention

Research in the United States with programs that have specialized early intervention programs has shown that early identification and effective intervention can result in significantly better outcomes (Moeller, 2000; Yoshinaga-Itano et al., 1998). The Zilmers should expect Amanda to make progress across all developmental domains given comprehensive services provided by well-qualified specialists. The early intervention program should provide the Zilmers with the information and guidance that will give Amanda the best opportunity to obtain age-appropriate outcomes in all developmental areas including language and communication.

Studies that have demonstrated strong communication development in their early-identified populations had early intervention providers with a high level of knowledge and expertise demonstrated by their professional training, their experience working with children who are deaf or hard of hearing and their families, and their on-going in-service education participation (Moeller, 2000; Yoshinaga-Itano et al., 1998). These programs provided mentoring from specialists for the early intervention providers, as well as ongoing progress monitoring with assessment tools that had normative data on children with typical development, provided strong family support, and could demonstrate a high level of family involvement. They also provided families with opportunities to interact with individuals and professionals who are deaf or hard of hearing. Children who have developed strong communication skills by the age of 3 years have developed these skills because of the high quality of their early intervention support and their family's involvement.

Early Intervention Services and Provider Qualifications

The goal of early intervention for deaf and hard-of-hearing infants and toddlers is to prevent developmental delay. Infants and toddlers with or without a cognitive or other developmental delay should be expected to achieve outcomes much like those of their hearing peers with similar characteristics (Yoshinaga-Itano et al., 1998), but only when appropriate and immediate early intervention services are provided by highly qualified providers knowledgeable in early childhood and the implications of being deaf or hard of hearing.

IDEA requires states to have available adequately trained personnel to serve children under Part C and their families. Part C of IDEA mandates that early intervention services "meet the standard of the State in which the services are provided" [20 U.S.C. § 1432 (4)(D)]. For example, a state may require early interventionists providing speech-language pathology services to meet certain licensure requirements.

IDEA provides a list of "qualified personnel," including special educators, speech-language pathologists and audiologists, occupational therapists, and others [34 C.F.R. § 303.13(c)]. IDEA also requires states to include, as a statewide system component, a "comprehensive system of personnel development" (34 C.F.R. § 303.18). This system must include the preparation of early intervention providers who are "fully and appropriately qualified to provide early intervention services" under Part C (34 C.F.R. § 303.118).

Qualified American Sign Language and Spoken Language Service Providers

Lou Ann wants to support the Zilmer's request for ASL instruction. However, she has learned that her state—and other states—do not have a formal designation or certification process for teaching ASL to families and is not sure how she will know if the teaching is effective. To follow best practice protocols for early intervention, states should introduce standards for the instruction of ASL to families and young children, especially if there is no professional designation for teaching ASL to infants, toddlers, and families.

The Joint Committee on Infant Hearing (JCIH) is composed of experts from audiology, pediatrics, otolaryngology, speech-language pathology, and deaf education in the United States and periodically issues best practices documents to guide the field. JCIH position statements and best practices documents are unique because they have received the endorsement of the educational, medical, audiological, and speech and language participating organizations. Although the recommendations are not binding, hearing screening and early intervention programs use them in establishing and improving their programs. The *Supplement to the Joint Committee on Infant Hearing (JCIH) 2007 Position Statement* (2013), a best practice document specific to early intervention services for infants who are deaf or hearing (see below), seeks to address the lack of qualified sign language instruction to families by establishing the following goal: "Intervention services to teach ASL will be provided by professionals who have native or fluent skills and are trained to teach parents/families and young children" (e1329). It further recommends that states (1) "identify collaborative partners who can assist in the development of statewide systems capable of providing competent sign language instruction to families and their infants/children"; (2) "establish a representative committee that develops guidelines related to the qualifications of sign language instructors" (e 1330); and (3) implement steps to establish a mechanism for monitoring quality.

Early intervention specialists from different disciplines, including audiologists, speech language pathologists, physicians, psychologists, and social workers, rarely possess the level of fluency in ASL to provide ASL instruction to families. The Zilmers live in a state in which there are no guidelines for competent sign language instructors and should request an ASL instructor for their family who is a native or fluent user of ASL.

Early intervention specialists also generally lack sufficient training in the development of listening and spoken language of infants and toddlers who are deaf or hard of hearing. The *Supplement to the JCIH 2007 Position Statement* (2013) states in Goal 3b, "Intervention services to develop listening and spoken language will be provided by professionals who have specialized skills and knowledge" (e1330). Unfortunately, most families with newly identified children who are deaf or hard of hearing have early intervention providers who do not have specialized skills in either listening and spoken language or in the early development of visual communication (Arehart, Yoshinaga-Itano, Gabbard, Stredler-Brown, & Thomson, 1998).

Early intervention systems should address gaps in training at all levels in the following manner: (1) establish professional development programs designed to upgrade the skills of early intervention providers in the areas of listening and spoken language; (2) hire early interventionists who are fluent in ASL and provide ongoing professional development to enhance the ASL skills of all professionals; and (3) implement a mentorship program with supervised observations to ensure quality of services in listening and spoken language and visual language learning.

Early Intervention System Accountability

As with EHDI, the specific way Part C is implemented varies from state to state. In some states the lead agency is a health department and in others it is an education department. However, the quality of the early intervention available to families is less dependent upon which is the lead agency and is related more to the expertise and knowledge of the personnel responsible for early intervention programming. As mentioned, each United States state has enacted its own regulations for Part C implementation resulting in different child eligibility criteria, specialized resources, and professional expertise available. Services may also vary from one local district to another. Parents' and children's rights under Part C are protected by a series of procedural safeguards, which include protection of confidentiality, right to consent to or decline services, notice explaining the actions of the Part C agency pertaining to the child, and dispute resolution options, including mediation and filing a formal complaint.

The United States Department of Education has established a system to monitor state compliance with IDEA Part C, requiring states to collect data and report on 14 indicators (United States Department of Education Office of Special Education Programs, n.d.).[2] Unfortunately, the indicators are quite broad, and provide very little information on or accountability for infants and toddlers who are deaf or hard of hearing and their families. States are not required to report data based on the child's hearing status or an identified disability category. Currently there is no national database tracking either long-term or short-term outcomes for these children.

However, research known as NECAP (National Early Childhood Assessment Project: Deaf/Hard of Hearing) is establishing state-wide databases on developmental outcomes. The purpose of this project was to establish state databases of the development of children receiving early intervention services. Currently, 15 states are actively attempting to create state outcome databases and to report it on their EHDI databases (Yoshinaga-Itano & Sedey, 2013). State outcome data will lead to the development of a national database and provide an important measure for how well states support the language development of their deaf or hard-of-hearing infant and toddler populations.

Transition from Early Intervention to Part B of IDEA

Once Amanda turns 3 years old, she may or may not be eligible for services under Part B of IDEA. Part B is the section of the law that covers children ages 3–21 years old. Similar to Part C, Part B is designed to address the academic, developmental, and functional needs of the child [34 C.F.R. §

300.324(a)(1)(iv)]. Part B requires that schools provide an eligible child with a *Free Appropriate Public Education (FAPE)* in the *Least Restrictive Environment (LRE)* based on an *Individualized Education Program (IEP)* that is assessment based. According to Part B, the rights of the child and family are protected by *procedural safeguards.*

To be eligible for special education and related services, Amanda must have "deafness" or a "hearing impairment" that adversely affects her educational performance and because of this, requires special education and related services (34 C.F.R. § 300.8). Adverse effect is typically measured through standardized testing based on milestones of children with typical development. The criteria (e.g., two standard deviations below the mean in two developmental areas) can vary by state. Knowledgeable providers understand the areas of development most at risk for developmental delay when a child is deaf or hard of hearing and choose developmental instruments accordingly. For example, the assessment of social–emotional and pragmatic language development should be included in the overall assessment protocol because these areas predict future academic performance (Goberis, Dalpes, Abrisch, Baca, & Yoshinaga-Itano, 2012). Deaf and hard-of-hearing children at 3 years of age, even when they have strong language skills in some areas, typically have delays in expressive syntax (Moeller et al., 2012), pragmatic language (Goberis et al., 2012), articulation (Yoshinaga-Itano & Sedey, 2000), and auditory skill development. (See Chapter 7, *Developmental Assessment.*)

More and more children are exhibiting age-appropriate development by 3 years of age in a number of areas, raising the probability that increasing numbers of children may be deemed ineligible for services under Part B. If a child who is deaf or hard of hearing has made a 1 year gain in development for each year of life, then it may be assumed that the child will continue this rate of development in the school-age period. Many children, however, require continued services to remain on age level academically. It is ironic that in some cases services are discontinued *because* the early intervention services the child received were successful. If a child who has been denied services falls behind, he or she may again become eligible for special education services, but by then may require more intensive programming to address deficits. Part B eligibility criteria should be interpreted or modified to permit the continuation of services or, at a minimum, provide close monitoring of progress for children who are deaf or hard of hearing to prevent or remedy any gaps or delays in development.

Thus, it is rarely appropriate for children who are deaf or hard of hearing to be denied special education services when they transition from early intervention. For most children at this young age, the failure to provide appropriate services can result in the emergence of significant developmental delays that did not exist in the early years. Appropriate educational services should be provided to ensure that children who are deaf or hard of hearing have the ability to make the same rate of developmental gain as they did in early intervention under Part C programs, that is, 1 year of language gain for 1 year of life. Children should not have to fail before they are eligible to receive appropriate services.

Relevant service agencies must work to facilitate a smooth transition to Part B services for the child and family. Early intervention under Part C outlines steps that must be taken and timelines that must be followed. If the child is not eligible for services under Part B, the lead agency should conduct a conference among the family and relevant agencies to discuss the services for which the child is eligible. In the United States a deaf or hard-of-hearing child—whether or not that child is eligible for IDEA—is eligible for accommodations under other laws: Section 504 of the Rehabilitation Act and the Americans with Disabilities Act.

Section 504 of the Rehabilitation Act (29 U.S.C. §794) prohibits discrimination by entities that receive federal financial assistance. A preschool or educational program may be required to provide an assistive listening system, sign language services, or other means of making the program accessible, depending on the needs of the child. This Act also applies to programs such as childcare centers that receive federal assistance.

The Americans with Disabilities Act (ADA) (42 U.S.C. §12101 *et seq.*) requires programs run by state and local governments, such as schools, and places of public accommodation, such as public or private childcare centers, to make themselves accessible and to provide "effective communication" to individuals who are deaf or hard of hearing. A key difference between IDEA and Section 504 and ADA is that IDEA requires individualized services to help the child progress developmentally and academically, while 504 and ADA focus simply on the communication access to the program provided to the child. Section 504 and the ADA do not require services to help the child progress developmentally or academically but provide access to programs available to all children.

More information about IDEA and educational advocacy can be found in the Recommended Resources.

Communication Planning

Some states have adopted use of a communication plan to ensure that supports are provided to maintain or enhance children's language and communication development. This is especially important when children transition from early intervention. Part B of IDEA includes several "special factors" provisions for educational placement and services, including some tailored to deaf or hard-of-hearing children and youth:

> in the case of a child who is deaf or hard of hearing, [the child's Individualized Education Program team must] consider the child's language and communication needs, opportunities for direct communications with peers and professional personnel in the child's language and communication mode, academic level, and full range of needs, including opportunities for direct instruction in the child's language and communication mode. [34 C.F.R. § 300.324(a)(2)(iv)]

A communication plan may be included in the child's Individualized Education Program (IEP) when the child transitions from early intervention. The plan documents the child's primary language and communication mode(s) and describes the specific needs for language and communication access throughout the school day. The plan also identifies the language and communication supports needed by the student to participate in and make progress in the general education curriculum.

(See, e.g., Pennsylvania Department of Education, 2011.) When Amanda is old enough to transition to preschool, her communication plan might include opportunities to interact with peers and adults who are deaf or hard of hearing, access to listening and spoken language services, support to ensure appropriate function and use of her assistive listening technology, and sign language instruction to enhance her knowledge of and ability to use ASL.

Parent Counseling and Training

Parent counseling and training, an IDEA service, is intended to help parents understand the special needs of their child; provide them with information about child development; and help them acquire the skills necessary to allow them to support the implementation of their child's IEP or IFSP [34 C.F.R. § 300.34(c)(8)]. The United States Department of Education has long recognized that sign language instruction can be provided to families under these provisions. In 1986, the Department stated ". . . an IEP for a deaf child could include training parents to use the mode of communication that their child uses as part of an educational program" (United States Department of Education, 1986). In 1991, a policy letter from the Department specifically mentioned sign language instruction as a matter of "entitlement to a related service" (United States Department of Education, 1991). And United States Department of Education guidance on the 1997 reauthorization of the Individuals with Disabilities Education Act stated "The IEP team may ... wish to consider whether there is a need for members of the child's family to receive training in sign language in order for the child to receive a Free Appropriate Public Education" (Appendix A to Part 300—Notice of Interpretation, p. 12472). If Amanda is later served by Part B the Zilmers will be entitled to request this type of training. Unfortunately, only a minority of programs offer sign language training to families after their child is 3 years old. Primary caregivers whose children are preschoolers or older and who use sign language with their children can use the procedural safeguard mechanisms in IDEA to request these services if they are not available. Because of the need for continued support for parents in learning ASL to support their child's education, educational programs should make sign language training more widely available.

Deaf Children's Bills of Rights

Thus far, 17 states have enacted a Deaf Children's Bill of Rights (DCBR),[3] which enhances IDEA's principles as applied to deaf or hard-of-hearing children. These bills of rights address the following, for example:

- specific languages and communication modes, such as American Sign Language and English, and manual and speech-based systems
- the availability of deaf and hard-of-hearing role models
- the language proficiency level of personnel in the deaf student's language and communication mode.

(See, e.g., Georgia Deaf Child's Bill of Rights, 2010.)

While most states' bills focus on school-age children, some also include considerations for early intervention. For example, Louisiana's DCBR states that children who are deaf or hard of hearing are "entitled to early intervention to provide for acquisition of solid language bases developed at the earliest possible age" (Louisiana Deaf Child's Bill of Rights, 1993). Maine's bill of rights for deaf children supports eligibility for early intervention services based on hearing status, regardless of whether the infant shows signs of developmental delay (Maine State Legislature, DCBR, n.d.).

The DCBR delineates important elements of a child's education program and setting. It can be an efficient way to support Amanda in her cognitive, linguistic, and social–emotional development. Referencing the DCBR in an IFSP meeting can help guide the discussion to focus on the factors most relevant for supporting Amanda's overall development and can minimize differences in agreement between the school and the family.

CONVENTION ON THE RIGHTS OF PERSONS WITH DISABILITIES

The United Nations' Convention on the Rights of Persons with Disabilities (CRPD) provides guidance designed to improve disability policies to nations around the world. Similar to the Americans with Disabilities Act (ADA), the principles of the CRPD include equality, nondiscrimination, inclusion in society, accessibility, and respect for inherent dignity. Many countries do not have a law preventing discrimination based on disability. The CRPD seeks to ensure that nations across the globe provide people with disabilities the same rights to live full, satisfying, and productive lives as people without disabilities. The CRPD was adopted by the United Nations in 2006, and since then more than 150 nations have ratified it.

Although the CRPD would not change existing law in the United States, it does require signatory nations to bring their nation's laws and practices into compliance with these principles; thus it could have a large impact on the education of deaf and hard-of-hearing children worldwide. (See the Recommended Resources.)

BEST PRACTICES AND POLICIES RECOMMENDATIONS

A number of organizations have issued statements regarding what constitute best practices in early intervention for deaf or hard-of-hearing children and their families. These statements include reference to roles and responsibilities of service providers (American Speech-Language-Hearing Association, 2010), informed decision making by parents and caregivers (Alexander Graham Bell Association for the Deaf and Hard of Hearing, 2008), communication access to the curriculum (National Association for the Deaf, n.d.), teacher qualifications (Conference of Educational Administrators of Schools and Programs for the Deaf, 2005), recognizing and supporting a "range of communication possibilities" and having "fluency and expertise using the communication approach selected by the family" (Moeller, Carr, Seaver, Stredler-Brown, & Holzinger, 2013), and advocating for the use of sign language in particular (World Federation of the Deaf, n.d.).

As mentioned earlier, the Joint Committee on Infant Hearing (JCIH) has developed guidelines that promote best practices in the early identification and early intervention for young deaf or hard-of-hearing children. The principles and guidelines of the JCIH are used by hospitals, audiologists, and early intervention programs to guide their policies and procedures. The Year 2007 Position Statement (Joint Committee on Infant Hearing, 2007) includes updated and expanded recommendations from previous position statements on newborn hearing screening, audiological evaluation, and early intervention.

While the JCIH position statements have focused primarily on hearing screening and evaluation, early hearing detection and intervention (EHDI) programs are charged with the responsibility of ensuring that infants and toddlers confirmed as deaf or hard of hearing have immediate access to early intervention programs that follow best practice principles. In 2013, the American Academy of Pediatrics published a supplement to the JCIH 2007 position statement focused on early intervention best practices (Joint Committee on Infant Hearing, 2013). The Supplement to the JCIH 2007 Position Statement describes 12 goals, recommendations, and benchmarks for early intervention services for families and infants and toddlers who are deaf or hard of hearing.

In June 2012, a group of international experts, including members of families and professionals who are deaf or hard of hearing, developed a consensus document of valid, evidence-based principles to guide family-centered early intervention with infants and toddlers who are deaf or hard of hearing (Moeller et al., 2013). The document provides an elaboration of many of the characteristics described in the supplement to the JCIH 2007 document described above.

These two documents provide an excellent review of the literature. Since the publication of the JCIH early intervention supplement, a number of states in the United States have used the document to set goals including the collection of baseline data. Families, such as the Zilmers, as well as professionals who serve them, can consult these documents and organizations for guidance and information to support their child's development and future success.

EFFICACY OF COMMUNICATION AND LANGUAGE PATHWAYS

One significant omission in both of these documents relates to the efficacy of one specific method of communication as compared to another. The Zilmers have requested services for Amanda's spoken language development and ASL. They believe that providing Amanda with both spoken language and sign language will be beneficial. Lou Ann has questions about this and has turned to the experts to help her understand how research can inform practice. She first wanted to know if there was evidence that one language and communication pathway was better than another.

There is no easy answer to this question. Currently, there is no comparative study with the statistical controls necessary to identify the efficacy of one method or approach to language and communication over another (e.g., bilingual/bimodal, simultaneous, cued speech, ora–aural). There are no comparative studies that have randomly assigned families and children to treatment groups, language (ASL or English), and mode (visual or auditory) to determine which pathway results in better outcomes. Several factors make this type of research impossible. First, ethical and legal issues give families the right to informed decision making and choice that make it inappropriate to assign children to treatment groups. Additionally, families often choose combinations of different modalities of communication, making it impossible to compare methods. Some families choose to learn American Sign Language from a native or fluent deaf sign language instructor, and may also be receiving listening and spoken language services. They may choose to speak more than one spoken language and may use sign language sometimes as ASL in a visual/manual only communication, or may use sign language simultaneously with spoken English in a manually coded form of communication. This makes it very difficult to compare language use among children and families.

In addition, individual characteristics of infants and toddlers and their families make comparisons difficult. Although it is unknown how many deaf or hard-of-hearing infants and toddlers have disabilities, approximately 35% to 40% of school-age children who are deaf have additional disabilities, ranging from cognitive delays or disabilities to developmental issues that impact motor development (Gallaudet Research Institute, 2008). Many of these children are at risk for accessing language through a single modality or approach (Yoshinaga-Itano et al., 1998).

With respect to the early childhood years all studies that have controlled the quality of the early intervention services (Moeller, 2000; Yoshinaga-Itano et al., 1998) have failed to find that one communication or language approach directly causes better outcomes than another. A recent study by Nittrouer (2009) compared children who were enrolled in oral–aural programs and those that were enrolled in sign-supported speech programs and found no difference in outcomes. Although the method or approach to communication in this study was defined, the quality and characteristics of the early intervention program were not controlled between the two groups. To date, no studies of early intervention programs *without a categorical deafness-specific specialized system for families with infants and children who are deaf or hard of hearing* have been able to demonstrate that children who are identified early have better outcomes than those who are identified later.

A survey of research on sign language and spoken language acquisition in deaf children concludes "[T]here is no evidence that using a signed language with deaf and hard of hearing children impedes spoken language development. Rather, spoken language skills increase as children learn more gestures and signs. Proficiency in ASL has been shown to positively influence spoken language development and the development of English literacy in deaf students. It is language that facilitates spoken language, not the mode of communication" (Baker, 2011).

Therefore, the research indicates that the use of sign language does not impair and is not detrimental to the development of age-appropriate language (either spoken or signed) by young children who are deaf or hard of hearing. There are some studies that indicate that sign language can facilitate the fast-mapping of spoken language after cochlear implantation when the children also receive high-quality listening and spoken language intervention services (Hassanzadeh, 2012). (See Chapter 8, *Collaboration for Communication, Language, and Cognitive Development.*)

The Zilmers want Amanda to acquire two languages, and there is increasing evidence that bilingual language acquisition supports improved cognitive function (Jasinska & Petitto, 2013; Kovelman, Baker, & Petitto, 2008). Children who are deaf or hard of hearing have demonstrated that they are capable of learning more than one spoken language, more than one sign language such as ASL or another signed language, both sign language and spoken language, Cued Speech, and can sing and play musical instruments. As long as the quality of the intervention services is high, early-identified children who are deaf or hard of hearing have demonstrated that they have the capability to be multilingual and multimodal. The logical conclusion is that bilingual or multilingual language acquisition, more than one signed language, more than one spoken language, or a signed and a spoken language, is beneficial to any child's cognitive development.

SUMMARY

Despite compelling research, legislation, and policies around early intervention, there continues to be a gap between recommended best practices and the quality of early intervention services for infants, toddlers, and their families. The Zilmer family can and should have access to high-quality services in ASL as well as high-quality services in listening and spoken language. The provision of these services should be immediate and at the earliest age possible. The family should be provided with a service coordinator who understands language and communication learning opportunities with infants and toddlers who are deaf or hard of hearing. This professional should coordinate services among the interdisciplinary team of early intervention service providers to ensure that Amanda's development in all areas is progressing at an appropriate rate and her family is equipped to meet her language and communication needs.

SUGGESTED ACTIVITIES

1. Interview parents or primary caregivers of newly identified children to learn about their experiences. What information is provided to them about their rights and legislation that supports the rights of deaf or hard-of-hearing children and adults?
2. Survey the early intervention programs available in your state or locality. What are the qualifications of the providers in regard to provision of services to deaf or hard-of-hearing infants and toddlers and their families? What services are available?
3. After reading the *Supplement to the JCIH 2007 Position Statement: Principles and Guidelines for Early Intervention Following Confirmation That a Child Is Deaf or Hard of Hearing* (Joint Committee on Infant Hearing, 2013), check out the early intervention program where you live to see if it conforms to those recommendations. If there are goals that are not addressed, what steps should be taken to improve the program?

RECOMMENDED RESOURCES

1. American Speech-Language-Hearing Association (ASHA).
   This website provides documents, references, resources, and products for audiologists and speech-language pathologists working in early intervention. See www.asha.org.
2. Cheryl DeConde Johnson, Janet DesGeorges, and Leeanne Seaver. (2013). *Educational Advocacy for Students Who Are Deaf or Hard of Hearing: The Hands & Voices Guidebook*. Boulder, CO: Hands & Voices, Inc.
   This book provides families and professionals with a resource focused on educational advocacy for deaf or hard-of-hearing children. See http://www.handsandvoices.org/resources/products.htm#astra.
3. IDEA Infant & Toddler Programs Coordinators Association (ITCA).
   ITCA is a nonprofit corporation to promote assistance, cooperation, and exchange of information in the administration of Part C. See http://www.ideainfanttoddler.org.
4. Joint Committee ASHA-CED (2006). *Natural environments for infants and toddlers who are deaf or hard of hearing and their families*.

This document provides guidance on how to select natural environments for deaf and hard-of-hearing infants and toddlers and their families, advocates for appropriate environments, and provides resources for further information. See http://www.asha.org/aud/Natural-Environments-for-Infants-and-Toddlers/.

5. Joint Committee on Infant Hearing.

The Joint Committee on Infant Hearing has position statements that include principles, guidelines, and best practices in early intervention. See http://www.jcih.org/posstatemts.htm.

6. National Association of the Deaf (NAD).

The NAD is a nonprofit organization that advocates for the rights of all people who are deaf or hard of hearing. The Law and Advocacy Center educates, advocates, and litigates on behalf of deaf people. See www.nad.org.

7. National Center for Hearing Assessment and Management.

This center is a national resource center for professionals and families on the implementation and improvement of Early Hearing Detection and Intervention systems. See www.infanthearing.org.

8. United Nations Convention on the Rights of Persons with Disabilities (CRPD).

The website provides information on topics related to disabilities and the work of the United Nations. See www.un.org/disabilities/.

9. United States Department of Education.

This website provides detailed information on IDEA—The Individuals with Disabilities Education Act, 2004, Part C and Part B. See http://idea.ed.gov.

10. Visual Language and Visual Learning Center (VL2).

This center studies the effects of visual processes, visual language, and social experience on the development of cognition, language, reading, and literacy. See http://vl2.gallaudet.edu.

REFERENCES

Alexander Graham Bell Association for the Deaf and Hard of Hearing. (2008). *Position statement: American sign language.* Washington, DC. Retrieved from http://listeningandspokenlanguage.org/Document.aspx?id=387.

American Speech-Language-Hearing Association (ASHA). (2010). *Roles and responsibilities of speech-language pathologists in schools* [Professional Issues Statement]. Retrieved from www.asha.org/policy.

American Speech-Language-Hearing Association (ASHA) and the Council on Education of the Deaf (CED) Joint Committee. (2006). *Fact sheet: Natural environments for infants and toddlers who are deaf or hard of hearing and their families.* Retrieved from http://www.asha.org/aud/ Natural-Environments-for-Infants-and-Toddlers/.

Americans with Disabilities Act, 42 U.S.C. § 12101 *et seq.* (1990).

Arehart, K. H., Yoshinaga-Itano, C., Gabbard, S., Stredler-Brown, A., & Thomson, V. (1998). State of the states: Status of universal newborn hearing screening, assessment and intervention in 17 states. *American Journal of Audiology, 7,* 101–111.

Baker, S. (2011, January). *Advantages of early visual language* (Visual Language and Visual Learning Science of Learning Center, Research Brief No. 2). Washington, DC.

Bruce, S., & Illinois State Univ., Normal. (1986). *The SKI-HI program: A descriptive update, 1986.* Washington, DC: ERIC Clearinghouse.

Buysse, V., Wesley, P. W., Snyder, P., & Winton, P. J. (2006). Evidence-based practice: What does it really mean for the early childhood field? *Young Exceptional Children, 9*(4), 2–11.

Conference of Educational Administrators of Schools and Programs for the Deaf (CEASD). (2005). *Position paper: Highly qualified teachers.* Retrieved from http://www.ceasd.org/advocacy/position-papers.

Early Detection, Diagnosis, and Treatment Regarding Hearing Loss in Newborns and Infants Act, 42 U.S.C. § 280g-1 (2010).

Gallaudet Research Institute. (2008). *Regional and national summary report from the 2007–2008 annual survey of deaf and hard of hearing children and youth.* Retrieved from http://research.gallaudet.edu/Demographics/2008_ National_Summary.pdf.

Georgia Deaf Child's Bill of Rights, O.C.G.A. 20-2-152.1 (2010). Retrieved from http://www.gadoe.org/Curriculum-Instruction-and-Assessment/ Special-Education-Services/Pages/Deaf-and-Hard-of-Hearing.aspx.

Goberis, D., Dalpes, M., Abrisch, A, Baca, R., & Yoshinaga-Itano, C. (2012). The missing link in language development of deaf and hard of hearing children: Pragmatic language development. *Seminars in Speech and Language, 33*(4), 297–304.

Hassanzadeh, S. (2012). Outcomes of cochlear implantation in deaf children of deaf parents: Comparative study. *The Journal of Laryngology & Otology, 126*(10), 989–994.

IDEA Infant and Toddler Coordinators Association and National Center for Hearing Assessment and Management. (2011). *Part C eligibility considerations for infants & toddlers who are deaf or hard of hearing.* Retrieved from http://www.infanthearing.org/earlyintervention/part_c_eligibility.pdf.

Individuals with Disabilities Education Act, 20 U.S.C. §1401 *et seq.* (2004).

Individuals with Disabilities Education Act (IDEA), Appendix A to Part 300—Notice of Interpretation. 64 Fed. Reg.12469–12480 (March 12, 1999).

Individuals with Disabilities Education Act (IDEA), Assistance to States for the Education of Children with Disabilities Regulations, 34 C.F.R. pt. 300 (2006).

Individuals with Disabilities Education Act (IDEA), Early Intervention Program for Infants and Toddlers with Disabilities Regulations, 34 C.F.R. pt. 303 (2011).

Jasinska, K. K., & Petitto, L. A. (2013). How age of bilingual exposure can change the neural systems for language in the developing brain: A functional near infrared spectroscopy investigation of syntactic processing in monolingual and bilingual children. *Developmental Cognitive Neuroscience, 6,* 87–101.

Joint Committee on Infant Hearing. (2007). Year 2007 position statement: Principles and guidelines for early hearing detection and intervention programs. *Pediatrics, 120,* 898–921. doi:10.1542/peds.2007-2333.

Joint Committee on Infant Hearing. (2013). Supplement to the JCIH 2007 position statement: Principles and guidelines for intervention after confirmation that a child is deaf or hard of hearing. *Pediatrics, 131*(4), e1324–1349. doi:10.1542/peds.2013-0008.

Kovelman I., Baker S. A., & Petitto, L. A. (2008). Bilingual and monolingual brains compared: An fMRI investigation of syntactic processing and a possible "neural signature" of bilingualism. *Journal of Cognitive Neuroscience, 20*(1), 153–169.

Louisiana Deaf Child's Bill of Rights; legislative recognition, RS 17:1960 *et seq.* (1993). Retrieved from http://statutes.laws.com/louisiana/rs/title17/rs17-1960.

Maine State Legislature: An act to establish the education bill of rights for deaf and hard-of-hearing children, 20-A MRSA c. 303 (n.d.). Retrieved from http://www.mainelegislature.org/legis/bills/bills_123rd/billpdfs/HP133501.pdf.

Maryland Health-General Code §13-601 *et seq.* (2013).

Moeller, M. P. (2000). Early intervention and language development in children who are deaf and hard of hearing. *Pediatrics, 106*(3), e43–51.

Moeller, M. P., Carr, G., Seaver, L., Stredler-Brown, A., & Holzinger, D. (2013). Best practices in family-centered early intervention for children who are deaf or hard of hearing: An international consensus statement. *Journal of Deaf Studies and Deaf Education, 18*(4), 429-445. doi:10.1093/deafed/ento34.

Moeller, M. P., McCleary, E., Putman, C., Tyer-Krings, A., Hoover, B., & Stelmachowicz, P. (2012). Longitudinal development of phonology and morphology in children with late-identified mild-moderate sensorineural hearing loss. *Ear and Hearing, 31*(5), 625–635.

National Association of the Deaf. (n.d.). *Education.* Retrieved from http://www. nad.org/issues/education.

Nittrouer, S. (2009). *Early development of children with hearing loss.* San Diego, CA: Plural Publishing.

Pennsylvania Department of Education. (2011). *Deaf and hard of hearing: Pennsylvania communication plan overview.* Retrieved from http://www. pattan.net/category/Educational%20Initiatives/Deaf%20-%20Hard%20 of%20Hearing/page/Communication_Plan.html.

Rehabilitation Act, Section 504, 29 U.S.C. §794 (1973).

Spencer, P. E., & Marschark, M. (2010). *Evidence-based practice in educating deaf and hard-of-hearing students.* New York, NY: Oxford University Press.

The White House, Office of the Press Secretary. (2010). *President Obama honors winners of the 2010 citizens medal.* Retrieved from http://www. whitehouse.gov/the-press-office/president-obama-honors-winners-2 010-citizens-medal.

Uhler, K., Thomson, V., Cyr, N., Gabbard, S., & Yoshinaga-Itano, C. (2014). State and territory EHDI databases: What we do and don't know about the hearing or audiological data from identified children. *American Journal of Audiology, 23,* 34–43. doi:10.1044/1059-0889(2013/13-0015).

United States Department of Education. (July 25, 1986). Letter to Dole from Assistant Secretary Madeleine Will.

United States Department of Education. (June 3, 1991). Letter to Dagley from Office of Special Education Programs Director Judy Schrag.

United States Department of Education Office of Special Education & Rehabilitative Services. (n.d.). Part C state performance plan (SPP) and annual performance report (APR). Retrieved from http://www2.ed.gov/policy/speced/guid/idea/capr/index.html?exp=0.

World Federation of the Deaf. (n.d.). *Policy—Education rights for deaf children.* Retrieved from http://wfdeaf.org/databank/policies/education-rights-for-d eaf-children.

Yoshinaga-Itano, C., & Sedey, A. (2000). Early speech development in children who are deaf or hard of hearing: Interrelationships with language and hearing. *The Volta Review, 100*(5) (monograph), 181–211.

Yoshinaga-Itano, C., & Sedey, A. (2013, May). *Outcomes of children who are deaf or hard of hearing.* Paper presented at the Connecticut Early Hearing Detection and Intervention (EHDI) Conference, Hartford, CT.

Yoshinaga-Itano, C., Sedey, A. L., Coulter, D. K., & Mehl, A. L. (1998). The language of early- and later-identified children with hearing loss, *Pediatrics*, *102*(5), 1161–1171.

NOTES

1. This law is due to expire in 2015. For it to continue beyond that, the U.S. Congress must reauthorize it.
2. At present, the Department is also considering the implementation of a Results Driven Accountability framework for Part C.
3. A leading proponent of the Georgia DCBR was awarded a Citizen's Medal—the "nation's second-highest civilian honor"—by President Obama in 2010 for "demonstrating the results one citizen can achieve for an entire community." The award was presented for her efforts to pass the Georgia Deaf Children's Bill of Rights (The White House, 2010).

5 Collaboration with Deaf and Hard-of-Hearing Communities

Paula Pittman, Beth S. Benedict, Stephanie Olson, and Marilyn Sass-Lehrer

Greg, a speech-language pathologist, is working with an infant who is deaf and his family who lives in a rural community in the United States. The Williams have never met another deaf or hard-of-hearing person and are struggling to understand what the future holds for their son, Dexter. The most recent audiological evaluation indicated that Dexter's hearing is in the severe to profound range. Greg, the primary early intervention provider to the family, has no contact with members of deaf or hard-of-hearing communities or any adults who are deaf or hard of hearing. He believes the family might benefit from meeting deaf or hard-of-hearing young people or adults, but has no idea how to make this happen.

GUIDING QUESTIONS

1. How might connecting families with an adult who is deaf or hard of hearing benefit a young child and family?
2. How might early intervention programs benefit when deaf or hard-of-hearing professionals and other adults are part of the interdisciplinary team?

3. What might an early intervention specialist do to provide meaningful connections for hearing families with deaf or hard-of-hearing adults?
4. How can early intervention programs overcome potential challenges to
   meaningful participation of adults who are deaf or hard of hearing in their
   programs?

COMPETENCIES ADDRESSED IN THIS CHAPTER

1. Socially, Culturally, and Linguistically Responsive Practices, Including
   Deaf/Hard-of-Hearing Cultures and Communities: Sensitivity to and
   Respect for an Individual Family's Characteristics
2. Language Acquisition and Communication Development: Typical
   Development, Communication Approaches Available to Children with
   Hearing Loss, and Impact of Hearing Loss on Access to Communication
3. Collaboration and Interdisciplinary Models and Practices

INTRODUCTION

The fact that Greg, the speech-language pathologist in the opening vignette, realized that it would be beneficial to introduce the Williams
to individuals who are deaf or hard of hearing was quite insightful.
Despite not knowing any deaf or hard-of-hearing adults himself, he
was interested in investigating how to make collaboration possible. As
a novice in this area, Greg knew that he needed to learn more about
people who are deaf or hard of hearing and understand who or what
the Deaf Community is. Greg also needed information about the role
of adults who are deaf or hard of hearing in early intervention, and the
potential value of connecting young deaf or hard-of-hearing children
and their families with them.

This chapter explores Greg's journey as he, in collaboration with the
other members of his professional team, examine the research, best practices, and the experiences of hearing families who have had meaningful relationships with members of deaf or hard-of-hearing communities.

Greg and Frances, a social worker on his team, discover ways to meet deaf and hard-of-hearing adults, and learn about early intervention programs that include deaf and hard-of-hearing adults as mentors, role models, or advisors. Greg's hope is that the information he gathers can be a catalyst for change and formalize the inclusion of adults who are deaf or hard of hearing in his state's early hearing detection and intervention (EHDI) program.

ROLE OF DEAF AND HARD-OF-HEARING ADULTS IN EARLY INTERVENTION

Early intervention specialists have backgrounds in a variety of academic disciplines in which people who are deaf or hard of hearing are greatly underrepresented. As a result, many specialists, such as Greg, lack experiences working side by side with colleagues who are deaf or hard of hearing and have limited understanding of what it means to be deaf (Benedict & Sass-Lehrer, 2007). The absence of people who are deaf or hard of hearing means that professionals who are hearing shape policies, positions, and services in early intervention programs. Hearing professionals often view being deaf or hard of hearing as a problem that needs to be fixed, primarily through medical interventions or therapies, whereas many adults who are deaf or hard of hearing have a different perspective. Being deaf is different from being hearing, but it is far from disabling (Padden & Humphries, 2006).

Early intervention programs have involved adults who are deaf or hard of hearing in informal ways for many years. Deaf and hard-of-hearing adults were, and still are, invited to participate on parent panels or share stories with young children using American Sign Language (ASL). Many programs enlist the help of adults who are deaf to teach hearing families how to communicate with their babies using a signed language and other visual strategies. Too often, early intervention programs have relied upon the good will of adults who are deaf or hard of hearing to voluntarily participate in these activities rather than hire them as members of the early intervention professional team. Informal opportunities for interactions with hearing families are helpful but provide only a glimpse into the lives of a small number of people who are deaf or hard of hearing, and rarely support ongoing relationships with families (Bodner-Johnson & Benedict, 2012).

The limited role of deaf or hard-of-hearing adults in early intervention began to change in the early 1990s when bilingual–bicultural education programs in the United States emerged and promoted the use of ASL with infants and ASL as the primary language of instruction in the classroom (Johnson, Liddell, & Erting, 1989). Bilingual–bicultural education, which today is known as American Sign Language (ASL)/English bilingual education, focuses on both ASL and English (in the spoken and written forms) and encourages programs to acquaint families with Deaf Culture and the Deaf Community. (See Chapter 8, *Collaboration for Communication, Language, and Cognitive Development.*) Early bilingual programs actively recruited deaf or hard-of-hearing professionals, especially those who were native or near native ASL users, as early intervention specialists and instituted more formal ways to involve people who are deaf or hard of hearing as mentors, role models, and ASL instructors. Prior to this time, the involvement of adults who were deaf or hard of hearing was limited, and it was unusual to find an early intervention professional who was deaf or hard of hearing. More adults who are deaf or hard of hearing are working in early intervention programs today than ever before, although their involvement is still limited in many programs in the United States and throughout the world.

MANY WAYS TO BE DEAF OR HARD OF HEARING

People who are deaf comprise an extremely heterogeneous community. Deaf and hard-of hearing people exist in every culture and every land around the globe. Although being deaf is considered "low incidence," people whose hearing is outside the audiological range of "normal" are plentiful. Deaf and hard-of-hearing babies are identified in roughly one to six births out of 1,000 (Cunningham & Cox, 2003), with lower rates in resource-rich countries and higher rates in developing countries (Olusanya, 2012). The number of children with limited hearing increases throughout the early childhood years. Many babies who were born with hearing in one or both ears (i.e., unilateral or bilateral) experience a gradual loss of hearing throughout their childhood years (Hoffman, Houston, Munoz, & Bradham, 2011).

Use of assistive listening technologies can influence access to hearing and communication modalities, which in turn affects a child's educational placement and their circle of friendships (Leigh, 2009; Wilkens & Hehir, 2008). People who do not use listening technologies or find them of limited use may use a visual language as their primary language of interaction, such as a native signed language, and may attend a school or educational program exclusively for deaf children. Their educational and social experiences are typically different from those who attend public schools designed primarily for hearing students.

Abilities, talents, and other differences also influence deaf people's pathways and choices. People, whether hearing, deaf, or hard of hearing, are influenced by many factors including their birth circumstances, their physical and emotional well-being, family and community support, socioeconomic factors, ethnicity, and education. Deaf or hard-of-hearing people are professionals and physical laborers. They may be doctors, lawyers, teachers, athletes, civil servants, or construction workers. Some are employed, some are underemployed, and some are looking for work. Deaf or hard-of-hearing people, like hearing people, reflect the range of human experience (Benedict et al., 2014). In short, there are many ways to be deaf and many factors that shape who deaf and hard-of-hearing people are and with whom they identify (Leigh, 2009).

Deaf and Hard-of-Hearing Communities

A person is considered a member of the Deaf Community if he or she ". . . identifies him or herself as a member of the Deaf Community, and other members accept that person as a part of the community" (Baker & Padden, 1978, p. 4). The Deaf Community is recognized as a sociocultural group of people whose identity is connected with being deaf and who value sign language for communication and interactions (Padden & Humphries, 2006).

There are many avenues for gaining access into the Deaf Community. Some children are born into families with deaf parents, raised using a signed language, and surrounded by others who share similar values and beliefs. More than 90% of children who are deaf or hard of hearing are born into hearing families (Mitchell & Karchmer, 2004). These children may learn a signed language and what it means to be deaf from interactions with other deaf or hard-of-hearing people, usually at school. Whereas most hearing children learn about their culture and community from their families, children who are deaf are more likely to learn about the Deaf Community from other individuals who are deaf. Identity and affiliations may change throughout a person's life. For example, someone not identified with the Deaf Community as a youth might connect with the Deaf Community later in life.

People who are deaf or hard of hearing, like those who are hearing, choose to identify with different social and cultural communities, and not all choose to identify with the Deaf Community. For example, people who are deaf or hard of hearing and communicate primarily through spoken language may choose to associate with others who use spoken language. They may use and understand sign language and choose instead to identify with the hearing community or others who use spoken language. Conversely, those who use a native signed language may prefer to associate with others who use a similar visual language and identify strongly with the Deaf Community. Many individuals who are deaf or hard of hearing identify with both the hearing and the Deaf Community because they have been raised in a bilingual environment and feel they have a place in both communities. The Deaf Community recognizes diversity in many areas including, but not limited to, language use, experiences, culture, religion, and sexual orientation.

Big "D" and Little "d"

When Greg started reading about the diversity among people who are deaf or hard of hearing, he discovered that some writers use "Deaf" written in upper case letters to refer to those who consider themselves to be culturally Deaf and members of the Deaf Community. The term "deaf" written in lower case letters was used to distinguish those people who are deaf or hard of hearing, audiologically, but who do not identify with the Deaf Community. While considering this distinction, Greg made a note to himself to investigate to what extent people who are deaf or hard of hearing use this "Deaf" versus "deaf" distinction and how or if this applies to infants or toddlers who have yet to discover their own identities.

Greg realized that the only way to answer these questions was to meet individuals who are deaf or hard of hearing and learn more about their lives. He contacted an agency in a city more than an hour away that serves and is run by individuals who are deaf or hard of hearing and requested an opportunity to meet with several people there. Greg listened to their stories and learned that some people do in fact identify themselves as culturally Deaf and would say they were "big D Deaf." Greg learned that the concept of cultural identity is somewhat fluid. Although some individuals fully identified with the Deaf Community and Deaf Culture, there were many who saw themselves as a part of both the hearing and the Deaf Community. It struck Greg that deaf or hard-of-hearing people, similar to hearing people, identify with different groups or subcultures that reflect their life experiences, attributes, and interests and that identity and involvement with different communities change over time. This information was helpful as Greg thought about how little Dexter's future life experiences will determine with whom he chooses to associate and to what extent he identifies with other people who are also deaf or hard of hearing.

DEAF CULTURE

Soon after the audiologist confirmed that Dexter was deaf, the Williams began their own search for information and found some websites on Deaf Culture. Most families, like the Williams, have never met another person who is deaf or hard of hearing, and have no idea that there is actually such a thing as Deaf Culture. The William's family shared some concerns with Greg about Dexter's identity, not only because Dexter is deaf, but also because he is African American. The Williams were concerned that if he chose to become a part of the Deaf Community and embrace Deaf Culture, that might mean that he would lose his African-American identity and cultural heritage.

Greg decided to contact the National Association of the Deaf (NAD) who referred him to the National Black Deaf Advocates. Their staffs were very helpful and gave him a list of reputable websites and books on Deaf Culture. (See Recommended Resources at the end of this chapter.) Greg realized that it would be helpful to connect the Williams with the National Black Deaf Advocates to learn more about how others who are African-American and deaf or hard of hearing preserve and cherish their cultural heritage and traditions. Based on his own readings and his recent interactions with deaf and hard-of-hearing adults, Greg could confidently share with the family that being affiliated with the Deaf Community does not exclude or homogenize other identities. He explained that the Deaf Community honors diversity, and that Dexter will be able to embrace his African-American heritage regardless of whether he chooses at some point in his life to identify with the Deaf Community.

Describing any culture is complex. Padden and Humphries (1988) define culture as a set of learned behaviors of a group of people who have their own language, values, rules of behavior, and traditions. Individuals who are deaf are the only "disability" group that has its own language. In the United States, that language is ASL. It is that language that provides a direct link to the Deaf Community and to Deaf Culture. American Sign Language, like other native signed languages, is a full and complex language, regulated by syntactical rules and grammar similar to other formal spoken languages (Stokoe, 2005). There is no universal sign language; native signed languages are distinct and reflect their respective countries and cultures. What makes signed languages unique is that they are visual languages with no written or spoken mode (Paul, 1996; Stokoe, 1996). ASL has traditionally been passed from generation to generation through residential schools for children who are deaf (Gannon, 1981). At the center of Deaf Culture is the value of knowing and using fluently the native signed language of the country where the individual lives.

In the Deaf Community, being deaf is a source of pride and identifying with a group of like individuals is at the heart of the culture. Social inter-action is an integral part of the Deaf Community. Although Deaf clubs were very popular years ago as a way to stay connected, social media, text messaging, and videophones have reduced their popularity (Power, Power, & Horstmanshof, 2006; Shoham & Heber, 2012). Opportunities to gather with other members of the Deaf Community remain a high priority for many people who are deaf (Atherton, 2009; Hadjikakou & Nekolaraizi, 2011; Lane, Hoffmeister, & Bahan, 1996).

RATIONALE FOR COLLABORATION WITH DEAF AND HARD-OF-HEARING COMMUNITIES

Greg, along with Frances and the early intervention program director, agreed that they needed information about the value of connecting adults who are deaf or hard of hearing with families and their young children. An internet search of best practices in early intervention for deaf or hard-of-hearing infants and toddlers led him to two evidence-based doc-uments that endorse the involvement of deaf and hard-of-hearing adults in early intervention.

Supplement to the JCIH 2007 Position Statement

The first document Greg reviewed was the *Supplement to the Year 2007 Position Statement: Principles and Guidelines for Early Intervention After Confirmation That a Child Is Deaf or Hard of Hearing* [Joint Committee on Infant Hearing (JCIH), 2013]. This document provides guidelines to EHDI programs to support effective provision of services to infants and toddlers who are deaf or hard of hearing and their families in the United States. The supplement includes three goals that specifically address this issue:

Goal 3a acknowledges the challenge for families of having access to adults who can teach ASL. The goal reinforces the importance of having early intervention providers who are fluent, native signers.

Goal 10 states: "Individuals who are D/HH [deaf or hard of hearing] will be active participants in the development and implementation of EHDI systems at the national, state/territory, and local levels; their participation will be an expected and integral component of the EHDI systems" (e1337). The document explains that "the goal is to have individuals who are D/HH woven into the fabric of EHDI systems at every level. Individuals who are D/HH know what works to meet their language and communication needs in a way that people who are hearing cannot. Because the support of language and communication of infants is intended to be the cornerstone of the EHDI systems, it is critical to include D/HH adults in these systems" (JCIH, 2013, e1337).

Goal 11 of this same document calls for "all children who are D/HH and their families [to] have access to support, mentorship and guidance from individuals who are D/HH" (e1338). The rationale for this goal points to research that affirms the benefits to children who are deaf or hard of hearing and their families when they interact with professionals and community members who are deaf or hard of hearing.

The JCIH Supplement to the 2007 Position Statement (JCIH, 2013) recommendations went beyond Greg's expectations by stating that adults who are deaf or hard of hearing should be fully included in all aspects of early intervention programming, not only as role models and mentors, but also as directors of EHDI programs, chairs of EHDI advisory committees, and other leadership positions. The JCIH guidelines emphasized the importance of providing families with access to deaf and hard-of-hearing adults who have a variety of life perspectives and experiences and called for more professional development and mentoring opportunities to provide deaf and hard-of-hearing adults with the knowledge and skills they need for different roles and positions in early intervention.

Best Practices in Family-Centered Early Intervention

The second document Greg found describes the consensus of a panel of international experts on the essential principles for family-centered early intervention (Moeller, Carr, Seaver, Stredler-Brown, & Holzinger, 2013). Greg was surprised when he discovered that including adults who are deaf or hard of hearing is not only valued in the United States, but in many other countries around the world. In this document, Principles 4, 7, and 8 mention the vital role of adults who are deaf or hard of hearing. Principle 4 addresses the importance of role models who are deaf or hard of hearing related to family social and emotional support. Principle 7 concerns qualified providers and notes that competent and fluent sign language models should be available to families that are learning to sign. Collaborative Teamwork is the focus of Principle 8 and states that service providers and programs should "Offer families opportunities for meaningful interactions with adults who are D/HH" (p. 144). They also state that "D/HH adults can serve as role models, consultants, and/or mentors to families, offering information and resources and demonstrate enriching language experiences" (p. 144). They recommend that providers and programs should "involve D/HH community members on the team in culturally and linguistically sensitive ways" (p. 441).

These documents provide Greg and his colleagues with substantial evidence and rationales to support including deaf and hard-of-hearing adults in their EHDI program. The fact that the documents have widespread support from a range of national and international professional groups and experts will strengthen the administrative efforts to improve the services in his state.

Benefits of Deaf and Hard-of-Hearing Adult Involvement in Early Intervention

Next, Greg and Frances decided to take a closer look at the research on the benefits to children and families when deaf and hard-of-hearing adults are included in early intervention programming. They decided to contact early intervention experts who were cited in the JCIH Supplement (2013) and Best Practices document (Moeller et al., 2013) to obtain more information about the benefits for children and their families.

Benefits to Young Children

Adults who are deaf or hard of hearing frequently share stories about how, as children, they believed they were the only deaf or hard-of-hearing person in the world. It is not unusual for a young child who is deaf or hard of hearing and attends a school with only hearing children to grow up with a sense of aloneness (Oliva & Lytle, 2014). Many people do not discover others who are like them until they reach high school or college. One man shared the following story:

> I grew up in a very small rural town to a hearing family. In fact, the whole town was hearing. I never met another person who was deaf or hard of hearing, or if I did, I had no idea that they were deaf. I knew I was different from everyone else. I knew I couldn't hear like they did, even with my hearing aids. No one else I knew wore hearing aids. No one else struggled to understand what was being said. For me, every day was a challenge, but I never let my lack of hearing equal a lack of love for my life, nor has it ever prevented me from doing exactly what I wanted to do. (D. Harman, personal communication, September, 1983)

Many individuals begin to develop an identity as a deaf person only after meeting other deaf people. For this man, it was after meeting other deaf people that he acknowledged:

> . . . this was the birth of my identity as a deaf man. That was the day that I began to realize that I was normal—a normal deaf person. And that was the day that I began to really understand the world around me. (D. Harman, personal communication, September, 1983)

Toddlers and preschoolers often "light up" when they see adults signing or when they see another person who has hearing aids or cochlear implants. When young children who are deaf or hard of hearing have opportunities to interact with deaf or hard-of-hearing adults and other children, they understand from an early age that the world is filled with many different kinds of people; some are hearing, some are deaf, and some are hard of hearing.

Communication and Language

For hearing families, deaf mentors, role models, or advisors can help them navigate their way through the experience of having a deaf or hard-of-hearing child. They can help put families' minds at ease as they learn about communication and language, technology and educational opportunities, and the actual life experiences of people who are deaf or hard of hearing.

The SKI-HI Deaf Mentor Program

In 1991, a model program was developed by the SKI-HI Institute at Utah State University called the Deaf Mentor Program (SKI-HI Institute, n.d.). The program included research to determine whether there was an impact on hearing families and their children when trained Deaf adults visited their homes weekly to help them learn how to communicate with their children. These professionals also exposed them to the Deaf Community and shared their life stories and experiences. At the completion of the study, there were significant improvements in the language skills of both the children and family. Mothers who were involved in the program reported using more than six times more signs with their child than families in a control group who did not have access to Deaf Mentors, and fathers reported using more than seven times more signs than fathers in the control group. In addition, parents in the experimental group reported that their child understood what they were communicating to them 84% of the time compared to 50% of the time as reported by families who did not have Deaf Mentors (Watkins, Pittman, & Walden, 1998).

As communication in the family improves, the quality of life for the entire family improves as well. There is a direct and positive correlation between linguistic responsiveness of the parent, the quality of interaction, and the level and speed of language development in the child (Nelson, Carskaddon, & Bonvillian, 1973; Newport, Gleitman, & Gleitman, 1977). Families who participated in the Deaf Mentor Program reported that when their language skills in ASL and signed English[a] improved, their child's behavior also improved. One parent commented:

> Our daughter would throw herself on the floor kicking and screaming several times a day. I will never forget when this happened for

---

[a] Signed English is an invented sign system that makes spoken English visually accessible. Other spoken languages (e.g., Spanish, Urdu) also have sign systems that, similar to signed English, are typically used simultaneously with the spoken language.

the first time when our Deaf Mentor was in our home. We were beside ourselves and asked our Deaf Mentor what we could do to stop these tantrums. She simply said, "You just need to help her understand what is happening." She went over to our daughter, began signing to her and pointing, and she figured out what our little girl wanted and in minutes, she was all smiles. As we learned more signs and could communicate more effectively with our daughter, her negative behaviors disappeared and she began asking for what she wanted instead of throwing herself on the ground. (N. Dexter, personal communication, July 14, 1995)

The Colorado Deaf and Hard-of-Hearing Role Model Program

The communication and language benefits of having deaf or hard-of-hearing adults involved in early intervention programming were also evidenced in Colorado (Beams & Olson, 2007). The Deaf and Hard of Hearing Role Model Program was established by the Colorado Home Intervention Program in 1995. This program provides families with opportunities to get to know deaf and hard-of-hearing adults who use a range of communication modalities and language(s), both ASL and spoken language. Adults who are trained to work as Role Models have different hearing levels and some use assistive listening technologies whereas others do not. Families that use sign language with their children can also receive sign language instruction and storytelling techniques from hearing and deaf ASL instructors . The SKI-HI Deaf Mentor Program and the Deaf and Hard of Hearing Role Model Program help families develop targeted skills to improve communication with their child.

Hearing families are often not aware of the adaptations they need to make to ensure that their child has direct access to communication. This became apparent to one parent who stated the following:

Our Deaf Role Model was also our early interventionist. It was in our weekly meetings that took place in our home that I learned how to naturally do everyday things in a new and better way that would give my son access to language. I met our early interventionist at the door and was chatting with her as we walked up the stairs. She was walking behind me holding my son's hand. When we got to the top of the stairs she told me that she could hear me talking but had no idea what I was saying. I looked at her, and then I looked at my son who was still holding her hand, and I realized that he had never heard me talking if he couldn't see my face. From then on when we walked up the stairs together I either turned my head back as I walking or we all walked together so we could see each other. (K. Bohan, personal communication, July 12, 2000)

Some parents stop talking or singing to their baby after they discover that they are deaf or hard of hearing. After meeting deaf or hard-of-hearing adults, they realize there can still be a place for sounds in their child's life. Deaf or hard-of-hearing adults experience the world in a multitude of ways; some experience it with and some without sound. Deaf or hard-of-hearing adults help families understand that a successful and fulfilling life does not depend upon the ability to hear. One parent said:

We learned that we didn't have to stop singing and playing! Our mentor shared how some deaf and hard of hearing people can and do enjoy music if it is something they are interested in. Just like hearing people, some people care a lot about music and others may not. (C. Bacher, personal communication, October, 2001)

Adults who are deaf or hard of hearing understand the language and communication needs of children who are deaf or hard of hearing and are in a unique position to support and facilitate early language development. Deaf or hard-of-hearing adults can interact with infants and toddlers in ways that make language both accessible and meaningful. Perhaps even more importantly, deaf or hard-of-hearing adults can teach families skills and strategies to help them make the most of every opportunity to promote their child's language development.

Benefits to Hearing Families

Hearing families who learn that they have a child who is deaf or hard of hearing often feel confused about what this will mean for their child and family. Families report a strong desire to have deaf or hard-of-hearing adults actively involved in their lives (Hintermair, 2000; Jackson, 2011). Those who have frequent contact with adults who are deaf or hard of hearing have greater confidence in raising their child who is deaf, feel less isolated, and have improved interactions with their child (Hintermair, 2000; Pittman, 2003).

Understanding Their Child's Potential

Individuals who are deaf or hard of hearing have much to offer children and their hearing families. Getting to know deaf or hard-of-hearing adults can help parents better understand their child's potential. One parent, who was involved in the Deaf Mentor Program in Utah, stated:

> I think that meeting and getting to know our Deaf Mentor made me feel less scared of her [our daughter's] future. Our Deaf Mentor has more of a college education than I have. You know she finished four years of college. I only finished two years of university. She's more skilled, more educated than I am. Meeting her and seeing all of her accomplishments helped me realize that my child could be more and do more than I ever dreamed. Here was this Deaf person who had surpassed me in school and was completely successful. Of course that changed how I felt about my child's future. (Pittman, 2003, p. 155)

Families can learn a great deal from hearing professionals, but they can learn what it is like to be a person who is deaf or hard of hearing only from individuals who are deaf or hard of hearing themselves. Families with little or no experience with people who are deaf or hard of hearing and learn that their baby is deaf or hard of hearing are often overwhelmed. They may experience many different emotions and without support have difficulty creating a secure, trusting, and nurturing relationship with their newborn (Pipp-Siegel, Sedey, & Yoshinaga-Itano, 2002). Meeting deaf or hard-of-hearing adults can help replace a family's concerns with hope and optimism as they focus on their child's strengths and abilities rather than the absence of hearing.

One family in Colorado shared these thoughts with a deaf professional on the early intervention team:

> When we first received our son's diagnosis, I looked at the doctor, he was hearing. I looked at the audiologist, she was hearing and as we walked out of the office, I looked back at the receptionist and she was hearing. I had no idea what this [raising a deaf child] would be like until you (deaf adult) walked in the door. (S. Strickfaden, personal communication, April, 2008)

Families that meet deaf or hard-of-hearing people during their child's early years realize what is possible for their own child. Families that have had the benefit of getting to know adults who are deaf rate their anxiety about raising a child who is deaf or hard of hearing lower than families who have never met an adult who is deaf or hard of hearing (Hintermair, 2006; Pittman, 2003; Watkins, Pittman, & Walden, 1998).

Benefits Extend to Other Family Members

The benefits of having deaf adults involved in the lives of young children and their families extend beyond parents and other primary caregivers. Grandparents and extended family members provide substantial support to families that have children who are deaf or hard of hearing (Jackson, 2011; Luckner & Velaski, 2004; Luterman, 1987; Meadow-Orlans, Mertens, & Sass-Lehrer, 2003; Morton, 2000). One parent explained:

> Our mentor helped us communicate and get our children communicating with her [our deaf daughter], and also to get our parents, our daughter's grandparents, into signing. . . . I think it was nice for the grandparents to see her [the Deaf Mentor], having never known a deaf person, and to see what she was like and to feel more comfortable with that. (Pittman, 2003, p. 145)

Technology

The selection and use of listening technologies can be difficult for families. Whereas hearing professionals provide information to families, it is only deaf or hard-of-hearing adults who can tell families how people who are deaf or hard of hearing actually use these technologies in everyday situations. Hearing families often pursue the use of auditory technology such as hearing aids, FM units, and cochlear implants to improve their children's ability to access spoken language. (See Chapter 6, *Getting Started: Hearing Screening, Evaluation, and Next Steps.*) However, families may not understand that even with the best technologies, hearing spoken language in noisy environments can be challenging. Individuals who are deaf or hard of hearing can help families better understand the benefits and challenges of technologies and suggest helpful strategies.

Although listening technologies are discussed with families soon after their infant's hearing evaluation has confirmed that he or she is deaf or hard of hearing, visual technologies are typically not mentioned. Visual technologies include videophones, texting, alarm clocks with vibration or flashing lights, captions, and flashing light alert systems. These technologies are not only part of the everyday lives of adults who are deaf or hard of hearing, but play an important role in the early years of children as they learn about the presence, source, and meaning of sounds in their environment.

Support for Families' Culture and Traditions

The Williams, similar to most families, want to share their values, traditions, and beliefs with their son. Understanding family traditions is a vital part of family life and helps children experience a sense of belonging. Greg believes that the Williams would benefit from the experiences of an African-American deaf or hard-of-hearing adult who could help the Williams explain their family traditions. Greg heard a story about one hard-of-hearing adult who worked with a Catholic family who observed Lent. The family decided not to eat meat on Fridays during Lent. Their daughter did not realize that when Lent was over, she would be able to eat meat again on Fridays. The hard-of-hearing adult working with the family realized this misunderstanding and discovered that her parents simply forgot to explain that the decision to eliminate meat from their diets on Fridays was only during Lent. Deaf and hard-of-hearing adults as mentors, role models, or advisors can provide families with ideas and strategies for how families can share their family traditions and help their children feel more connected to their families.

Benefits for Early Intervention Systems, Programs, and Professionals

There are many advantages to having deaf and hard-of-hearing professionals and other adults meaningfully involved in all aspects of EHDI programs. Greg learned, to his surprise, that there are deaf professionals who are audiologists, superintendents of schools for deaf children, counselors, educators, psychologists, and social workers. These professionals have the ability to make changes in systems that might not have been realized without their input. For example, when newborn hearing screening programs began, families whose newborns did not pass were often told that their babies had "failed" the newborn hearing screening. The message relayed to families was laced with "doom and gloom." Professionals told families that they were very sorry that their baby had a "hearing loss" and families reported that some professionals would tell them that their child would never be able to talk, or read, or go to college. The influence of professionals and other adults who are deaf or hard of hearing, along with families and others who understand the experiences of deaf people, has helped to change the tone and content of these early messages families received. Today, families are "referred" for further evaluation when their newborn does not receive "a pass" on the hearing screening. Families are more often being told that their newborn has a bright future ahead and that families should have high expectations. Many families are meeting deaf and hard-of-hearing adults soon after they learn that their baby is deaf or hard of hearing and are learning first hand what people who are deaf can do.

TYPES OF INVOLVEMENT

Deaf or hard-of-hearing adults working in early intervention programs include professionals with expertise in a variety of areas (e.g., ASL instruction, audiology, speech-language pathology, counseling, education, psychology, social work). Many of these professionals are also parents themselves with deaf or hard-of-hearing children. They may have grown up in families in which they were the only deaf person, or have grown up in families with deaf parents and deaf siblings. They can and do assume the same roles and responsibilities as professionals who are hearing. Appropriate training and support are critical to effectiveness regardless of whether the individual is deaf, hard of hearing, or hearing.

Deaf Mentor and Role Model Programs

Through their research, Greg and Frances discovered that several states in the United States have adapted elements of the SKI-HI Deaf Mentor Program at Utah State University and the Deaf and Hard of Hearing Role Model Program from Colorado to fit the needs of families and children in their programs. For example, New Mexico has established a statewide Deaf Mentor Program. See Gallegos and Abrams (2011) for a description of their program.

Both of these programs (e.g., Deaf Mentor Program and Deaf and Hard of Hearing Role Model Program) have different strengths, and both place a high value on ensuring that families have opportunities to meet deaf or hard-of-hearing adults.

PROGRAMS PROMOTING MEANINGFUL COLLABORATIONS

Based on what they had learned so far, Greg and his colleagues developed a list of factors that appear to promote effective and meaningful collaboration with deaf or hard-of-hearing adults and their communities (see Table 5.1).

Components of the SKI-HI Deaf Mentor Program

The early intervention administrative team needs significant guidance to ensure that the program they implement is not only effective but also sustainable. Greg was able to share with them the five foundational components of the SKI-HI Deaf Mentor Program (DMP) to use as a model. Many of these components are also incorporated in the Colorado Deaf/

Table 5.1 *Factors Promoting Meaningful Collaborations with Deaf and Hard-of-Hearing Adults and Their Communities*

---

1. Deaf or hard-of-hearing professionals are involved in every component of the early hearing detection and intervention process from screening through provision of services.
2. Professionals provide opportunities for families to meet deaf or hard-of-hearing people with a variety of backgrounds and characteristics:
   - Different levels of hearing
   - Different language and communication preferences and abilities
   - Deaf or hard of hearing from birth and those who have become deaf or hard of hearing later in life
   - Use of assistive listening technologies (e.g., hearing aids, cochlear implants) and those who use visual and tactile technologies
   - Identify with the Deaf community and those who do not
   - Well educated and hold professional positions and those who do not
   - Are culturally, linguistically, and ethnically diverse
   - Have none, one or more developmental delay or difference
3. Programs provide families with opportunities to establish ongoing and meaningful relationships.
4. Programs provide opportunities for deaf or hard-of-hearing professionals to be equal and respected members of the interdisciplinary team.
5. Programs provide training, mentoring, and support for deaf or hard-of-hearing professionals to acquire the knowledge and skills they need to work with infants, toddlers, and their families.

Hard of Hearing Role Model Program. These include (1) training; (2) direct service; (3) supervision and collegial support; (4) administration and support; and (5) involvement of the local Deaf Community.

Training

Deaf mentor programs must provide effective training opportunities initially and as an organized and ongoing process. Working in a home setting with families requires specialized skills to provide effective services. Initial training includes best practices in early intervention including how to work with families and early childhood development. Mentors who are native or near native-signers who work with families who use ASL with their children also learn how to teach ASL to families and how to involve families in the Deaf Community.

Direct Service

At the heart of the DMP are weekly visits with families that take place in the family's home or other natural environments for the child and family. For families learning ASL, the visits have three components: teaching the family ASL, interaction with the child using ASL, and sharing information regarding Deaf Culture and the Deaf Community. Families are taught ASL through formal ASL lessons that fit the needs of the family and informally through conversational interactions. Interactions with the child always include the family and new ASL skills that the family is learning are embedded into the family and child's daily routines through modeling on the part of the Deaf Mentor and active involvement from the family. The Deaf Mentor acts as a "guide" to the family as they explore and learn more about the Deaf Community and meet individuals within the community. Families have reported that seeing their Deaf Mentor in everyday situations has brought them immediate comfort as well as a glimpse into their child's future. One mother reported:

> We would occasionally go to get ice cream or go to the grocery store, and I just learned so much from our Deaf Mentor, seeing how she used gestures, spoken language, sign language and print to communicate with everyone around her. It was just so easy for her that all of my concerns for my daughter just melted away. It really helped me to understand that my daughter needs all kinds of communication and language skills, but most importantly, she needed confidence to communicate in any situation. That was a powerful realization for me. (A. Pack, personal communication, April, 2002)

Families who communicate with their children through spoken language receive visits from a Deaf Mentor who also uses spoken language.

During these visits families learn how to communicate more clearly with their child and obtain ideas to make communication in everyday situations easier for the child and family. The Mentor remains available to the family to answer questions or respond to concerns they might have.

Visits with Deaf Mentors and families should be enjoyable. Learning a new language, learning about a new culture and about a new community, or discovering adaptations that individuals who are deaf or hard of hearing make to participate fully in a world of sound can be challenging, but when visits with the Deaf Mentor are fun, families tend to be more engaged.

Supervision and Collegial Support

Supervision and support from colleagues are essential for any early intervention service to be effective. Supervision provides an opportunity for Deaf Mentors to obtain feedback about their work with families and young children and to learn new strategies. Deaf Mentor Program supervisors should be individuals who have been highly effective Deaf Mentors or Deaf Role Models themselves. Effective supervision requires training, and all supervisors should have the opportunity to develop the knowledge and skills needed to provide effective supervision.

Administration and Support

Deaf Mentor Programs require support from program administrators who appreciate the value of the program and believe it is essential. Regardless of the communication approach that is used by a family, the benefit of having deaf or hard-of-hearing adults involved as an integral member of the early intervention team is vital. Administrators can sustain these programs by providing sufficient resources to hire effective staff, providing appropriate compensation, and ensuring quality training, supervision, and support.

Deaf Community Involvement

Deaf Mentor Programs require strong and positive relationships with their local deaf and hard-of-hearing communities. Collaboration encourages a sense of shared ownership and responsibility for the quality of the program. Success will depend in large part on the ability to recruit outstanding deaf and hard-of-hearing mentors and provide Deaf Community events for families. The Deaf Mentor Program can be a model for how deaf, hard-of-hearing, and hearing people work together. As families learn about deaf and hard-of-hearing communities, they are likely to develop a sense of comfort knowing that the community of deaf and hard-of-hearing adults will lend its support and encouragement. As these individuals develop positive relationships with families and the early intervention program specialists, they recognize that regardless of the paths families choose for communication and education, or the technologies they select for their children, a positive relationship with individuals who are deaf or hard of hearing is essential. One parent, when reflecting on her experiences with the Deaf community, had this to share:

> We have a very high regard for the Deaf community, and because we've chosen to put our kids in mainstream educational programs, we know they need to socialize with Deaf people. We feel that the Deaf community can teach our children things that are important to them because they are Deaf and we are not. We know that they need other people who are like them to share those feelings and experiences that only Deaf people can share, and we want to be a part of that too. (Pittman, 2003, p. 164)

CHALLENGES TO COLLABORATION

Greg and Frances are very enthusiastic about setting up a Deaf Mentor Program in their area, but they are not naive concerning the challenges that lie ahead. They wonder: Where will we find qualified individuals who are willing to be trained as Deaf Mentors? Who will provide training for the Deaf Mentors? How will we be able to provide the Williams with a deaf or hard-of-hearing mentor or role model? These issues are challenging, especially for families such as the Williams who live in rural areas where it is difficult to find people who are deaf or hard of hearing.

Finding and Training Mentors, Role Models, and Guides

Deaf or hard-of-hearing individuals who are interested in becoming mentors or role models must have the dispositions needed to work with families and very young children and be willing to acquire new knowledge and skills. They must be open-minded and flexible and they must be willing to put aside their personal beliefs and biases to understand and respect the family's perspective and the decisions they make for their child. Families have beliefs and values that reflect their experiences, their cultures, and their traditions, and Deaf Mentors or Deaf/HH role models must be willing to learn how to work with families whose values and beliefs may be very different from their own.

Locating adults who are deaf or hard of hearing and who are interested in working with babies and families in rural areas can be difficult. Deaf adults tend to settle in urban or suburban areas where more services and supports are available. To address the lack of individuals who are deaf or hard of hearing in rural areas, some programs use distance technology (e.g., Skype, Face Time). Although this can be successful, the quality and cost of internet services available can create a challenge. Greg and his team must figure out ways to provide families with opportunities to engage with adults who are deaf or hard of hearing that require limited cost and travel time. Greg will contact their state school for the deaf and association of the deaf to investigate the availability of community and outreach services that may be able to help. Commitment to funding for these valuable opportunities is a priority for Greg's team.

SUMMARY

Families with deaf or hard-of-hearing children consistently note that adults who are deaf or hard of hearing provide an important source of support (Hintermair, 2000; Jackson, 2011; Meadow-Orlans et al., 2003; Pittman, 2003). The benefit of a deaf mentor, role model, or guide ranks among the highest needs identified by parents of children who are deaf or hard of hearing (Jackson, 2011).

It is clear that the influence of adults who are deaf or hard of hearing in the lives of hearing families and their children who are deaf or hard of hearing is positive and can impact the child and family for the rest of their lives. Including deaf and hard-of-hearing adults in a range of positions, including leadership roles, is essential to the success of a quality early intervention program (JCIH, 2013). Despite the known benefits, Greg and his colleagues know that establishing and sustaining a deaf mentor, role model, or guide program and recruiting and hiring deaf or hard-of-hearing adults will be challenging. They are convinced of the value of these experiences for families and children and are confident that the information and resources they have collected will guide them as they develop and incorporate this critical component of services into their early intervention programming.

SUGGESTED ACTIVITIES

1. When is the right time for a family to meet an adult who is deaf or hard of hearing? Prepare to defend your position by providing a rationale and describing the purpose of connecting with deaf and hard-of-hearing adults.
2. After families learn that their child is deaf or hard of hearing, they often report that everything changes. Professionals can help families reclaim what is still the same for their family and their new baby. Role play inter-actions with a family that has recently learned their baby is deaf. Here are some suggestions to get you started: (1) ask the family about their dreams and hopes for their child; (2) talk about the expectations they have for their child related to friendships, education, interests, or careers; (3) ask them what they believe will be the same or different for their child because their child is deaf.
3. *The Passionate Lives of Deaf and Hard of Hearing People* by Karen Putz features stories of deaf and hard-of-hearing people doing what they love, for example, climbing mountains, racing cars, championing causes, trav-eling the world, and more. Discuss a story that seemed "impossible" to you or to a family with whom you work. Discuss what made these dreams possible for the people in this book.

4. Watch the following: Navigating Deafness in a Hearing World: Rachel Kolb at TEDxStandford https://www.youtube.com/watch?v=uKKpjvPd6Xo. Rachel shares several obstacles she faced in her life. What strategies worked for her or for her family in overcoming those obstacles?

RECOMMENDED RESOURCES

1. American Sign Language
   - *ASL Nook* A resource for families learning American Sign Language. It includes ASL words, pictures, and stories. www.ASLnook.com.
   - *ASL University* An online ASL curriculum resource center. www. ASLUniversity.com.
2. American Sign Language Storybook Apps
   - *VL2 Storybooks* The storybook apps produced by the Visual Language and Visual Learning Science of Learning Center (VL2) at Gallaudet University include children's stories in both American Sign Language and English. http://vl2storybookapps.com.
   - *Zoey Goes* This is a series of ASL stories about a Deaf dog, Zoey, and her human partner. They are written and signed by Rachel Berman Blythe and illustrated by Jena Floyd. http://zoeygoes.com/about/.
3. American Society for Deaf Children (ASDC)
   ASDC is a national organization that provides support, encouragement, and information to families of deaf and hard-of-hearing children. ASDC educates families about education for deaf and hard-of-hearing children, Individualized Education Plan (IEP) rights, bilingualism, English and ASL, and what it means to be deaf or hard of hearing. www.deaf-children.org.
4. Gallaudet University
   Gallaudet University was founded in 1864 as the first school where students who were Deaf or hard of hearing could received an advanced education. It was a federally chartered school for the deaf and hard of hearing in Washington, D. C. Today, it remains the only liberal arts university in the world that has been designed for the Deaf. The university strives to make every possible accommodation for individuals who are deaf or hard of hearing to ensure their academic and career success.

The university is bilingual, ensuring that course instruction is accessible in both ASL and English. https://www.gallaudet.edu.

5. ASLIZED!

An online video library of ASL literature and ASL linguistics research (www.aslized.org). See *Early Intervention: The Missing Link* for a presentation about the inclusion of deaf and hard of hearing professionals in early intervention (http://aslized.org/ei/).

6. Holcomb, T. (2012). *Introduction to American deaf culture*. New York, NY: Oxford University Press.

This book provides a historical review and current view of Deaf culture; it includes topics such as Deafhood, disability versus culture, American Sign Language, and social interaction. Multiple references and resources to other works can be found.

7. The Integrated Reading Project

The Integrated Reading Project is designed to help families learn to read and enjoy books with their children who are deaf or hard of hearing. It is specifically for families that have chosen a simultaneous communication approach (signing and voicing at the same time). http://www.csdb.org/Default.aspx?DN=dc05dda4-a81e-4792-bc54-f79d4812ba16.

8. National Association of the Deaf (NAD)

The NAD is a nonprofit organization that advocates for the rights of all people who are deaf or hard of hearing in a variety of areas including early intervention, education, employment, health care, technology, telecommunications, youth leadership, and more. www.nad.org.

9. National Deaf Black Advocates (NDBA)

The NDBA is an advocacy organization for Black Deaf and Hard of Hearing Americans and includes not only Black Deaf and Hard of Hearing individuals, but also parents, professionals who work with Black Deaf and Hard of Hearing youth and adults, sign language interpreters, and others. www.nbda.org.

10. National Deaf Children's Society

The National Deaf Children's Society (NDCS) is the leading charity in the United Kingdom that provides resources, programs, and services for deaf and hard-of-hearing children, adults, and their families. The NDCS website offers information about their Deaf Role Model project and British Sign Language (BSL). http://www.ndcs.org.uk.

11. Sensual Cultures

    This mobile app is a visual guide to cross-cultural conflicts and provides an introduction into how Deaf and hearing cultures value sight, touch, and sound. [Benedict, L. (2013). Sensual Cultures (Version 1.0). [Mobile application software. Retrieved from https://itunes.apple.com/us/app/sensual-cultures/id643961910?mt=8.]

12. Shared Reading Project

    The Shared Reading Project is designed to teach parents and caregivers how to read to their deaf and hard-of-hearing children using American Sign Language, and to use strategies to make book sharing more effective.

    http://www.gallaudet.edu/clerc_center/information_and_resources/info_to_go/language_and_literacy/literacy_at_the_clerc_center/welcome_to_shared_reading_project.html.

13. World Federation of the Deaf

    The World Federation of the Deaf (WFD) includes approximately 130 member countries that represent 70 million people who are deaf internationally. The WFD mission is to expand the acceptance of sign language and to improve educational opportunities and human rights for deaf people throughout the word. Http://wfdeaf.org.

REFERENCES

Atherton, M. (2009). A feeling as much as a place: Leisure, Deaf clubs, and the British Deaf community. *Leisure Studies, 28*(4), 443–454.

Baker, C., & Padden, C. (1978). *American Sign Language: A look at its story, structure and community.* Dallas, TX: T.J. Publishers.

Beams, D., & Olson, S. (2007, March). *Partnering with deaf adults: Creating positive outcomes for children and families.* Paper presented at the Early Hearing Detection and Intervention Conference, Salt Lake City, Utah.

Benedict, B., Crace, J., Holmes, T., Hossler, T., Oliva, G., Raimondo, B., … Vincent, J. (2014). Deaf community support for families: The best of partnerships. In L. Schmeltz (Ed.), *The NCHAM eBook: A resource guide for early hearing detection and intervention (EHDI).* Retrieved from http://www.infanthearing.org/ehdi-ebook/2013_ebook/21Chapter20DeafCommunity2013.pdf.

Benedict, B. S., & Sass-Lehrer, M. (2007). Deaf and hearing partnerships: Ethical and communication considerations. *American Annals of the Deaf, 152*(3), 275–282.

Bodner-Johnson, B., & Benedict, B. S. (2012). *Bilingual deaf and hearing families: Narrative interviews.* Washington, DC: Gallaudet University Press.

Cunningham, M., & Cox, E. O. (2003). Hearing assessment in infants and children: Recommendations beyond neonatal screening. *Pediatrics, 111,* 436–440.

Gallegos, R., & Abrams, S. (2011). Deaf role models making a critical difference in New Mexico. *Odyssey: New Directions in Deaf Education, 12,* 24–27.

Gannon, J. (1981). *Deaf heritage: A narrative history of deaf America.* Silver Spring, MD: National Association of the Deaf.

Hadjikakou, K., & Nekolaraizi, M. (2011). Deaf clubs today: Do they still have a role to play? The cases of Cyprus & Greece. *American Annals of the Deaf, 155*(5), 605–617.

Hands and Voices (n.d.). *Deaf and hard of hearing mentors and role models.* Retrieved from http://www.handsandvoices.org/comcon/articles/mentorsRolemodels.htm.

Hintermair, M. (2000). Hearing impairment, social networks, and coping: The need for families with hearing-impaired children to relate to other parents and to hearing-impaired adults. *American Annals of the Deaf, 145*(1), 41–53.

Hintermair, M. (2006). Parental resources, parental stress, and socioemotional development of deaf and hard of hearing children. *Journal of Deaf Studies and Deaf Education, 11*(4), 493–513.

Hoffman, J., Houston, K. T., Munoz, K. F., & Bradham, T. S. (2011). Periodic early childhood hearing screening: The EHDI perspective. *The Volta Review, 111*(2), 195–208.

Jackson, C. (2011). Family supports and resources for parents of children who are deaf or hard of hearing. *American Annals of the Deaf, 156*(4), 343–362.

Johnson, R., Liddell, S., & Erting, C. (1989). *Unlocking the curriculum: Principles for achieving access in deaf education.* Washington, DC: Gallaudet Research Institute.

Joint Committee on Infant Hearing. (2013). Supplement to the JCIH 2007 position statement: Principles and guidelines for intervention after confirmation that a child is deaf or hard of hearing. *Pediatrics,131*(4), e1324–1349. doi:10.1542/peds.2013-0008.

Lane, H., Hoffmeiser, R., & Bahan, B. (1996). *Journey into the DEAF-WORLD.* San Diego, CA: Dawn Sign Press.

Leigh, I. (2009). *A lens on deaf identities.* New York, NY: Oxford University Press.

Luckner, J., & Velaski, A. (2004). Healthy families of children who are deaf. *American Annals of the Deaf, 149*(4), 324–335.

Luterman, D. (1987). *Deafness in the family.* Boston, MA: College Hill Press

Meadow-Orlans, K. P., Mertens, D. M., & Sass-Lehrer, M. A. (2003). *Parents and their deaf children: The early years*. Washington, DC: Gallaudet University Press.

Mitchell, R., & Karchmer, M. (2004). When parents are deaf versus hard of hearing: Patterns of sign use and school placement of deaf and hard of hearing children. *Journal of Deaf Studies and Education, 9*(2), 133–152.

Moeller, M. P., Carr, G., Seaver, L., Stredler-Brown, A., & Holzinger, D. (2013). Best practices in family-centered early intervention for children who are deaf or hard of hearing: An international consensus statement. *Journal of Deaf Studies and Deaf Education, 18*(4), 429–445. doi:10.1093/deafed/ent034.

Morton, D. D. (2000). Beyond parent education: *The impact of extended family dynamics in deaf education. American Annals of the Deaf, 145*(4), 359–365.

Nelson, K. E., Carskaddon, G., & Bonvillian, J. D. (1973). Syntax acquisition: Impact of experimental variation in adult verbal interactions with the child. *Child Development, 44*, 497–504.

Newport, E., Gleitman, H., & Gleitman, L. (1977). Mother, I'd rather do it myself: Some effects and noneffects of maternal speech style. In C. Snow & C. Ferguson (Eds.), *Talking to children: Language input and acquisition*. Cambridge, England: Cambridge University Press.

Oliva, G., & Lytle, L. (2014). *Turning the tide: Making life better for deaf and hard of hearing schoolchildren*. Washington, DC: Gallaudet University Press.

Olusanya, B. O. (2012). Neonatal hearing screening and intervention in resource-limited settings: An overview. *Archives of Disease in Childhood, 97*, 654–659.

Padden, C., & Humphries, T. (1988). *Deaf in America: Voices from a culture*. Cambridge, MA: Harvard College.

Padden, C., &. Humphries, T. (2006). *Inside deaf culture*. Cambridge, MA: Harvard University Press.

Paul, P. V. (1996). First and second language English literacy. *Volta Review, 1*, 3–15.

Pipp-Siegel, S., Sedey, A., & Yoshinaga-Itano, C. (2002). Predictors of paternal stress in mothers of young children with hearing loss. *Journal of Deaf Studies and Deaf Education, 7*(1), 1–17.

Pittman, P. (2003). *Starting small: A qualitative study of families of deaf children who have experienced early intervention services*. Retrieved from *Dissertation Abstracts International, 64*(05), 1600A. (UMI No. 3091770.)

Power, M. R., Power, D., & Horstmanshof, L. (2006). Deaf people communicating via SMS, TTY, relay service, fax, and computers in Australia. *Journal of Deaf Studies and Deaf Education, 12*(1), 80–92.

Shoham, S., & Heber, M. (2012). Characteristics of a virtual community for individuals who are d/Deaf and hard of hearing. *American Annals of the Deaf, 157*(3), 251–263.

SKI-HI Institute. (n.d.). *Deaf mentor program.* Retrieved from www.skihi.org/deafment.html.

Stokoe, W. (1996). *Sign language studies.* Silver Spring, MD: Linstok Press.

Stokoe, W. (2005). Sign language structure: An outline of the visual communication systems of the American deaf. *Journal of Deaf Studies and Deaf Education, 10*(1), 3–37.

Watkins, S., Pittman, P., & Walden, B. (1998). The deaf mentor experimental project for young children who are deaf. *American Annals of the Deaf, 143*(1), 29–34.

Wilkens, C. P., & Hehir, T. P. (2008). Deaf education and bridging social capital: A theoretical approach. *American Annals of the Deaf, 153*(3), 275–284.

PART II

Early Intervention Practices

6 Getting Started: Hearing Screening, Evaluation, and Next Steps

Rachel St. John, Linda Lytle, Debra Nussbaum, and Angela Shoup

Following a routine birth and prior to leaving the hospital, Abby Cullen had a newborn hearing screening that she did not pass in either ear. The hearing screener told the Cullen family that this sometimes happens and not to be too concerned, but stressed the importance of bringing Abby back to the hospital in 1 week to repeat the screening. Abby did not pass the second screening, and was referred to Dr. Davis, a pediatric audiologist, for a comprehensive audiological evaluation to confirm her hearing status. After completing comprehensive audiological testing, Dr. Davis confirmed that 5-week-old Abby was deaf. He briefly discussed the evaluation findings and scheduled a follow-up appointment to start the process of getting hearing aids for Abby. He indicated that he would send the evaluation results to the Cullen's pediatrician, Dr. Lacey, and asked the family to sign a consent form to refer their daughter for early intervention services.

GUIDING QUESTIONS

1. What information is important for the audiologist and other professionals to share with families immediately following confirmation that a child is deaf or hard of hearing?
2. How can medical and educational professionals collaborate to impart information to families to positively impact their experience getting started in raising a child who is deaf or hard of hearing?
3. How can professionals effectively collaborate to support families through the initial identification that their child is deaf or hard of hearing?

COMPETENCIES ADDRESSED IN THIS CHAPTER

1. Screening, Evaluation and Assessment: Interpretation of Hearing Screening and Audiological Diagnostic Information; Ongoing Developmental Assessment; and Use of Developmental Assessment Tools to Monitor Progress
2. Family-Centered Practice: Family–Professional Partnerships, Decision Making, and Family Support
3. Technology: Supporting Development by Using Technology to Access Auditory, Visual, and/or Tactile Information
4. Collaboration and Interdisciplinary Models and Practices

INTRODUCTION

A family's journey with their child who is deaf or hard of hearing begins at the time of the baby's hearing screening and subsequent referral for further hearing evaluation. Unless a family has some reason to suspect that their child might be deaf, this is usually the first time that they have even considered hearing as an issue for their child. The initial screening result is the beginning of a series of many medical appointments. Following the actual confirmation that their child is deaf or hard of hearing, a family will encounter many decisions regarding their child's development.

Even with the most efficient early hearing screening and intervention programs, there is a gap between the time of identification by the audiologist and the point at which a family formally begins early intervention services. This is a crucial time because families often have many questions and need quality support. This period, from hearing screening to referral for early intervention services, is the primary focus of this chapter. The chapter will address many issues that families and the professionals working with them should consider when an infant is identified as deaf or hard of hearing, as well as how professionals can effectively collaborate to make the identification and intervention process a positive one.

THE HEARING SCREENING AND EVALUATION PROCESS

The Hearing Screening Process

The Cullens received the results of the newborn hearing screening in the hospital, but were not sure what it meant. One week later, they brought Abby back to repeat the hearing screening and learned that the screening test used was called Otoacoustic Emissions. When Abby did not pass the second screening, the Cullens were told to follow-up as soon as possible with a pediatric audiologist for detailed comprehensive hearing testing to confirm Abby's hearing abilities.

There are two types of commonly used hearing screening technologies: Otoacoustic Emissions (OAE) and Automated Auditory Brainstem Response (AABR). OAE is a quick and easy test that presents a sound to the ear through a soft probe that is placed in the infant's ear canal. A typically functioning ear responds to sound in a specific way. If this response is not observed, it indicates that there is a possibility that the hearing system is not functioning. The OAE indicates only whether an infant's ear is responding to the sounds presented during the screening. If a child does not pass the hearing screening, it indicates that further evaluation is necessary.

For the AABR screening, small electrodes are placed on the baby, typically on the back of the neck, forehead, and cheek or shoulder. Sounds are presented through earphones, and sensors pick up brain waves that occur in response to the sounds. Similar to the OAE, a screening AABR does not identify a child's precise hearing level; it indicates only whether further testing is necessary.

For both the screening OAE and the screening AABR, the result is automatically processed and calculated by a computer, and is recorded as either a "pass" or a "did not pass/refer." The terms "did not pass" or "refer" are suggested as an alternative to the term "failed" to avoid the implication of "failure" on the part of a newborn. There is no universal agreement among professionals, however, about which terms should be used. Providers should be aware that families might be exposed to these terms interchangeably.

The professional who shares the hearing screening results with the family needs to communicate very clearly both the importance and limitations of the information that has been obtained. It is important for a family to realize that a hearing screening is not a definite test of hearing level and that a detailed follow-up assessment is needed. The hearing screener must strike a balance between creating unnecessary anxiety about a hearing screening that is not passed and minimizing the results to the point that the family loses sight of the importance and urgency of follow-up testing.

If a newborn does not pass the initial hearing screening, this does not mean that the baby is deaf or hard of hearing. A baby may not pass the screening for a variety of reasons. Sometimes issues may resolve in the first weeks of life, and sometimes the issues are permanent. For example, debris in the ear canal just after birth, also known as vernix, or fluid in the middle ear may cause a "did not pass" result on the newborn hearing screening. The American Academy of Pediatrics (AAP) recommends that all infants who do not pass their hearing screening, for any reason, receive a full audiological evaluation by 3 months of age.

The Hearing Evaluation Process

The Cullens made an appointment for Abby to see Dr. Davis, a pediatric audiologist, for a complete hearing evaluation. Dr. Davis explained that he would conduct a battery of tests. Some of the tests would be objective tests and would not require a behavioral response from Abby, whereas other tests would require an observation of how Abby responds to sound. He explained that a combination of these tests would be used to confirm Abby's hearing ability.

It is recommended that a pediatric audiologist specifically trained to test the hearing of infants and toddlers conduct the comprehensive audiological evaluation. One of the tests central to confirming whether a child is deaf or hard of hearing is an Auditory Brainstem Response (ABR) test. The ABR test provides information about the inner ear (cochlea) and brain pathways for hearing. For diagnostic ABR testing, similar to the AABR screening, the audiologist attaches sensors/electrodes to the infant to record the brain responses to sounds. Different from the screening AABR, the diagnostic ABR uses sounds of varying loudness and frequency to record brain wave activity in response to sound. This helps determine the level at which the child responds to sounds at specific frequencies. The ABR test can be completed only if the child is sleeping or lying perfectly still with his or her eyes closed. When a baby is younger than 6 months of age, the ABR test often can be done while he or she naps. However, this test may need to be completed under mild sedation for infants who cannot maintain natural sleep long enough for testing to be completed.

Additional tests, such as Behavioral Observation Audiometry (BOA), examine how a child responds to sound (e.g., changes in breathing patterns, sucking, reflexes), and can also be used to help confirm ABR findings. These tests are not as definitive as ABR testing because they are based on observations of the infant's behavior, but the results of BOA can serve as an important adjunct to other testing by the audiologist as part of the testing process. Testing of middle ear status should also be completed to confirm that there are no middle ear issues confounding the findings of the hearing tests that are completed [American Speech-Language-Hearing Association (ASHA), 2004].

Dr. Davis informed the Cullens that Abby's tests demonstrated her hearing level was in the profound range in both ears, and that her hearing condition, described as sensorineural, was permanent and was related to the part of the ear called the inner ear. Dr. Davis explained that this meant that she is deaf in both ears and could hear only very loud sounds, such as an airplane or a lawn mower.

THE HEARING SYSTEM

When a family learns that their child is deaf or hard of hearing, they are faced with unfamiliar, and potentially confusing, medical and audiological information. It is helpful for them to have a basic understanding of the hearing system to sort out this new information. There are four main components of the auditory pathway or hearing system: the outer ear, the middle ear, the inner ear, and the auditory (8th) nerve and brain. Recommendations for intervention services relate to which of the four components, or combinations of components, may be involved, and may be important for determining eligibility for services under state programs directed by Part C of the Individuals with Disabilities Education Act (IDEA Infant and Toddler Coordinators Association and National Center for Hearing Assessment and Management, 2011). The types of hearing conditions reflect the specific point in the hearing system at which function is atypical. See Table 6.1 for a description of the Types of Hearing Conditions.

Families will also learn that children who are deaf or hard of hearing have a range of hearing levels. The goal of the audiological evaluation is to identify a child's hearing levels at various frequencies (pitches) of sound, and to determine the pattern of a child's hearing across frequencies. In the field of audiology, hearing levels are described as ranging from "within normal range" to "profound" and there are various descriptions of hearing patterns in terms of how a child may process the sounds of speech. It is important for families to learn about the audiological information regarding their child and how this information guides the fitting of hearing aids and recommendations for developing language and communication.

A child's hearing ability can change over time. The incidence of infants who are born deaf or hard of hearing in the United States is between one and three in 1,000 live births [Centers for Disease Control and Prevention (CDC), 2013] and even higher in developing countries. (See Chapter 10,

Table 6.1 *Types of Hearing Conditions*

Conductive	This occurs when sound is not effectively transmitted through the outer and middle ear to the inner ear. This can happen for a variety of reasons: the ear canal is blocked, something is interfering with the function of the middle ear, or the ear itself does not form correctly during pregnancy. Depending on the reason, conductive hearing conditions are often responsive to treatment and may resolve.
Sensorineural	This occurs when sound does not effectively travel through the inner ear, up the auditory nerve, and to the brain for processing and understanding. This type of hearing condition is generally permanent in nature.
Mixed	Sometimes conductive and sensorineural hearing conditions can occur together. A child, for example, who has sensorineural involvement could also have fluid in the middle ear, which would result in an overlapping conductive hearing component. The conductive component may or may not be temporary.
Auditory Neuropathy	Also referred to as Auditory Dys-synchrony or Auditory Neuropathy Spectrum Disorder (ANSD), this unique type of hearing condition occurs when the transmission of sound from the inner ear to the brain is not effective. Infants who are born extremely prematurely, or require extensive life-saving interventions at birth, are at higher risk for developing auditory neuropathy. For some infants with auditory neuropathy at birth, developmental maturation of the auditory system may partially or fully resolve the neuropathy. For others, it will be permanent (Uus, 2011). Auditory neuropathy can be challenging for both families and health care providers, as it varies from person to person, and does not consistently respond to any one treatment opportunity. Some children may benefit from traditional hearing aids, and others may not (Roush, Frymark, Venediktov, & Wang, 2011; Santarelli, Rossi, & Arslan, 2013).

Early Intervention in Challenging National Contexts.) This number increases significantly as a child gets older, and by the time a child is school-aged, it is estimated that 9–10 children in 1,000 will be identified as deaf or hard of hearing [American Academy of Audiology (AAA), 2011]. Health care providers can assist families in understanding the importance of regular hearing evaluations, and monitor for possible changes in hearing ability over time. In fact, it is estimated that among school-aged children whose hearing levels significantly impact their learning, up to half passed their initial newborn hearing screenings (AAA, 2011).

FAMILY REACTIONS AND PROFESSIONAL RESPONSES

Families' Reactions to the Initial Screening and Identification Process

The Cullens thought Abby's hearing was going to be just fine and were shocked to learn that she was deaf. Dr. Davis told the Cullens that he would send the test results to Abby's pediatrician. After he shared the test results with the Cullen family, he asked them to sign a consent form so that he could refer them to other professionals who were skilled in early intervention for young children who are deaf or hard of hearing. The Cullens left the audiology clinic in disbelief, with many questions about what this would mean for their child.

Although a family may be actively involved in the screening and identification process, it is not until the full evaluation is complete and the results are shared that the family is confronted with the reality that their baby is deaf or hard of hearing. Unless a family has had previous experience either having or knowing another child who is deaf or hard of hearing, they probably never thought this could be a possibility for their child. This places the audiologist in the position of being a first responder responsible for informing families of the test findings, as well as what to expect from the audiological follow-up and early intervention processes.

The way in which audiological evaluation findings are conveyed to families plays an important role in a family's reaction and the intervention steps taken (ASHA, 2008). Audiologists may struggle with providing either too much or not enough information to families. It is important that they be sensitive to the individual characteristics and needs of families and monitor the pace and process for sharing audiological findings and their implications (Meadow-Orlans, Mertens, & Sass-Lehrer, 2003). Laugen (2013) suggests that audiologists consider the following in the process of sharing information with families: (1) clearly explain whether there is ambiguity in the test findings as well as the professional recommendations related to the test findings; (2) provide comprehensive information; (3) provide information both in writing and through conversation; (4) have all essential family members present; (5) provide connections to professionals for follow-up (not only recommendations specific to audiology); and (6) support independent information seeking in families.

Families receive confirmation that their baby is deaf or hard of hearing from health care professionals, who understandably tend to focus on the medically related actions, such as fitting of hearing aids, genetic counseling, or an appointment with an ear, nose, and throat (ENT) doctor (Matthijs et al., 2012). Families may not understand how the medical aspects of the audiological evaluation process relate to their child's language, cognitive, and psychosocial development. It is important that health care professionals understand that an optimal early identification and intervention process involves the collaboration of all providers including audiologists as well as early intervention professionals (Fitzpatrick, Angus, Durieux-Smith, Graham, & Coyle, 2008; Laugen, 2013).

If the early intervention process is to start well, audiologists will take into consideration the many key points detailed in the *"What Else" Checklist: Guiding Audiologists in Their Role with Families* (Grimes & DesGeorges, 2013). This checklist, developed in collaboration between the Center for Disease Control Provider Education and Parent-to-Parent Committees, addresses considerations for audiologists as they share information that goes beyond basic descriptions of a child's hearing abilities. The guidelines specifically ask audiologists to self-reflect on questions such as the following:

- Did I allow the parent to guide me in what they need?
- Have I considered the family's perspective regarding their child's needs?

- Have I considered the family's priorities in our discussion?
- Did I talk about this experience in a "nonmedical" way?

The checklist also includes guidance for audiologists on providing information and resources to families about the various approaches to language and communication typically used with young children who are deaf or hard of hearing as well as information to support families in connecting with resources in their region.

Families' Information Processing

After learning from the audiologist, Dr. Davis, that Abby is deaf, Mrs. Cullen went home and immediately did an internet search for "deaf children." Mr. Cullen preferred to wait until their next appointments when they would have the opportunity to talk with Dr. Davis and Abby's pediatrician, Dr. Lacey, again.

Acquiring and digesting information are ongoing processes for families. Professionals may struggle with the desire to provide important information to families without overwhelming them. Each family is unique, and will acquire and process information in their own way and at their own speed. To assume a universal "timeline of readiness" for every family is unrealistic. Although some families want information available as soon as possible, other families prefer to receive information on an "as needed" basis. Professionals may do well by asking families what information they want, guiding them through the vast array of resources, and being responsive to their questions and requests for more information. Being responsive and sensitive to families' information needs establishes a strong foundation of mutual respect (Meadow-Orlans et al., 2003)

There is no "one size fits all" when it comes to making information meaningful for families of very young children who are deaf or hard of hearing. Although every family is unique, there are some common ways in which parents tend to learn new information. Les Schmeltz (2013) describes four overarching learning styles for how parents take in and process new information. See Table 6.2, How Families Take in and Process Information.

Table 6.2 *How Families Take in and Process Information*[a]

Dynamic Learners	Learn by hands-on doing ("trial and error")
Analytic Learners	Want all information and research available
Common Sense Learners	Want just the basic facts
Imaginative Learners	Acquire information best through social interactions, talking, and consulting with others

[a]Adapted from Schmeltz (2013).

These different learning styles influence individual preferences for acquiring information. Although some family members want to read peer-reviewed research articles, others prefer having the information summed up succinctly for them. Internet users may prefer a list of websites to access information. Others may prefer watching a video or discussing a topic with a professional.

There are also diverse ways professionals share information with families. The art of delivering information is ideally honed by the individual provider through years of experience working with families, and adapted to meet the unique needs of each family (Laugen, 2013). Although each provider develops his or her own best sense of how to connect meaningfully with families, there are some ineffective styles of communication that can create problems for the provider–family relationship. Schmeltz (2013) illustrates seven ineffective communication styles: (1) overwhelm them with the facts; (2) the hit-and-run professional; (3) the busybody; (4) sympathy, not empathy; (5) the canned presentation; (6) the nonstop talker; and (7) don't worry we can fix it (p. 9). None of these approaches promotes a family–professional relationship.

Professionals need to be prepared to share information with families in a structured and balanced way (Matthijs et al., 2012). They should be able to

- share test results in a positive and constructive manner with families after they have first received the news that their child is deaf or hard of hearing;

- provide information, guidance, and emotional support to facilitate the development of informed, independent, and empowered families (ASHA, 2008);
- guide families in filtering the vast amount of information available on the internet (ASHA, 2008);
- share assessment findings and recommendations with families who are deaf in a culturally sensitive manner;
- share information using the family's preferred language, comfortably using interpreters as needed;
- share language and communication opportunities in a manner that goes beyond providing a "menu" of approaches, and acknowledges the importance of capitalizing on a child's natural skills and characteristics (Young et al., 2006);
- help families recognize that all decisions are subject to change over time and that initial choices are not set in stone (ASHA, 2008).

COLLABORATION AMONG PROFESSIONS AND PROFESSIONALS

The Medical Home

The Cullens were fond of Abby's pediatrician, Dr. Lacey. She admitted upfront to the Cullens that she had not had the opportunity to take care of many children like Abby who are deaf or hard of hearing. The Cullens were impressed that Dr. Lacey was quick to consult the guidelines for caring for deaf and hard-of-hearing children established by the American Academy of Pediatrics (2014), and was honest with them about what she knew and did not know. The Cullens appreciated that Dr. Lacey was willing to work with them to help coordinate all of Abby's care.

In 1967, the term "medical home" first appeared in a publication by the AAP. This referred specifically to the centralizing of medical records as a way to address overlaps and gaps in medical care for children with special health care needs (Sia, Tonniges, Osterhaus, & Taba, 2004). The definition of the medical home evolved over the next several decades, and in 1992 the AAP published its first policy statement defining medical home as a philosophy of care applying to all infants, children, and adolescents.

Children with multiple medical conditions benefit from an effective medical home that facilitates decisions about their care and development. Traditionally, the medical home role is taken on by the primary care provider (PCP). The child's pediatrician, a family practitioner, the physician's assistant, or a nurse practitioner may fill the medical home PCP role. The medical home provider is the "front line" in working with a family and child to coordinate and interpret the multiple recommendations and opportunities for care. As described in the 2007 Joint Committee on Infant Hearing (JCIH) position statement, "The primary health care professional acts in partnership with parents in the medical home to identify and access appropriate audiology, intervention, and consultative services that are needed to develop a global plan of appropriate and necessary health and habilitative care for infants identified with hearing loss and infants with risk factors for hearing loss" (p. 6). According to the most recent AAP policy statement revision in 2002, an ideal medical home has seven defined characteristics, in that it is accessible, family centered, continuous, comprehensive, coordinated, compassionate, and culturally effective. For an in-depth description of effective medical home characteristics, see the AAP Medical Home weblink in the Recommended Resources section at the end of this chapter. Because educators and intervention specialists do not fall under the category of health care providers, medical home providers and early intervention professionals cannot communicate with each other without permission from the family. Although it is not practical or necessary to communicate every aspect of the intervention process with medical home providers, it can be helpful to share information from time to time with the medical home.

Coordinated Care for Children with Developmental or Physical Conditions

While the Cullens were at Dr. Lacey's office for a follow-up visit, they noticed another family whose son was connected to equipment and monitors and who appeared to have a number of medical issues. In talking with the family, the Cullens learned that their son was born extremely prematurely. In addition to medical complications involving his heart, lungs, and other body systems, he also had a hearing level similar to Abby's. The Cullens, who until this time have been very preoccupied with Abby's needs, had a difficult time imagining how these parents could handle all of their son's medical issues in addition to being deaf.

Some families may have critically ill children, whose medical concerns take priority over the issues related to hearing. These families may be initially less concerned about their child's hearing, and have different questions from other families. Families of children who have complex medical needs may experience patterns of stress that are qualitatively different from families whose children are deaf only (Hintermair, 2000; Meadow-Orlans et al., 2003). With continuing advancements in modern technology, premature infants and children with complex medical syndromes and illness are surviving and living longer than in years past. According to the national survey of children and youth from the Gallaudet Research Institute, nearly 40% of deaf or hard-of-hearing students had at least one identified condition in addition to being deaf or hard of hearing (Gallaudet Research Institute, 2010). Researchers have found that families with a medically complex child can experience additional strain in caring and making decisions for their child (Hintermair, 2000; Pipp-Siegel, Sedey, & Yoshinaga-Itano, 2002).

Family members and friends, though well intentioned, may minimize or invalidate a parent or caregiver's emotional response in an attempt to make the parent feel better. Families may experience feelings of fear, loss of control, or frustration. Others may feel guilt for a perceived wrong that somehow led to their child's medical situation (Luterman, 2004). Families with medically complex infants and children often need help from the medical home and other interdisciplinary team members to access appropriate services and support.

Some families, particularly those with children who have multiple complex medical needs, elect to set up a *formalized* medical care coordination plan that can be documented and shared among providers and caregivers. A family member, social worker, formal care coordinator, nurse, or other individual who has knowledge of the child and the family can do this. Care coordination planning ideally includes plans for both emergency and routine situations and can be shared with the family's permission at Individualized Family Service Plan (IFSP) meetings so all key providers can work from the same construct. Sample templates for care coordination plans can be easily accessed online through the Medical Home Portal website, and are included in the Recommended Resources.

The Interdisciplinary Team of Specialists

The Cullens put together a notebook containing information and medical records from different specialists providing care and support for Abby. In her first few months of life, Abby had already seen an audiologist, an otolaryngologist (ENT physician), an ophthalmologist (eye physician), and a geneticist. The Cullens were not sure why all of these specialists had to be involved.

All children and families benefit from a collaborative approach to care, whether the focus is medical, educational, or psychosocial. From the initial screening and identification process, the infant is typically under the care of an audiologist. The family with a deaf or hard-of-hearing child may then be referred to multiple health care specialists. The Joint Committee on Infant Hearing recommends appropriate subspecialty referrals immediately after identification, and not later than 6 months of age [Joint Committee on Infant Hearing (JCIH), 2007]. For all infants and children who are deaf or hard of hearing, there are a minimum of three specialty services that should be included in coordinated care with the medical home provider: an otolaryngologist, an ophthalmologist, and a geneticist.

Otolaryngology (ENT) physicians provide a full medical examination of the head and neck and help explain the reason a child may be deaf or hard of hearing. The ENT also makes recommendations to the family and primary care physician regarding possible medical and/or surgical treatments. The otolaryngologist, in collaboration with the medical home provider and the family, monitors long-term treatment outcomes and participates in assessments to determine whether the infant or toddler is a candidate for hearing aids, cochlear implants, or bone-anchored hearing devices (JCIH, 2007).

Medical home providers do not always realize the importance of including the ophthalmologist on the care team for infants and toddlers who are deaf or hard of hearing. The prevalence of vision problems in these children is approximately 40–60%, significantly higher than the general population (Nikolopoulos, Lioumi, Stamataki, & O'Donoghue, 2006). Vision problems, in addition to being deaf or hard of hearing, can impact the development and the services recommended for these children. The ophthalmologist may be the first professional to identify a condition such as Usher Syndrome, which is characterized by a progressive decrease in hearing as well as vision. The communication of results of annual eye examinations to the medical home provider is crucial to maintaining coordinated care for a child who is deaf or hard of hearing.

The option to visit a genetic specialist should be offered to all families of children who are identified as deaf or hard of hearing. The medical geneticist may be able to help families understand why their child is deaf or hard of hearing. Genetic counseling may help families understand the possibilities of future children being deaf or hard of hearing (JCIH, 2007). It is important to let families know that a genetics evaluation does not guarantee finding a genetic reason for why their child is deaf or hard of hearing, and not every family wants a genetics assessment. Nonetheless, the primary care provider should offer a referral for genetic counseling, and help set realistic expectations for the kind of information that may be discovered. See the Gallaudet University website under the Recommended Resource section for more information on genetic counseling.

As the child and family are referred to early intervention services, it is beneficial for an audiologist to have an ongoing and clearly defined role on the team working with the family and child. See Table 6.3 for Roles of the Pediatric Audiologist.

IMPORTANCE OF AN EARLY START

The Cullens want to make the best possible choices for Abby, and are doing their best to follow the advice that they are being given. They wonder why all of the professionals caring for Abby have been encouraging things to move forward so quickly.

Table 6.3 *Roles of the Pediatric Audiologist*

Monitoring hearing levels

Fitting and monitoring hearing aid(s) benefit and use

Interpreting audiological findings with families and other members of the early intervention team regarding the potential impact on the child's ability to understand and use spoken language

Collaborating with other early intervention professionals to educate families regarding cochlear implant technology, whether their child is a candidate, and the various factors impacting spoken language outcomes with a cochlear implant

Counseling families as to the varied spoken language outcomes possible for each child regardless of hearing levels and technologies used

Counseling families regarding the benefits of early language access in any modality to minimize language delay and maximize cognitive outcomes

Collaborating with other early intervention professionals in assessing and monitoring a child's listening and spoken language progress with his or her hearing aid(s) and/or cochlear implant(s)

Recognizing when families may have significant distress in processing information and connecting them with counseling resources as appropriate

---

For infants who do not share a common language with their families, being born deaf or hard of hearing is considered a developmental emergency (Wyckoff, 2013). It is important to convey to families why time is critical in following up on recommendations for services. Infancy and early childhood are the times at which brain pathways are created and cemented, and lack of meaningful input can lead to significant and permanent developmental delays (Easterbrooks & Baker, 2002; Harris, 2010; Stredler-Brown, 2010; Yoshinaga-Itano, 2006). All children need to establish early language foundations, and for children who are deaf or hard of hearing, this may include spoken language, visual language, or some combination of both (Young et al., 2006). (See Chapter 8, *Collaboration for Communication, Language, and Cognitive Development.*)

To reinforce the urgency of getting an early start, professionals can refer to the recommendations of experts and stakeholders such as the

Joint Committee on Infant Hearing (JCIH, 2007). The JCIH 2007 Position Statement is endorsed by the AAP and recommends that the screening process, including outpatient rescreening, should be completed no later than 1 month of age. For infants who do not pass their hearing screening, the identification and confirmation of hearing ability should occur no later than 3 months of age, and appropriate intervention opportunities should be initiated no later than 6 months of age. These are often referred to in the area of Early Hearing Detection and Intervention (EHDI) as the "1-3-6 guidelines." Families may also benefit from research findings and best practices in early intervention for children who are deaf and hard of hearing, familiarity with the implications for their child and family, and resources that can impact development (Russ, Dougherty, & Jagadish, 2010).

Transitioning from Early Identification to Early Intervention

The Cullens were contacted by an early intervention service coordinator, Ariana Sykes, from their local Part C agency. She asked to visit their home to answer questions they had, conduct an initial developmental assessment, and discuss the next steps.

A service coordinator from the local Part C agency is typically assigned to coordinate the intervention part of the EHDI process. In many states, Part C agencies have dedicated service coordinators who are knowledgeable about the needs of children who are deaf or hard of hearing. Unfortunately, this is not always the case in every community. The goal is to connect families quickly with early intervention service providers who have expertise in working with families who have deaf or hard-of-hearing infants or toddlers. Fortunately, for the Cullens, Ariana has experience, knowledge, and skills in working with infants who are deaf or hard of hearing and their families.

The early intervention process typically starts with an initial assessment to gather information about the child as well as about the family's priorities and needs. This leads to the development of an IFSP. The IFSP occurs under the scope of Part C of the Individuals with Disabilities Education Act, commonly referred to as IDEA. The IFSP is designed to coordinate the many services and supports recommended for the child and family. (See Chapter 7, *Developmental Assessment,* and Chapter 9, *Individualized Family Service Plans and Programming.*)

There are a variety of early intervention service providers that may work with a family according to the needs identified during the IFSP. Depending upon the needs of the child, the early intervention team may want to ask the family for permission to share the IFSP with their primary care provider. Many early intervention professionals play a critical role in providing supports and services to families. These services include (1) educating the family on a range of topics related to raising a child who is deaf or hard of hearing; (2) providing families with the skills to facilitate language and communication; and (3) connecting families to resources such as parent organizations, agencies, and other families who have a child who is deaf or hard of hearing. Early intervention service providers should also connect families and their children with adults who are deaf or hard of hearing. (See Chapter 5, *Collaboration with Deaf and Hard-of-Hearing Communities.*)

LANGUAGE, COMMUNICATION, AND TECHNOLOGY

Dr. Lacey reinforced the importance of Abby acquiring language so that she could progress in all areas of development. The Cullens were naturally concerned about Abby's ability to communicate. They wondered how she would learn to talk, or if she would be able to talk at all. They wanted to know how to support Abby's language and communication development and connect with other people in her life.

Families often face a host of recommendations and professional opinions on how to encourage their child's language and communication development. Soon after it is determined that a child is deaf or hard of hearing, audiologists generally recommend that families begin the process for obtaining hearing aids. This process typically begins with an appointment with the ENT, as mentioned earlier. It is natural for many families, particularly hearing families, to want their children to develop listening and spoken language. Although it is impossible to predict with absolute certainty how much an individual child will benefit from hearing aids and develop spoken language skills, most resource-rich countries, such as the United States, tend to recommend hearing aids or other listening technologies (such as cochlear implants) for children who are deaf or hard of hearing.

When a child is deaf and does not appear to benefit from hearing aids, families are often introduced to the technology of a cochlear implant as a possibility for their child. Cochlear implants, which provide electrical stimulation directly to the hearing system, provide access to sound that may be more beneficial for some children than traditional hearing aids (Geers & Nicholas, 2013). Cochlear implantation usually requires a trial period with hearing aids as part of the implantation candidacy process. Not all children are candidates for cochlear implants, and it is important for families and professionals to acknowledge the possibility of variable outcomes when setting expectations for spoken language development (Geers, 2006; Nicholas & Geers, 2006; Niparko et al., 2010; Peterson, Pisoni, & Miyamoto, 2010).

Listening technologies and spoken language are only one component of maximizing early language development (Young et al., 2006). As families are introduced to strategies for communicating with their child, it is critical that they also understand the role of visual and tactile avenues such as eye contact, touch, body language, gestures, and sign language to facilitate meaningful connections and promote cognitive development (Bailes, Erting, Erting, & Thumann-Prezioso, 2009; Mayberry & Eichen, 1991; Meadow-Orlans et al., 2003; Meadow-Orlans, Spencer, Koester, & Steinberg, 2004).

Families need to be fully informed of the evidence demonstrating how visual language can support early language development for children who are deaf or hard of hearing, including children who may access sound through hearing aids or cochlear implants [Visual Language and Visual Learning Science of Learning Center (VL2), 2011, 2012]. Early intervention specialists can connect families with resources to learn how to support the visual aspects of their child's language and communication development, as well as visual technologies available (Visual Language and Visual Learning Science of Learning Center, 2013). At the same time families need to know that auditory and visual approaches to developing language are not mutually exclusive, and both visual and auditory strategies should be addressed and evaluated for each child. In the special case of dual sensory involvement, for example, a child who is deaf and also has low vision or is blind, providers need to be prepared to connect families with appropriate deaf–blind organizations that can provide services such as tactile language skills development, collaborative educational planning, and eventual independence training, among others.

EMOTIONAL WELL-BEING

Mr. and Mrs. Cullen wonder if their child will be able to lead a "normal" life. During Mrs. Cullen's pregnancy, they had hopes and dreams for their child, plans for the kind of things they would do together as a family, and visions of what their child would become when an adult. Now these and many other expectations they had feel threatened.

The weeks and months after identification may be a mix of emotions for families. Some may experience guilt in thinking that they did, or did not do, something to cause their child to become deaf. Others may grieve, believing they have lost hope of having a "perfect" child. Still others may be motivated to move forward quickly. The time period immediately following a family learning their child is deaf or hard of hearing presents professionals with the opportunity to provide support to families and help them see their child in a positive way. Promoting a hopeful, optimistic outlook can move a family toward possibilities that they might not have initially imagined, and away from a perspective focused on loss. It can be a time during which professionals can begin to support families in thinking about the overall development of their child, instead of focusing solely on their child not being able to hear. Emotional support during this time period is critical. Families need providers who can listen actively, show families that they understand their point of view, and exercise patience and empathy as the family absorbs new information.

It is important for families not to lose sight of outcomes beyond language, including the need for children to (1) possess a strong sense of self and positive self- esteem; (2) develop meaningful relationships with others; (3) communicate their needs and wants as well as complex thoughts and ideas; (4) achieve academically and vocationally; and (5) find a place of significance in the world (Calderon & Greenberg, 2011). It is critical that families understand that cognitive development and social competence are connected, and growth in each of these areas influences the growth of the other. Children need language in order to develop social skills. Growth in a child's ability to communicate effectively and think critically promotes opportunities for more social interactions, which in turn increases a child's opportunity to acquire more information and use language in meaningful ways.

The Cullens have a weekly home visit scheduled with their early intervention service coordinator, Ariana Sykes. She is available to answer the Cullen's questions about Abby's development, and share the many resources about working with children who are deaf or hard of hearing. They have an appointment scheduled with the audiologist, Dr. Davis, to get hearing aids for Abby, and realize that this is only one step toward helping Abby learn language. They are looking forward to meeting a family who lives in a neighboring town who also has a daughter who is deaf. They are also scheduled to meet with a professional who works in the early intervention program who is deaf herself and mentors families about what it means to be deaf. The Cullens remain anxious about Abby's future, but now believe that they are connected with the appropriate supports and services to guide them.

SUMMARY

Families benefit from providers who are open to collaboration across disciplines. It is not realistic to think that any one audiologist, primary care provider, specialist, or service provider will be able to provide complete information on opportunities for language, as well as cognitive and social emotional development. Families need providers who know their own areas of expertise as well as their limitations, and are willing to connect with other professionals and resources to help families support their child's overall development.

Although reactions to discovering a child is deaf or hard of hearing differ from family to family, professionals can support families to frame their perspectives in ways that help them view their journey positively, focusing on what their child *can* achieve rather than what he or she *cannot*. Particularly in the time period immediately following the determination that a child is deaf or hard of hearing, an attitude of caring and collaboration, and a focus on the opportunities available to all children who are deaf or hard of hearing, can help set high expectations as families and professionals work together in partnership.

SUGGESTED ACTIVITIES

1. Review your state's Early Hearing Detection and Intervention website. Become more familiar with your state system, paying attention to more than just the information presented. Ask yourself questions such as the following: What is the prevalent tone of the site and does this represent my approach with families? Is this site accessible to all, considering issues such as culture, language, and disability? How are deaf individuals/families portrayed, and again, does this portrayal match my thinking? Apply this same line of thinking to brochures and information provided by local hospital hearing screening programs, as well as information provided to parents from your own practice or agency.

2. If you are an early intervention specialist, identify the members of the medical team caring for the families and children in your program. With permission from families, make a professional connection with each of them.

3. Interview an early intervention provider. Include questions such as the following: Why did you become interested in this field? What was your training like? What is the scope of your work—do you work with a variety of families? Focus on asking questions related to the provider's first contact with families, and what happens after families are initially referred for early intervention services.

4. Invite a family of a child who is deaf or hard of hearing to share their story with you. Let the family's story unfold without imposing an agenda. Do not focus only on the child. Learn about the family's origin, home language(s), family members, and hopes, dreams, successes, and failures. Does what you learned challenge any preconceived concepts? Are you surprised by anything you learned?

RECOMMENDED RESOURCES

1. American Academy of Pediatrics (AAP): Early Hearing Detection and Intervention (EHDI) by State http://www.aap.org/en-us/advocacy-and-policy/aap-health-initiatives/PEHDIC/pages/Early-Hearing-Detection-and-Intervention-by-State.aspx.

   This webpage, part of the website of the American Academy of Pediatrics, provides valuable information for professionals related to the AAP EHDI Chapter Champions initiative (which identifies an individual or individuals who can lead and respond to provider concerns regarding newborn hearing screening in each state) as well as links to EHDI information from the Centers for Disease Control and Prevention (CDC) and the National Center for Hearing Assessment and Management (NCHAM).

2. Guidelines for Audiologists Providing Informational and Adjustment Counseling to Families of Infants and Young Children with Hearing Loss Birth to 5 Years of Age http://www.asha.org/policy/GL2008-00289.htm.

   This ASHA document shares practical strategies and considerations for audiologists when counseling families of newly identified children who are deaf or hard of hearing.

3. Hearing Loss in Children http://www.cdc.gov/ncbddd/hearingloss/index.html.

   This comprehensive website developed by the CDC covers a variety of topics for both professionals and families related to screening and intervention, including research and family stories. Links are provided to free, downloadable resources useful for counseling families of children who are deaf or hard of hearing, including fact sheets, posters, and brochures. Many resources are available in Spanish.

4. The "State" of Early Hearing Detection and Intervention in the United States http://www.infanthearing.org/states/index.html.

   This webpage from NCHAM links professionals to information about EHDI programs in each state. It maintains important contact information, as well as links to useful EHDI resources (both print and online) developed within each state.

5. Genetics Program: Gallaudet University http://www.gallaudet.edu/genetics/about_us_-_services_and_research.html.

   This webpage shares information for professionals about the genetics program at Gallaudet University in Washington, DC. It includes links to numerous national resources related to genetics and children who are deaf or hard of hearing.

6. Medical Home Portal: http://www.medicalhomeportal.org/clinical-practice/building-a-medical- home/care-coordination.

   A comprehensive website for physicians and other professionals working with children who have special needs and their families. It addresses many important considerations related to coordinated care as well as links to numerous resources on how to establish an effective "Medical Home."

7. Interactive Notebook for Families with a young child who is deaf or hard of hearing http://www.infanthearing.org/states/documents/other/parent-notebook.pdf.

   A downloadable resource notebook developed collaboratively by professionals and parents. It provides information for families on a variety of topics related to raising a child who is deaf or hard of hearing.

8. Infant Hearing Guide http://www.infanthearing.org/slideshow/ihg/index.html.

   A family training CD developed with funding by the National Institute on Deafness and other Communication Disorders (NIDCD) at the National Institutes of Health. It covers three general topic areas: Diagnosis, Taking Action, and Family Support. Each of these sections includes videos and/or interactive multimedia activities to facilitate family learning.

9. Video Overview of How Hearing Works: Auditory Transduction http://www.youtube.com/watch?v=46aNGGNPm7s.

   This comprehensive video provides a 7-minute 3-D animation of a trip through the ear. It is a useful tool for professionals when counseling families about the hearing mechanism. Professionals should be aware that this video is not captioned, which means that it is not accessible to deaf individuals.

10. Part C Eligibility Considerations for Infants and Toddler Who Are Deaf or Hard of Hearing http://www.infanthearing.org/earlyintervention/part_c_eligibility.pdf.

   This document, developed by a committee convened by the IDEA Infant & Toddler Coordinators Association and the National Center for Hearing Assessment and Management, provides important information for professional consideration when determining Part C eligibility. It includes a comprehensive chart describing the relationship between hearing levels and a child's development.

11. National Center on Deaf-Blindness https://nationaldb.org/.

This comprehensive website provides practical information for both professionals and families to increase awareness, knowledge, and skills related to intervention for children who are deaf–blind. The website includes links to an extensive library of publications, as well as other initiatives from this Center.

12. Science of Learning Center on Visual Language and Visual Learning (VL2) http://vl2.gallaudet.edu/.

VL2 has a variety of resources for educators and parents regarding visual language that are based on relevant scholarship and make recommendations for practice. The many resources available include a Parent Information Package, a series of research briefs (some available in Spanish and Mandarin), American Sign Language assessment tools, and ASL storybooks.

REFERENCES

American Academy of Audiology. (2011). *Childhood hearing screening guidelines*. Retrieved from http://www.cdc.gov/ncbddd/hearingloss/documents/aaa_childhood-hearing-guidelines_2011.pdf.

American Academy of Pediatrics. (2014). *Early hearing detection and intervention (EHDI)*. Retrieved from http://www.aap.org/en-us/advocacy-and-policy/aap-health-initiatives/PEHDIC/Pages/Early-Hearing-Detection-and-Intervention.aspx.

American Speech-Language-Hearing Association. (2004). *Guidelines for the audiologic assessment of children from birth to 5 years of age*. Retrieved from http://www.asha.org/policy/.

American Speech-Language-Hearing Association. (2008). *Guidelines for audiologists providing informational and adjustment counseling to families of infants and young children with hearing loss birth to 5 years of age*. Retrieved from http://www.asha.org/docs/html/GL2008-00289.html.

Bailes, C. N., Erting, C. J., Erting, L. C., & Thumann-Prezioso, C. (2009). Language and literacy acquisition through parental mediation in American Sign Language. *Sign Language Studies, 9,* 417–456.

Calderon, R., & Greenberg, T. (2011). Social and emotional development of deaf children: Family, school, and program effects. In M. Marschark &

P. E. Spencer (Eds.), *The Oxford handbook of deaf studies, language, and education* (Vol. 1, 2nd ed.). Oxford, England: Oxford University Press.

Centers for Disease Control and Prevention. (2013). *Summary of 2011 National CDC EHDI Data.* Retrieved from http://www.cdc.gov/ncbddd/hearingloss/2011-data/2011_ehdi_hsfs_summary_a.pdf.

Easterbrooks, S., & Baker, S. (2002). *Language learning in children who are deaf and hard of hearing: Multiple pathways.* Boston, MA: Allyn & Bacon.

Fitzpatrick, E., Angus, D., Durieux-Smith, A., Graham, I. D., & Coyle, D. (2008). Parents' needs following identification of childhood hearing loss. *American Journal of Audiology, 17,* 38–49.

Gallaudet Research Institute. (2010). *Regional and national summary report of data from the 2009-2010 annual survey of deaf and hard of hearing children and youth.* Washington, DC: Gallaudet University.

Geers, A. E. (2006). Spoken language in children with cochlear implants. In P. E. Spencer & M. Marschark (Eds.), *Advances in the spoken language of deaf and hard-of-hearing children* (pp. 244–270). New York, NY: Oxford University Press.

Geers, A. E., & Nicholas, J. (2013) Enduring advantages of early cochlear implantation for spoken language development. *Journal of Speech, Language, and Hearing Research, 56,* 643–653.

Grimes, A., & DesGeorges, J. (2013, April). *The "what else?" checklist: Guiding audiologists in their role with families.* Paper presented at the Early Hearing Detection and Intervention Conference, Phoenix, AZ. Retrieved from http://ehdimeeting.org/System/Uploads/pdfs/992JanetDesGeorges.pdf.

Harris, M. (2010). Early communication in sign and speech. In M. Marschark & P. E. Spencer (Eds.), *Oxford handbook of deaf studies, language, and education* (pp. 316–330). New York, NY: Oxford University Press.

Hintermair, M. (2000). Hearing impaired children with additional disabilities and related aspects of parental stress: Results of a study carried out by the University of Education in Heidelberg. *Exceptional Children, 66,* 327–332.

IDEA Infant and Toddler Coordinators Association and National Center for Hearing Assessment and Management. (2011). *Part C eligibility considerations for infants & toddlers who are deaf or hard of hearing.* Retrieved from http://www.infanthearing.org/earlyintervention/part_c_eligibility.pdf.

Joint Committee on Infant Hearing. (2007). Year 2007 position statement: Principles and guidelines for early hearing detection and intervention programs. *Pediatrics, 120,* 898–921. doi:10.1542/peds.2007-2333.

Laugen, N. (2013). Providing information to families in newborn hearing screening follow-up: Professional Challenges. *Seminars in Hearing, 34,* 11–18.

Luterman, D. (2004). Counseling families of children with hearing loss and special needs. *The Volta Review, 104*(4), 215–220.

Matthijs, L., Loots, G., Mouvet, K., Van Herreweghe, M., Hardonk, S., Van Hove, G., . . . Leigh, G. (2012). First information parents receive after UNHS detection of their baby's hearing loss. *Journal of Deaf Studies and Deaf Education, 17*(4), 387–401.

Mayberry, R. I., & Eichen, E. B. (1991). The long-lasting advantage of learning sign language in childhood: Another look at the critical period for language acquisition. *Journal of Memory and Language, 30*, 486–512.

Meadow-Orlans, K., Mertens, D., & Sass-Lehrer, M. (2003). *Parents and their deaf children: The early years*. Washington, DC: Gallaudet University Press.

Meadow-Orlans, K. P., Spencer, P. E., Koester, L. S., & Steinberg, A. C. (2004). Implications for intervention with infants and families. In K. P. Meadow-Orlans, P. E. Spencer, & L. S. Koester (Eds.), *The world of deaf infants* (pp. 218–228). New York, NY: Oxford University Press.

Nicholas, J. G., & Geers, A. E. (2006). The process and early outcomes of cochlear implantation by three years of age. In P. E. Spencer & M. Marschark (Eds.), *Advances in the spoken language of deaf and hard-of-hearing children* (pp. 271–297). New York, NY: Oxford University Press.

Nikolopoulos, T. P., Lioumi, D., Stamataki, S., & O'Donoghue, G. M. (2006). Evidence-based overview of ophthalmic disorders in deaf children: A literature update. *Otology and Neurotology, 27*(2 Suppl 1), S1–24.

Niparko, J. K., Tobey, E. A., Thal, D. J., Eisenberg, L. S., Wang, N. Y., Quittner, A. L., . . . The CDaCI Investigative Team. (2010). Spoken language development in children following cochlear implantation. *Journal of the American Medical Association, 303*, 1498–1506.

Peterson, N., Pisoni, D., & Miyamoto, R. (2010). Cochlear implants and spoken language processing abilities: Review and assessment of the literature. *Restorative Neurology and Neuroscience, 28*(2), 237–250.

Pipp-Siegel, S., Sedey, A. L., & Yoshinaga-Itano, C. (2002). Predictors of parental stress in mothers of young children with hearing loss. *Journal of Deaf Studies and Deaf Education, 7*, 1–17.

Roush, P., Frymark, T., Venediktov, R., & Wang, B. (2011). Audiologic management of auditory neuropathy spectrum disorder in children: A systematic review of the literature. *American Journal of Audiology, 20*, 159–170.

Russ, S.A., Dougherty, D., & Jagadish, P. (2010). Accelerating evidence into practice for the benefit of children with early hearing loss, *Pediatrics, 126*(Suppl. 1), S7–S18.

Santarelli, R., Rossi, R., & Arslan, E. (2013). Assistive devices for patients with auditory neuropathy: Hearing aid use. *Seminars in Hearing, 34*, 51–64.

Schmeltz, L. (2013). Parent counseling in the internet age: The rules & roles have changed. In L. Schmeltz (Ed.), *The NCHAM eBook: A resource guide for early hearing detection and intervention (EHDI).* Retrieved from http://www.infanthearing.org/ehdi-ebook/2012_ebook/Chapter7.pdf.

Sia, C., Tonniges, T., Osterhaus, E., & Taba, S. (2004). History of the medical home concept. *Pediatrics, 113,* 1473.

Stredler-Brown, A. (2010). Communication choices and outcomes during the early years: An assessment and evidence-based approach. In M. Marschark & P. E. Spencer (Eds.), *Oxford handbook of deaf studies, language, and education* (pp. 292–315). New York, NY: Oxford University Press.

Uus, K. (2011). Transient auditory neuropathy in infants: How to conceptualize the recovery of auditory brain stem response in the context of newborn hearing screening? *Seminars in Hearing, 32,* 123–128.

Visual Language and Visual Learning Science of Learning Center. (2011, January). *Advantages of early visual language* (Research Brief No. 2). Washington, DC: Sharon Baker.

Visual Language and Visual Learning Science of Learning Center. (2012, June). *The implications of bimodal bilingual approaches for children with cochlear implants* (Research Brief No. 6). Washington, DC: Julie Mitchiner, Debra Berlin Nussbaum, and Susanne Scott.

Visual Language and Visual Learning Science of Learning Center. (2013, June). *Family involvement in ASL acquisition.* (Research Brief No. 9). Washington, DC: Charlotte Enns and Liana Price.

Wyckoff, A. (2013). American Academy of Pediatrics endorses early intervention for children who are deaf, hard of hearing. *AAP News.* Retrieved from http://aapnews.aappublications.org/content/34/4/23.

Yoshinaga-Itano, C. (2006). Early identification, communication modality, and the development of speech and spoken language skills: Patterns and considerations. In P. Spencer & M. Marschark (Eds.), *Advances in the spoken language development of deaf and hard-of-hearing children* (pp. 298–327). New York, NY: Oxford University Press.

Young, A., Carr, G., Hunt, R., McCracken, W., Skipp, A., & Tattersall, H. (2006). Informed choice and deaf children: Underpinning concepts and enduring challenges. *Journal of Deaf Studies and Deaf Education, 11*(3), 322–336.

7 Developmental Assessment

Amy Szarkowski and Nicole Hutchinson

Jessica Harper is a speech-language pathologist working in early intervention providing family-centered care to young children and their family members. The early intervention program in which Ms. Harper works is moving to incorporate better assessment tools and procedures in the developmental assessment process. The program currently utilizes an interdisciplinary approach for the provision of early intervention services and wants to extend this model to assessment practices.

The team will be working with Adam and his family. Adam is a 16-month-old boy whose hearing levels are in the moderate to severe range. His parents, who are both first-generation Brazilian-Americans, are concerned about his delayed acquisition of motor skills and his limited language skills. Adam's parents have never worked with early intervention professionals before and are unsure what it means for Adam to be involved in a developmental assessment. Ms. Harper and her team would like to facilitate a comprehensive and meaningful assessment so that they can better identify needed services and closely monitor Adam's progress. The team will also need to explain to Adam's family what the process will entail and how they can be involved.

GUIDING QUESTIONS

1. What does a comprehensive and meaningful assessment entail for an infant or toddler who is deaf or hard of hearing?
2. What assessment strategies should be used?
3. Who should be involved in the assessment?
4. How can assessment information be used to guide the Individualized Family Service Plan (IFSP) and to monitor the progress of an infant who is deaf or hard of hearing?

COMPETENCY AREAS ADDRESSED IN THIS CHAPTER

1. Screening, Evaluation and Assessment: Interpretation of Hearing Screening and Audiological Diagnostic Information; Ongoing Developmental Assessment; and Use of Developmental Assessment Tools to Monitor Progress
2. Factors Influencing Infant and Toddler Development
3. Collaboration and Interdisciplinary Models and Practices

INTRODUCTION

This chapter describes why and how to conduct developmental assessments of infants and toddlers who are deaf or hard of hearing. It will emphasize best practices, as identified in the professional literature and endorsed by relevant bodies that govern, inform, and/or provide leadership in this area. For the general early intervention population, best practices have been defined by organizations in the United States such as the National Center for Infants, Toddlers, and Families (Zero to Three); the Council for Exceptional Children (CEC)—in particular, the Division for Early

Childhood (DEC); the Early Childhood Technical Assistance Center (ECTA) within the Office of Special Education Programs in the United States Department of Education; the National Association for the Education of Young Children (NAEYC); the Early Head Start National Resource Center (EHSNRC); and the National Scientific Council on the Developing Child (NSCDC).

Assessment policies for all children from birth to 3 years of age, including those who are deaf or hard of hearing, are guided by Part C of the Individuals with Disabilities Education Improvement Act (IDEA, 2004). The Joint Committee on Infant Hearing (JCIH) has also developed principles and guidelines for the assessment of infants and toddlers who are deaf or hard of hearing [Joint Committee on Infant Hearing (JCIH), 2007, 2013] (see Chapter 4, *Legislation, Policies, and Roles of Research in Shaping Early Intervention,* for more information on the JCIH). Additionally, a recent international document on best practices for children who are deaf or hard of hearing endorses these principles and offers useful suggestions for conducting developmental assessments (Moeller, Carr, Seaver, Stredler-Brown, & Holzinger, 2013).

Assessment protocols have changed over time and are likely to continue to evolve as our understanding of the developmental process of infants and toddlers continues to grow. This chapter will not focus on particular assessment tools; it will instead explore the principles of developmental assessment, the approaches used to assess infants and toddlers, and how assessment can be used to inform programming. It will also address the importance of having skilled professionals on the assessment team and how to share assessment results with families. By striving to incorporate the best of what we know with regard to the assessment of young children, Ms. Harper can be sure that she is honoring the principles of providing family-centered care highlighted throughout this book.

THE IMPACT OF BEING DEAF ON DEVELOPMENT

After identification of his hearing status, Adam's family is eager to learn more about how it might affect his learning as he grows. Ms. Harper explains that the development of children who are deaf or hard of hearing, as with all children, is influenced by early experiences, particularly those that occur between birth and 3 years of age. Early experiences, including the exposure the infant or toddler has to social and learning opportunities, lay the foundation for a child's future by literally altering the architecture of the brain and influencing how a child learns, behaves, and interacts with others [National Scientific Council on the Developing Child (NSCDC), 2007].

Ms. Harper also explains to Adam's family that hearing status, in and of itself, does not necessarily have a negative impact on a child's development. Barring any complicating factors (such as additional disabilities or cognitive limitations), when early identification and early intervention are in place, expectations for cognitive and linguistic development for deaf or hard-of-hearing children need not differ from that of their peers with typical hearing (Marschark & Hauser, 2011; Thagard, Hilsmier, & Easterbrooks, 2011; Yoshinaga-Itano, Baca, & Sedey, 2010). This requires, however, that the child be afforded consistent access to communication, whether through continuous auditory access (with the assistance of hearing aids or cochlear implants) or through visual access (such as when infants and toddlers are exposed to consistent use of a signed language). Ms. Harper explained that although Adam had not previously received early intervention, there is strong evidence that families who are highly involved in their child's early intervention services can make a positive difference in their development over time (Calderon, 2000; Moeller, 2000).

Because Adam has developed only a few spoken words, his grandparents have expressed their concern that Adam may be cognitively challenged. Back in Brazil, one of Adam's cousins was found to have significant delays and was sent away to a special school. Ms. Harper explained that many deaf or hard-of-hearing children are at greater risk for delays or interruptions in their communication and language development as a result of decreased access to their environment (Marschark & Hauser, 2011). Children with typical hearing inadvertently acquire information by overhearing others, a phenomenon known as *incidental learning* (Marschark & Hauser, 2008, 2011). For children who are deaf or hard of hearing and who do not have full access to language from their caregivers, incidental learning tends to be reduced. These children also have less access to communicative interactions with others (Easterbrooks & Baker, 2002). Without early intervention and appropriate supports, decreased access to information and communication opportunities can have a negative influence on a child's cognitive, linguistic, and social development (Marschark & Hauser, 2011; Moeller, 2000; NSCDC, 2007). This information increases the need for Adam's family to establish effective communication as soon as possible.

DEFINING DEVELOPMENTAL ASSESSMENT

In early intervention terminology, the term *evaluation* is typically used to describe the process by which a determination is made regarding eligibility for services [Early Head Start National Resource Center (EHSNRC), 2013; Zero to Three, 2014]. This chapter will focus on *developmental assessment* rather than evaluation. "Assessment can be broadly defined as an ongoing and comprehensive process of collecting information about children and families for the purpose of making informed instructional decisions" (Notari-Syverson & Losardo, 2008, p. 161). Developmental assessment refers to the collective activities that are involved in gathering information about a child's developmental strengths and needs, functional capacities, as well as the resources and priorities of the family (Bruder, 2010; EHSNRC, 2013; Guralnick, 2005; Zero to Three, 2014).

Developmental assessments with deaf or hard-of-hearing children should be socially, culturally, and linguistically responsive and should show respect for communication opportunities and approaches (JCIH, 2007, 2013). This would include equal opportunities for infants and toddlers using a signed language or a spoken language to demonstrate their language and communication skills. To address different hearing levels, professionals may need to adjust their approaches. Examples could include repeating information if an infant or child seems to have not heard or misheard something, using a personal FM system, or being sure to obtain the child's attention before presenting information in a signed language. It might also involve the inclusion of professionals who are deaf or hard of hearing as part of the assessment team. Appropriate developmental assessment can inform professionals and the family about the most effective and efficacious communication modalities for the child (JCIH, 2013; Moeller et al., 2013) as well as the services needed to promote communication development.

PRINCIPLES OF DEVELOPMENTAL ASSESSMENT

Family Involvement

Developmental assessment should utilize family-centered principles; families are an integral part of the process (Division for Early Childhood, 2014; Zero to Three, 2014). The information that families share will guide the assessment in many ways (Brotherson et al., 2010). Families are encouraged to provide information about their child's abilities and share any concerns they may have about their child's development. A child's capabilities must be understood in the context of the child's family and culture (EHSNRC, 2013; Guralnick, 2005; Hanson & Lynch, 2013). Ms. Harper and her team will need to consider the cultural perspectives of Adam's family, their views on development, and what it means for Adam to be hard of hearing.

The assessment process should be adjusted to meet the needs of the family (Neisworth & Bagnato, 2004). Consideration should be given to the time and location of the assessment as well as to the composition of the team members. Ms. Harper will need to consider the cultural and linguistic preferences of Adam's family and, together with the family, consider how language interpreters can ensure that the information shared among the family members and professionals is accurate and is understood by all parties (Hanson & Lynch, 2013). Attending to the family's needs is likely to enhance the collaboration between the professionals and the family and increase the validity of the information collected.

Family Assessment

Part C of the Individuals with Disabilities Education Act (2004) §303.321(c)(2) requires that a family-directed assessment be conducted to ". . . identify the families' resources, priorities and concerns and the supports and services necessary to enhance the family's capacity to meet the developmental needs of the family's infant or toddler with a disability". The family assessment should be conducted by qualified personnel and is likely to include interview(s) as well as the use of assessment tools. The family assessment must be voluntary on the part of the family, based on the information obtained through the interview or other assessments, and include a description of the family's resources, priorities, and concerns related to supporting their child's development. For Adam's family, one identified area of need is the ability to understand the results of his audiogram. Some family members have expressed confusion because it appears that Adam is sometimes able to hear, and they would like to understand what Adam can and cannot hear. It is a priority for the family to learn more about Adam's audiological status in order to better meet his needs.

Natural Environments

Assessments of infants and toddlers should consider the child's natural environments. These are environments that are familiar to the child and include the adults with whom the child interacts frequently. Natural environments provide opportunities for the child to demonstrate how he or she functions in real-life contexts and in places in which he or she is likely to feel secure and comfortable (EHSNRC, 2013; Zero to Three, 2014). For Adam, these could include his home, the home of his grandparents, his daycare, or the park in which he frequently plays.

Authentic Assessment

Developmental assessments for young children should utilize the principles of authentic assessment in order to obtain a realistic picture of a child's abilities (Losardo & Notari-Syverson, 2011). Authentic assessment uses observation of a child's behaviors and functional skills in the child's natural environments and during daily routines in order to capture a child's abilities in real-life contexts. (Bagnato, Neisworth, & Pretti-Fronteczak, 2010). By helping to identify an infant or toddler's strengths and needs, authentic assessments yield information that can help to identify appropriate, functional goals.

The Whole Child Approach

When planning Adam's developmental assessment, Ms. Harper and her team need to consider his abilities in many domains. Typically, the domains that are assessed include: (1) cognitive; (2) communicative/linguistic; (3) motoric; (4) social–emotional; and (5) adaptive functioning/self-help skills. Examining abilities in each domain will help the professionals and family members better understand areas of strength and vulnerability.

Although domain-specific assessment is important, so too is the consideration of the *whole child*. An infant's or toddler's development in one domain can limit or facilitate development in other domains (Center on the Developing Child, 2007; Kostelnik, Soderman, & Whiren, 2007). For example, a toddler learning to walk will have greater opportunities to explore the world, which will influence the child's cognitive development. Although concerns for Adam's development are now focused on his language and motor development, Ms. Harper and the interdisciplinary team will also be concerned about Adam's overall development and well-being.

Team-Based Assessment

Best practices also suggest team-based approaches to assessment (Bruder, 2010; DEC, 2014). Ms. Harper has determined that she would like to know more about how early intervention teams work together. Rather than assume that a group of professionals will just simply "get along," she has opted to read about how teams have defined the roles of their members. She was fascinated by what she learned about the many ways in which team members can work collaboratively.

Early intervention programs that use team-based services show objective benefits for the children and families with whom they work (Kassini, 2008; King et al., 2009). A number of terms are used to describe how professionals can work together to conduct an assessment. Table 7.1 describes three types of professional teaming: multidisciplinary, interdisciplinary, and transdisciplinary.

Table 7.1 *Professional Teaming Models for Developmental Assessment*

Multidisciplinary	Professionals from various disciplines are involved in the assessment process; however, each professional is responsible for the assessment only in his or her own professional domain. There is not a great deal of interaction among the professionals; rather, each person performs a piece of the evaluation and offers insights to the group based on his or her area of expertise (Bruder, 2010).
Interdisciplinary	Professionals from various disciplines coordinate efforts and work collaboratively to perform the assessment. The framework for the assessment remains profession specific, yet there is greater interaction among the team (King et al., 2009).
Transdisciplinary	Professional roles are shared across disciplinary boundaries so that communication, interaction, and cooperation are maximized. Team members make use of their own expertise while assimilating the knowledge and expertise of other team members (King et al., 2009).

Teams work best when professionals demonstrate honesty and openness, share information and responsibility, prove themselves to be trustworthy and consistent, show empathy, and work collaboratively with families (Park & Turnbull, 2003). Team performance is also improved when professionals understand the role of each team member, possess good communication skills, have time available to collaborate, share clear goals and objectives, and have the resources needed to meet the needs of the child and his or her family members (King et al., 2009). The Joint Committee on Infant Hearing (2013) recommends that early intervention professionals understand and participate in assessment procedures using these team-based frameworks.

SKILLED PROFESSIONALS

Early intervention specialists must possess interpersonal skills that reflect their respect, responsiveness, and support to families (Gilkerson & Taylor

Ritzler, 2014; see Chapter 1, *What Every Early Intervention Professional Should Know*). Effective professionals must be able to listen carefully, demonstrate concern and empathy, and respond thoughtfully. They must be able to understand the child and make themselves understood by the child and family. Additionally, professionals should be knowledgeable about child development as well as family functioning and should possess strong collaborative consultative skills (Rapport, McWilliam, & Smith, 2004).

IDEA Part C requires that personnel conducting evaluations and assessments be qualified in the area(s) in which they are conducting evaluations or assessments [Individuals with Disabilities Education Act (IDEA), 2011 §303.31]. Ms. Harper is aware that the professionals involved in Adam's assessment will need to accurately describe his social skills, attention, communicative competence, learning style, and behaviors (Rowland, 2009). Indicating which tasks require support and which can be done independently provides important information. Does the child explore new objects or appear disinterested? Does the child show a preference for certain people or objects? What does it take to gain or regain the child's attention? Answers to questions such as these can be quite useful in generating a profile of the child's abilities.

Role of Professionals with Specific Areas of Expertise

For children with specific developmental needs, such as problems with movement, learning challenges, low vision, or who are deaf or hard of hearing, the team should be composed of individuals with particular expertise (DEC, 2014). Making accommodations to the assessments may be necessary, and those with expertise in specific areas are more likely to be knowledgeable about the types of assessments, alterations, and adjustments that can be made while maintaining the integrity of the assessment process. For example, if the child being assessed uses assistive technology, such as a picture communication system, the assessment team should include a professional who is both knowledgeable about the type of assistive technology used and comfortable making adaptations to the assessment tools used in order to adequately evaluate the child's functioning.

Professionals who have expertise with young children who are deaf or hard of hearing as well as those with other disabilities are important members of the assessment team (JCIH, 2013; Moeller et al., 2013). Approximately 40% of infants and toddlers who are deaf or hard of hearing have an "educationally relevant additional need" (Gallaudet Research Institute, 2009; Picard, 2004). The assessment team should include professionals with specialized training from diverse disciplines in order to most effectively serve this unique population of children (Orelove, Sobsey, & Silberman, 2004).

Historically, the abilities of deaf or hard-of-hearing children have frequently been underestimated as a result of (1) insufficient training and knowledge on the part of the professional and (2) inappropriate interpretation of assessment results (Wood & Dockrell, 2010). Professionals working with children who are deaf or hard of hearing require training and knowledge regarding infant development and the implications of being deaf or hard of hearing on communication and language skills. See Table 7.2 for the knowledge and skills shared by early intervention

Table 7.2 *Knowledge and Skills of Early Intervention Specialists Related to Assessment*

---

1. Deep knowledge of infant and toddler development and the implications of being deaf or hard of hearing including being deaf or hard of hearing with developmental concerns or disabilities

2. Strong appreciation of the factors that can significantly influence development, including cultural factors

3. Excellent observational skills

4. The ability to aptly describe what they see and put it into an appropriate context

5. The capacity to succinctly convey their findings, with compassion

6. Understanding of family systems and sensitivity in working with families

7. The ability to understand the child's communicative behaviors and be understood by the child

8. Knowledge of and familiarity with specific assessment tools, as well as the ability to select appropriate assessments for each child

---

professionals who can effectively assess infants and toddlers who are deaf or hard of hearing.

Inclusion of Deaf Adults in the Assessment Process

One of the professionals who will join Adam's assessment team is a physical therapist who works primarily with deaf and hard-of-hearing children and is fluent in American Sign Language as well as spoken English. The other is a teacher of the deaf who is deaf herself, and is able to offer insight regarding Adam's communication abilities and access to information. She may be able to assist the team in interpreting Adam's nonverbal communication and other visual communication that might not be evident to hearing professionals. (See Chapter 5, *Collaboration with Deaf and Hard-of-Hearing Communities*.)

ASSESSMENT APPROACHES

Developmental assessment information can be collected using formal and informal assessments including: (1) norm-referenced assessments; (2) criterion-referenced assessments; (3) observation checklists and questionnaires; (4) portfolios; (5) functional behavioral assessments; and (6) play-based assessment strategies (Bruder, 2010; EHSNRC, 2013; Guralnick, 2005).

Norm-Referenced Assessments

Norm-referenced assessment instruments measure a child's abilities relative to the abilities of other children of the same chronological age. Incorporating norm-referenced assessment protocols in the developmental assessment allows for precise measurement of progress (Stredler-Brown, 2010), as long as the tools and assessment approaches used are appropriate for the child. When cognition is within normal limits, norm-referenced assessments can track the progress made in the development of particular skills or abilities and can compare this with expectations for same-aged peers. When cognitive limitations are present, expectations for progress should, instead, be based on a child's cognitive age (Bagnato, Neisworth, & Pretti-Frotczak, 2010). Areas of strength and vulnerability can be determined based on comparisons of the child's current functioning to documented norms (EHSNRC, 2013; Stredler-Brown, 2010). This information can inform the types of services that are appropriate to promote the child's growth (DEC, 2014; Zero to Three, 2014).

Ms. Harper knows that using standardized measures can help professionals identify present levels of performance and results can be quantified. By doing so, she can aid the family in understanding Adam's strengths and areas of vulnerability as they relate to age-based expectations. Analysis of a child's performance on a standard measure (such as identifying which tasks a child can do readily, which types of tasks can be completed but are challenging for the child, and which tasks require skills that are beyond those that the child possesses at a given time) can yield good information and serve as an important tool for the team in identifying intervention goals. Standardized assessments, however, are only a snapshot of the child's abilities demonstrated at a particular time and place. The results are only as valid as the effectiveness of the professional administering the assessment and the child's state. For example, at times young children are too sleepy, hungry, upset, or ill to demonstrate the skills or abilities that they possess. It is also important to note that the availability of standardized measures that are appropriate for use with young children who are deaf or hard of hearing is quite limited.

Criterion-Referenced Assessments

Developmental assessment should also include assessment tools that help families and professionals document a child's growth over time, such as criterion-referenced assessments. In contrast to norm-referenced assessments, criterion-referenced assessments do not compare a child's scores with that of other children of the same age. Instead, they monitor a child's development compared to established benchmarks such as those found in early learning standards and early intervention program curricula. These assessments can provide a picture of a child's developmental progress over time (DEC, 2014; Hafer & Stredler-Brown, 2003). Ms. Harper might use a criterion-referenced assessment, for example, to illustrate Adams progress toward a specific motor milestone such as walking independently. A criterion-referenced assessment could be used to show Adam's progress, even if incremental, toward accomplishing this milestone.

Observation Checklists and Questionnaires

One method for gathering authentic assessment information is through the use of questionnaires and checklists. Assessments that involve family input provide authentic information about the child (Bagnato, 2005; Bagnato et al., 2010). Family members may be asked to independently complete questionnaires about the infant or toddler's functioning. Alternatively, information may be obtained through an interview format with the early intervention professional asking family members and other primary caregivers about the child's skills or behaviors. For example, the Infant Toddler Meaningful Auditory Integration Scale (ITMAIS) (2008) is a parent questionnaire designed to assess a deaf or hard-of-hearing child's responses to sound in their everyday environment, and the MacArthur Bates Communicative Development Inventory (2013) is a checklist completed by the parent or caregiver to identify the words in their child's lexicon.

Questionnaires and checklists tend to provide information about an infant's or toddler's functioning that may not be obtained through other assessment measures. Though some professionals may question the accuracy of parent-based assessments, researchers have shown that parents are reasonably good reporters of their child's skills (Feldman et al., 2005; Miller, Sedey, & Miolo, 1995), and the use of parent-completed checklists and interview questionnaires is a valuable way to encourage family involvement in the assessment process (Hafer & Stredler-Brown, 2003).

Portfolio Assessment

Portfolio assessment is a method for obtaining a comprehensive and authentic picture of a child's abilities across multiple settings and environments (Hafer & Stredler-Brown, 2003; Losardo & Notari-Syverson,

2011). There is no single accepted way to compile a portfolio. Rather, it is a flexible, individualized method for collecting and storing information about the child's progress across various domains (LaBoskey, 2000). A portfolio assessment consists of a collection of the child's work (e.g., photos, videos, artwork), anecdotal observations made by the parents and caregivers, as well as early intervention specialists who work with the child (Losardo & Notari-Syverson, 2011). The content of the portfolio is determined by the specific goals identified by the family and professionals on the early intervention team, with items being added frequently (Puckett & Black, 2008). Adam's family, for example, is video recording his interactions with cousins. Although the communicative exchanges are in Portuguese, the videos provide real-life examples of how Adam makes his needs known and interacts with other young children.

Portfolios can be a valuable tool for supplementing and supporting assessment findings obtained through other measures (Puckett & Black, 2008). They can be used to monitor a child's progress after the initial developmental assessment has been conducted. Portfolios tend to be sensitive to incremental progress over time (Losardo & Notari-Syverson, 2011), and are particularly useful in tracking progress toward specific goals. Portfolio assessments can also be used to track progress with children for whom traditional assessments may not yield meaningful results (Jarrett, Browne, & Wallin, 2006).

Functional Behavioral Assessments

Functional behavioral assessments can provide information about how Adam functions, how he interacts with others, and how he responds to various stimuli in the environment (Sugai, Lewis-Palmer, & Hagan-Burke, 2000). In utilizing a functional approach to behavioral assessment, professionals and families work collaboratively to describe a child's behaviors, including strengths and areas of concern. The professionals and the family can then examine the context in which particular behaviors occur in order to identify the purpose of a child's behavior and better predict when these behaviors might happen (Drecktrah & Marchel, 2014). Functional behavior analysis is a problem-solving strategy that involves identifying a problem, collecting and analyzing information about the problem, planning an intervention(s) to address the problem, and then monitoring and evaluating the outcome (Gresham, Watson, & Skinner, 2001; Sugai et al., 2000).

Play-Based Assessment

Many child development experts recommend the use of play-based assessments as a complement to standardized measures (Kelly-Vance & Ryalls, 2004; Lifter, Foster-Sanda, Arzamarski, Briesch, & McClure, 2011; Lifter, Mason, & Barton, 2011). Lifter and colleagues (2011) described play as the "demonstration of what children know" and a "demonstration of what they are currently thinking about" (p. 228). Linder (2008) proposes transdisciplinary play-based assessment to gather information across a child's domains of functioning.

Play-based assessment is used to examine a child's play skills. Play skills, in turn, can be a valid measure of cognition and other skills, such as social problem solving and language abilities (Lifter et al., 2011; Linder, 2008). Play-based assessment tends to be authentic in that a child's performance reflects skills that are not represented on standardized measures (Kelly-Vance & Ryalls, 2004; Linder, 2008). During the administration of more formal measures, Adam was rather shy; yet while he was playing, he was more interactive, engaging and communicative with members of the assessment team. Assessment through play also tends to be culturally sensitive, as it often occurs in a natural context, such as the child's home, and includes familiar people and objects (Lifter et al., 2011).

USING ASSESSMENT DATA FOR PROGRESS MONITORING

Assessments are conducted for a variety of reasons: (1) to identify a child's present level of performance and track progress; (2) to inform early intervention programming; (3) to monitor family outcomes; (4) to assess program outcomes; and (5) to monitor program accountability. Progress monitoring allows professionals, in tandem with the family, to reflect on the strategies that are shown to be effective, modify interventions accordingly, and better promote desired or optimal outcomes (EHSNRC, 2013;

Moeller et al., 2013). Information gathered through progress monitoring might include the quality and quantity of family and child services provided, the learning strategies employed, as well as behavioral management supports used (Bruder, 2010).

Monitoring a Child's Progress

IDEA, the Individuals with Disabilities Education Act (2004), recommends comprehensive, interdisciplinary assessment at specific intervals—every 6 months for the child's first 3 years of life. Yet in the life of a young child, 6 months is a long time to "wait and see" if a child is making progress. Systematically and continuously documenting an infant or toddler's progress through regular and ongoing assessment practices is vitally important to ensure that the intervention is effective and that the child is making the expected progress (JCIH, 2013; Moeller et al., 2013; Stredler-Brown, 2010). Adam's family was relieved to learn that the assessment process is on-going in nature. They were pleased that Adam's progress would be documented and that services could be adjusted as needed to help the family support Adam in meeting specific goals.

Monitoring an Early Intervention Plan

Progress monitoring allows professionals to utilize assessment data to guide, adjust, or alter goals (Niparko et al., 2010; Stredler-Brown, 2010). It can promote the ability of professionals to reflect on their own practices and to try new techniques. Progress monitoring can also enhance problem solving in situations that are particularly challenging (Moeller et al., 2013). Progress monitoring in working with children who are deaf or hard of hearing can further professionals' understanding of "what works" to support young children who are deaf or hard of hearing (Hafer & Stredler-Brown, 2003; Yoshinaga-Itano, 2003).

Monitoring Family Outcomes

Progress monitoring provides a means for early intervention specialists and family members to assess progress toward goals established by the family (Moeller et al., 2013; Stredler-Brown, 2010). Typical family outcomes include identifying resources, accessing new information (often related to a child's condition), acquiring techniques to foster the child's development of particular skills, and implementing strategies in the home environment in an effort to optimize the child's growth (ECTA, 2015; EHSNRC, 2013).

Monitoring Program Outcomes

Progress monitoring can also introduce accountability into a program's infrastructure. Using the same assessment protocols with all children enrolled in a program provides information about the overall effectiveness of the program (Stredler-Brown, 2004, 2010). When the same data on many children are analyzed, program administrators can reflect on the efficacy of program services (ECTA, 2015; Stredler-Brown, 2004, 2010). This can have wide-reaching implications for program planning and management. These data can also inform program administrators about training needs of the early intervention team.

Monitoring Early Intervention Program Accountability

In the United States, the Office of Special Education Programs encourages states to report child and family outcomes in an effort to track and monitor the effectiveness of early intervention at the national level (ECTA, 2015). States are now asked to report the progress made by children in the following areas: (1) positive social–emotional skills (including social relationships); (2) acquisition and use of knowledge and skills (including early language and communication); and (3) use of appropriate behaviors to meet their needs (ECTA, 2015). Early intervention programs are also encouraged to report how the early intervention services have helped families make progress in the following areas: (1) knowing their rights; (2) effectively communicating their children's needs; and (3) helping their children develop and learn. Studies of models of early intervention have found that teams who implement rigorous assessment, monitor the quality of the services provided, and provide training and technical assistance to providers are generally more successful (National Scientific Council on the Developing Child, 2007).

SPECIAL CONSIDERATIONS FOR ASSESSING INFANTS AND TODDLERS WHO ARE DEAF OR HARD OF HEARING

The specific methods employed will depend upon the particular needs of a given child in the context of that child's family. There is no perfect, one-size-fits-all assessment protocol. Flexibility in conducting assessments is paramount. Whereas real-world demands may dictate some aspects of the assessment, professionals should tailor the assessment to ensure that the information obtained paints an accurate picture of the skills of the child and the strengths and priorities of the family. Ms. Harper wonders about the best way to conduct an assessment that will be useful and informative for Adam's family.

It is important for the team to know how to design, alter, or supplement an assessment protocol in light of the child's hearing ability or developmental delays or disabilities. For example, although a linguistically based measure of cognitive ability may be appropriate to administer to a child who is deaf or hard of hearing (Marschark & Hauser, 2008, 2011), professionals need to be cognizant of how a child's hearing abilities may influence performance. For example, asking a child to place the blue blocks inside the red cup may actually be assessing factors other than cognition (or knowledge of colors), such as whether: (1) the child understands the directions; (2) the child is able to perform the task; (3) the child hears and understands the instructions if presented through spoken language, or sees and understands the instructions if presented through a signed language; or (4) the child has had experience with the materials (e.g., he has played with blocks and knows what they are). This becomes particularly relevant when using assessment materials with children who may not have been exposed to "everyday objects" readily found in the dominant culture.

During the assessment process, Ms. Harper may find that accommodations to the standard administration of a test protocol are needed.

For example, if she determines that Adam's language is delayed, she may choose to incorporate nonverbal or less linguistically challenging materials during evaluation in order to appropriately ascertain his skills in other areas, such as his problem-solving abilities. According to the Division for Early Childhood (2014), common modifications in assessment include: (1) using alternative measures; (2) allowing the child flexibility in how a skill is performed or demonstrated; (3) measuring prerequisite or underlying skills; and (4) limiting the number of items administered. When modifications are made in the administration of assessments, these need to be noted, as they will influence the interpretation of the results.

Assessment of Communication and Language

Understanding how a child communicates and uses language is a crucial aspect of assessment (Yoshinaga-Itano, 2003). Communication between infants and their caregivers is essential for their relationship and can be assessed by examining how they share attention, demonstrate turn-taking, and respond to each other (Brazelton & Nugent, 2011). In older babies and toddlers, assessment often focuses on receptive and expressive language skills, and measures the words or signs that the child understands and uses. It was helpful for the team to discuss the difference between communication and language with Adam's family. With this knowledge, family members have begun to notice the many ways in which Adam is communicating his needs and desires to them, despite his apparently reduced repertoire of spoken words.

Many infants and toddlers who are deaf or hard of hearing benefit from visual access to information, whether through the use of a formal signed language, such as American Sign Language, through the incorporation of conceptually accurate signs in conjunction with spoken language, or through the use of other visual communication. Assessment of language and communication abilities should address a variety of areas, including: (1) listening skills; (2) adult–child communication; (3) vocabulary; (4) pragmatics; and (5) spoken and/or signed language skills.

Implications of Communication and Language on Functioning across Domains

Language development has far reaching implications for the overall functioning of the child. The development of social–emotional skills is significantly correlated with language development (Yoshinaga-Itano, 2003), as is development of cognition (Marschark, 2007). As an infant grows into a toddler, the ability of the child and family to share ideas, express needs, and describe internal states by having a shared means by which to communicate is important in fostering positive familial relationships (Barker et al., 2009).

SELECTION OF ASSESSMENT MATERIALS

Bagnato and colleagues (2010, pp. 23–32) suggest eight standards to consider when selecting assessments that can help to ensure developmentally appropriate assessment. The first, *acceptability*, suggests that skills being assessed are considered important and that improvements in child competence are evident to the family. The materials should yield *authentic* information that provides a real-life picture of the child's skills at a given time, gathered *collaboratively* by the professionals and family members. There should be some *evidence* of appropriateness for each of the measures used. For example, some instruments are widely regarded as good tools, or "gold standards" for assessing particular skills, yet they may not be the best choice for infants and toddlers with different hearing levels; if studies have been conducted and have documented that use of those measures is appropriate with infants and toddlers who are deaf or hard of hearing, then professionals can be more confident about the selection of that measure for assessment. Emphasizing that *multiple factors* influence how an infant or toddler demonstrates his or her skills, information should be gathered across several setting, occasions, and methods. Assessment items should be *sensitive* enough to detect even small changes in a child's functioning. Measures should be *universal,* in that they can be adapted to infants and toddlers with a wide range of needs or challenges. Finally, assessments must have *utility*—they need to be useful and helpful.

Documents issued by the National Association of State Directors of Special Education (2014) and the Clerc Center at Gallaudet University (2013) offer information about particular instruments that can be used to assess the skills of deaf or hard-of-hearing infants and toddlers. (See the Recommended Resources at the end of this chapter.)

USABILITY OF ASSESSMENT RESULTS

Professionals should be mindful of the numerous factors that can influence the assessment process and the usability of the results. These factors may include (1) the child's disposition; (2) the environment; (3) the level of involvement of the family; and (4) the caregiver's report of the child's functioning. For example, during the formal evaluation of his gross motor skills, it was important to select tasks that challenged Adam, in order to show his optimal abilities, yet were not too difficult, so as not to frustrate him. Adam became highly frustrated when asked to perform motor tasks that were challenging for him. Often, providing multiple opportunities to observe the child that include different settings or times during the day will elicit targeted behaviors. Environmental disruptions may also interfere with the assessment process; auditory and visual distractions may impact the child's performance. For infants or toddlers who use assistive listening technologies, professionals need to ensure that the technologies are functioning optimally and that background noise is controlled. For children who communicate using a signed language, factors such as distance and lighting may impact the child's performance. When sharing assessment results, professionals should indicate the extent to which the findings are believed to be accurate and representative of the child's abilities.

PROVIDING FEEDBACK TO FAMILIES

Ms. Harper wants Adam's family members to be comfortable as they discuss the results of the developmental assessment. She and her team consider how they will deliver the information, knowing that each family member may respond differently. Adam's mother tends to want "the facts"; Adam's father is less interested in details and tends to "focus on the big picture." The team must determine how to share the assessment findings, offer their professional recommendations, and solicit input from family members, while respecting each family member's goals. The team will include a Portuguese/English interpreter in the feedback session to facilitate communication.

Ms. Harper is particularly interested in how the family would like to receive the information. What medium is best for them (e.g., a written outline, a visual graphic of the child's results, a chart listing the child's scores)? Ms. Harper believes that it may be helpful if the team prepared a summary of the results of the assessment in advance of the feedback meeting with the family as well as some concrete recommendations to share with the family during the meeting. She wonders if this might help prompt a positive exchange of ideas about how the information they have obtained can inform the services provided.

Strategies for Framing Assessment Results

The discussion should begin by focusing on what Adam is able to do, including his strengths and abilities. Presenting findings in this way highlights skills rather than deficits. Professionals can remind families that assessment findings are not necessarily predictive. A comprehensive assessment will gather data from various sources and across different contexts, yet it still captures a child's skills within a specific time frame. Professionals should be careful to avoid definitive statements about a child's future abilities; after all, the intention of early intervention is to improve those outcomes.

Begin with the Family

Encourage family members to describe what they have observed and what they know about their child's abilities in different areas. Before offering any results, ask family members about the questions they have pertaining to the assessment. The perceptions of the family members and their questions can guide the feedback session, help professionals to gain a sense of what the family members have understood about the assessment, and correct any misinterpretations (Postal & Armstrong, 2013).

To Number or Not to Number

Data derived from assessments usually yield numerical results. Professionals can report a child's abilities based on the percentage of same-aged children who can perform a task or the age at which mastery of a particular skill is expected, for example. This can help families know where their child stands with respect to developmental expectations and can provide the "evidence" that many families seek. This type of information may also be necessary to justify services.

Some family members, however, prefer descriptions of the child's skills rather than numerical scores. When reporting in descriptive terms, professionals may use visuals, such as a graph that can show which skills are at expectation for chronological age or developmental age (the latter is especially useful for children with cognitive limitations). A graph can help some family members to understand the child's overall developmental profile.

Determining How Much Is Enough

Some family members want to know the "big picture." Others may want domain-specific reports. Feedback can occur over time. Some family members will be able to digest only a portion of the information and may need additional sessions for feedback. Sometimes it is appropriate to appoint one professional to deliver the results.

Individualizing Feedback

The professional can use the family's own stories to personalize the feedback. When feedback to tailored to the family, they are better able to understand and accept it (Postal & Armstrong, 2013). For example, Ms. Harper may state, "Do you remember when you told me about the difficulties Adam has in walking up stairs? You mentioned that it was confusing, because he is a master at using a spoon, so it seems his motor skills are OK. That is a good example of what I mean by gross motor versus fine motor skills."

Adam's family members, having been highly involved throughout the assessment process, were not surprised when the results were shared with them. They appreciated the fact that the intervention team described the purposes of various aspects of the developmental assessment as it proceeded. They were particularly grateful that Ms. Harper and her team had the family identify their own questions before launching into the results, and that they used visual graphs to share the information. Additionally, Adam's family greatly appreciated the efforts of the team to make the results meaningful by providing many real-life examples and describing the findings in the context of Adam's home environment. Along with the presence of an interpreter for the initial feedback session, these strategies ensured that Adam's parents and grandparents could all access the information.

SUMMARY

Early intervention specialists are responsible for ensuring that the assessment is authentic and reflects the child's real-life competencies (Moeller et al., 2013; Neisworth & Bagnato, 2004). An authentic assessment (Moeller et al., 2013; Neisworth & Bagnato, 2004) informs the interdisciplinary team, and the family, as they select and prioritize goals for the child's programming (e.g., see Chapter 9, *Individualized Family Service Plans and Programming*). Striving to incorporate best practices into developmental assessment will help ensure that the essence of each child is understood. With that understanding, professionals and families can work collaboratively to support the child in reaching his or her optimal potential.

Evaluation results are often described in terms of domains of functioning, yet this alone is not enough to fully capture the various attributes of a child. Each child is more than the sum of his or her abilities. Consideration should be given not only to what a child *can do*, but also to how the child *is doing*. Beyond assessing for skills that a child demonstrates, professionals should attend to other important factors, such as the child's emergent sense of self, mastery, comfort in interacting with others, and esteem.

In considering best practices for developmental assessment, early intervention professionals should be cognizant of the overarching aims of assessment and should employ the techniques that best allow them to understand the whole child and the family in the context of their environment. Being mindful of the need for *comprehensive, meaningful,* and *authentic* assessments, professionals can understand, as fully as possible, how the child is functioning and what that functioning means in terms of the life of the child and the family.

Acknowledgments: The authors gratefully acknowledge Arlene Stredler-Brown for her contributions to the development of this chapter.

SUGGESTED ACTIVITIES

1. Based on the vignette of Adam, assume that his gross motor skills, as well as his communication and language skills, are significantly below age expectation. His abilities in all other domains are within the normal range for his age. Generate a visual handout that could be used when discussing the assessment results with Adam's family. See the Child Development Review website for an example of a chart demonstrating progress across several developmental domains. http://www.childdevrev.com/index.html; http://www.childdevrev.com/page3/page56/files/idi-chart-17monthchecked.pdf.

2. Review three commonly used infant and toddler assessment tools (i.e., assessments used widely in early intervention, not with deaf or hard-of-hearing children in particular). Identify assessment items or protocols (i.e., assessment procedures) that may not accurately measure the skills of an infant or toddler who is deaf or hard of hearing.

3. Using the assessments identified in activity 2 above, make two lists of accommodations that might be necessary if administering these tools with infants and toddlers who are deaf or hard of hearing. In the first list, assume that the child's hearing levels are in the moderate to moderate–severe range and that the child communicates via spoken language. In the second list, assume that the child's hearing levels are in the profound range and that the child communicates through a signed language. What accommodations would be needed given the two different profiles? Would the standardized tools still measure what they are

intended to measure? How might you describe the limitations of these protocols for the hard-of-hearing and the deaf populations?

4. Make a list of the various assessment tools used in your early intervention program or a program that you know. Determine which assessment tools include family input in the assessment process. Reflect on ways you may be able to increase the involvement of families in their child's assessment process.

RECOMMENDED RESOURCES

1. Clerc Center at Gallaudet University: Suggested Scales of Development and Assessment Tools

   This website provides a list of assessment tools that might be useful in assessing children who are deaf or hard of hearing. Six categories of assessment tools are listed: (1) auditory perception/listening skills; (2) speech/intelligibility; (3) speech reading; (4) language; (5) basic concepts; and (6) sign language. (http://www.gallaudet.edu/clerc_center/information_and_resources/cochlear_implant_education_center/resources/suggested_scales_of_development_and_assessment_tools.html.)

2. Massachusetts Child Care Resources—Common Assessment Tools for Infants and Toddlers

   A list of commonly used, research-based assessment tools used for infants, toddlers, and young children. (http://machildcareresourcesonline.org/for-providers/common-assessment-tools/.)

3. National Association for the Education of Young Children (NAEYC): Position Statement on Early Childhood Curriculum, Assessment, and Program Evaluation

   NAEYC is a national organization that is dedicated to the needs, rights, and well-being of all young children. This position statement was developed based on the 2003 Joint Position Statement of the NAEYC and the National Association of Early Childhood Specialists in State Departments of Education (NAECS/SDE). (https://www.naeyc.org/files/naeyc/file/positions/CAPEexpand.pdf.)

4. National Center for Hearing Assessment and Management (NCHAM): Assessment Tools for Communication/Language and Auditory Development

NCHAM is a national organization that is dedicated to ensuring that all infants and toddlers who are deaf or hard of hearing are identified as early as possible, and receive appropriate audiological, educational, and medical interventions. NCHAM has developed a list of assessment tools for communication, language, and auditory development that have been recommended for use with infants, beginning at birth. (http://www.infanthearing.org/earlyintervention/assessment.html.)

5. National Association of State Directors of Special Education (NASDSE)—Assessment Tools for Students Who Are Deaf or Hard of Hearing

The NASDSE recommended list of assessment tools for deaf or hard-of-hearing children of all ages, with many appropriate for infants and toddlers. It includes assessments in nine categories: (1) cognitive/intellectual; (2) psychosocial; (3) behavior; (4) occupational therapy; (5) expressive and receptive language; (6) auditory/listening skills; (7) speech skills; (8) vocabulary, basic concepts; and (9) sign language. (https://www.nasdse.org/Portals/0/Documents/AssessmentTools.pdf.)

6. Texas Women's University—Selected Evaluation and Assessment Instruments for Early Intervention

An extensive list of assessment tools used for infants and toddlers provided in six categories: (1) developmental screening; (2) standardized developmental and intellectual assessments; (3) behavioral/social emotional functioning; (4) communication; (5) listening comprehension; and (6) criterion-referenced instruments. (http://www.twu.edu/downloads/early-intervention/mi.pdf.)

REFERENCES

Bagnato, S. J. (2005). The authentic alternative for assessment in early intervention: An emerging evidence-based practice. *Journal of Early Intervention*, *28*(1), 17–22.

Bagnato, S., Neisworth, J., & Pretti-Frotczak, K. (2010). *LINKing authentic assessment and early childhood intervention: Best measures for best practices* (2nd ed.). Baltimore, MD: Brookes Publishing Co.

Barker, D. H., Quittner, A. L., Fink, N. E., Eisenberg, L. S., Tobey, E. A., Niparko, E. A., & the CDaCI Investigative Team. (2009). Predicting behavior problems in deaf and hearing children: The influences of language, attention, and parent–child communication. *Developmental Psychopathology, 21*(2), 373–392.

Brazelton, T. B., & Nugent, J. K. (2011). *The Neonatal Behavioral Assessment Scale.* Cambridge, England: Mac Keith Press,

Brotherson, M. J., Summers, J. A., Naig, L. A., Kyzar, K., Friend, A., Epley, P., ... Turnbull, A. P. (2010). Partnership patterns: Addressing emotional needs in early intervention. *Topics in Early Childhood Special Education, 30*(1), 32–45.

Bruder, M. B. (2010). Early childhood intervention: A promise to children and families for their future. *Exceptional Children, 76*(3), 339–355.

Calderon, R. (2000). Parental involvement in deaf children's educational programs as a predictor of child's language, early reading, and social-emotional development. *Journal of Deaf Studies and Deaf Education, 5*(2), 140–155.

Center on the Developing Child at Harvard University. (2007). *A science-based framework for early childhood policy: Using evidence to improve outcomes in learning, behavior, and health for vulnerable children.* Retrieved from http://www.developingchild.harvard.edu.

Division for Early Childhood. (2014). *DEC recommended practices in early intervention/early childhood special education 2014.* Retrieved from http://www.dec-sped.org/recommendedpractices.

Drecktrah, M. E., & Marchel, M.,A. (2014). *Functional assessment: Analyzing child behavior.* Retrieved from http://www.earlychildhoodnews.com/early-childhood/article_view.aspx?ArticleID=255.

Early Childhood Technical Assistance Center (ECTA). (2015). *Outcomes Measurement.* Retrieved from http://ectacenter.org.

Early Head Start National Resource Center. (2013). *Developmental screening, assessment and evaluation: Key elements for individualizing curricula in early head start.* Technical Assistance Paper No. 4.

Easterbrooks, S. R., & Baker, S. (2002). *Language learning in children who are deaf and hard of hearing: Multiple pathways.* Boston, MA: Allyn & Bacon.

Feldman, H. M., Dale, P. S., Campbell, T. F., Colborn, D. K., Kurs-Lasky, M., Rockette, H.E., & Paradise, J. L. (2005). Concurrent and predictive validity of parent reports of child language at ages two and three years. *Child Development, 76*(4), 856–868.

Gallaudet Research Institute. (2009). *Regional and national summary report of data from the 2007-08 annual survey of deaf and hard of hearing children and youth.* Retrieved from http://research.gallaudet.edu/Demographics/2008_National_Summary.pdf.

Gilkerson, L., & Taylor Ritzler, T. (2014). The role of reflective process in infusing relationship-based practice into an early intervention system. In K.

M. Finello (Ed.), *The handbook of training and practice in infant and pre-school mental health*. Manuscript submitted for publication.

Gresham, F. M., Watson, T. S., & Skinner, C. H. (2001). Functional behavioral assessment: Principles, procedures and future directions. *School Psychology Review, 30*(2),156–172.

Guralnick, M. J. (2005). An overview of the developmental systems model for early intervention. In M. J. Guralnick (Ed.), *The developmental systems approach to early intervention* (pp. 3–28). Baltimore, MD: Brookes Publishing Co.

Hafer, J. C., & Stredler-Brown, A. (2003). Family-centered developmental assessment. In B. Bodner-Johnson & M. Sass-Lehrer (Eds.), *The young deaf or hard of hearing child: A family centered approach to early education* (pp. 127–149). Baltimore, MD: Brookes Publishing Co.

Hanson, M. J., & Lynch, E. W. (2013). *Understanding families: Approaches to diversity, disability, and risk*. Baltimore, MD: Brookes Publishing Co.

Individuals with Disabilities Education Act, Early Intervention Program for Infants and Toddlers with Disabilities Regulations, 34 C.F.R. pt. 303 (2011).

Infant Toddler Communicative Development Inventory (ITMAIS). (2008). Sylmar, CA: Advanced Bionics.

Jarrett, M. H., Browne, B. C., & Wallin, C. M. (2006). Using portfolio assessment to document developmental progress of infants and toddlers. *Young Exceptional Children, 10*(1), 22–32.

Joint Committee on Infant Hearing. (2007). Year 2007 position statement: Principles and guidelines for early hearing detection and intervention programs. *Pediatrics, 120*, 898–921. doi:10.1542/peds.2007-2333.

Joint Committee on Infant Hearing. (2013). Supplement to the JCIH 2007 position statement: Principles and guidelines for intervention after confirmation that a child is deaf or hard of hearing. *Pediatrics, 131*(4), e1324–1349. doi:10.1542/peds.2013-0008.

Kassini, I. (2008). Professionalism and coordination: Allies or enemies? *American Annals of the Deaf, 153*(3), 309–313.

Kelly-Vance, L., & Ryalls, B. O. (2004). Best practices in play assessment and intervention. In A. Thomas & J. Grimes (Eds.), *Best practices in school psychology* (5th ed., pp. 549–560). Bethesda, MD: National Association of School Psychologists.

King, G., Strachan, D., Tucker, M., Duwyn, B., Desserud, S., & Shillington, M. (2009). The application of a transdisciplinary model for early intervention services. *Infants & Young Children, 22*(3), 211–223.

Kostelnik, M. J., Soderman, A. K., & Whiren, A. P. (2007). *Developmentally appropriate curriculum: Best practices in early childhood education*. Upper Saddle River, NJ: Pearson.

LaBoskey, V. K. (2000). Portfolios here, portfolios there: Searching for the essence of 'educational portfolios.' *Phi Delta Kappan*, *81*(8), 590–595.

Lifter, K., Foster-Sanda, S., Arzamarski, C., Briesch, J., & McClure, E. (2011). Overview of play: Its uses and importance in early intervention/early childhood special education. *Infants & Young Children*, *24*(3), 225–245.

Lifter, K., Mason, E. J., & Barton, E. E. (2011). Children's play: Where we have been and where we could go. *Journal of Early Intervention*, *33*, 281–297.

Linder, T. (2008). *Transdisciplinary play-based assessment* (2nd ed.). Baltimore, MD: Brookes Publishing Co.

Losardo, A., & Notari-Syverson, A. (2011). *Alternative approaches to assessing young children* (2nd ed.). Baltimore, MD: Brookes Publishing Co.

MacArthur Bates Communicative Development Inventory (CDI). (2013). Baltimore, MD: Brookes Publishing Co.

Marschark, M. (2007). *Raising and educating a deaf child: A comprehensive guide to the choices, controversies, and decisions faced by parents and educators* (2nd ed.). New York, NY: Oxford University Press.

Marschark, M., & Hauser, P. (2008). *Deaf cognition: Foundations and outcomes*. New York: Oxford University Press.

Marschark, M., & Hauser, P. (2011). *How deaf children learn: What parents and teachers need to know*. New York, NY: Oxford University Press.

Miller, J. F., Sedey, A. L., & Miolo, G. (1995). Validity of parent report measures of vocabulary development for children with Down syndrome. *Journal of Speech and Hearing Research*, *38*(5), 1037–1044.

Moeller, M. P. (2000). Early intervention and language development in children who are deaf and hard of hearing. *Pediatrics*, *106*(3), e43.

Moeller, M. P., Carr, G., Seaver, L., Stredler-Brown, A., & Holzinger, D. (2013). Best practices in family-centered early intervention for children who are deaf or hard of hearing: An international consensus statement. *Journal of Deaf Studies and Deaf Education*, *18*(4), 429–445.

National Scientific Council on the Developing Child. (2007). *The timing and quality of early experiences combine to shape brain architecture.* Retrieved from http://developingchild.harvard.edu/resources/reports_and_working_papers/working_papers/wp5/.

Neisworth, J. T., & Bagnato, S. J. (2004). The mismeasure of young children: The authentic assessment alternative. *Infants and Young Children: An Interdisciplinary Journal of Special Care Practices*, *17*(3), 198–212.

Niparko, J. K., Tobey, E. A., Thal, D. J., Eisenberg, L. S., Wang, N. Y. Quittner, A. L., . . . CDaCI Investigative Team. (2010). Spoken language development in children following cochlear implantation. *Journal of the American Medical Association*, *303*(15), 1498–1506.

Notari-Syverson, A., & Losardo, A. (2008). Assessment for learning: Teaching about alternative assessment approaches. In P. Winton, J. McCullom, & C. Catlett (Eds.), *Practical approaches to early childhood professional development*. Baltimore, MD: Brookes Publishing Co.

Orelove, F. P., Sobsey, D., & Silberman, R. K. (2004). *Educating children with multiple disabilities: A collaborative approach*. Baltimore, MD: Brookes Publishing Co.

Park, J., & Turnbull, A. P. (2003). Service integration in early intervention: Determining interpersonal and structural factors for its success. *Infants and Young Children, 16*(1), 48–58.

Picard, M. (2004). Children with permanent hearing loss and associated disabilities: Revisiting current epidemiological data and causes of deafness. *The Volta Review, 104*, 221–236.

Postal, K., & Armstrong, K. (2013). *Feedback that sticks: The art of effectively communicating neuropsychological assessment results*. New York, NY: Oxford University Press.

Puckett, M. B., & Black, J. K. (2008). *Meaningful assessments of the young child: Celebrating development and learning* (3rd ed.). Upper Saddle River, NJ: Pearson.

Rapport, M. J. K., McWilliam, R. A., & Smith, B. J. (2004). Practices across disciplines in early intervention: The research base. *Infants & Young Children, 17*(1), 32–44.

Rowland, C. (2009). *Assessing communication and learning in young children who are deafblind or who have multiple disabilities (targeted for ages 2–8)*. Retrieved from http://www.ohsu.edu/xd/research/centers-institutes/institute-on-development-and-disability/design-to-learn/completed-projects/upload/Assessing-Communication-Learning.pdf.

Stredler-Brown, A. (2004). Family-centered intervention: Proven strategies to assure positive outcomes. In R. Seewald & J. Bamford (Eds.), *A sound foundation through early amplification 2004: Proceedings of the third international conference* (pp. 185–195). Bungay, Suffolk, England: Immediate Proceedings Limited.

Stredler-Brown, A. (2010). Communication choices and outcomes during the early years: An assessment and evidence-based approach. In M. Marschark & P. E. Spencer (Eds.), *Oxford handbook of deaf studies, language, and education* (pp. 292–315). New York, NY: Oxford University Press.

Sugai, G., Lewis-Palmer, T., & Hagan-Burke, S. (2000). Overview of the functional behavioral assessment process. *Exceptionality, 8*(3), 149–160.

Thagard, E. K., Hilsmier, A. S., & Easterbrooks, S. R. (2011). Pragmatic language in deaf and hard of hearing students: Correlations with success in general education. *American Annals of the Deaf, 155*(5), 526–534.

Wood, N., & Dockrell, J. (2010). Psychological assessment procedures for assessing deaf or hard-of-hearing children. *Educational & Child Psychology, 27*(2), 11–22.

Yoshinaga-Itano, C. (2003). From screening to early identification and intervention: Discovering predictors to successful outcomes for children with significant hearing loss. *Journal of Deaf Studies and Deaf Education, 8*(1), 11–30.

Yoshinaga-Itano, C., Baca, R., & Sedey, A. L. (2010). Describing the trajectory of language development in the presence of severe to profound hearing loss: A closer look at children with cochlear implants versus hearing aids. *Otology and Neurotology, 31,* 1268–1274.

Zero to Three. (2014). Tips for surviving child development assessment. Retrieved from http://www.zerotothree.org/child-development/mental-health-screening.

8 Collaboration for Communication, Language, and Cognitive Development

Maribel Gárate and Susan Lenihan

Ms. Stevens, an early intervention specialist, has been working with Mindy and her family since Mindy was 6 months old. Mindy is deaf and has had a cochlear implant since she was 13 months old. She is now 15 months old and has very limited receptive and expressive vocabulary. Her family's goal is for her to acquire spoken language. Ms. Stevens has provided Mindy's family with access to resources, connecting the family with parent support groups and guiding Mindy's caregivers in language and learning strategies for daily routines. Ms. Stevens has also encouraged the family to meet other families with deaf or hard-of-hearing children. This chapter will follow Mindy and her family's journey by describing two different paths they might take to achieve their goal.

GUIDING QUESTIONS

1. What information does the early intervention specialist need to guide and support the age-appropriate language and communication skills for Mindy?
2. What developmental factors, programs, and services need to be considered?
3. How can the interdisciplinary team provide support and guidance for this family?

COMPETENCIES ADDRESSED IN THIS CHAPTER

1. Family-Centered Practice: Family–Professional Partnerships, Decision Making, and Family Support
2. Socially, Culturally, and Linguistically Responsive Practices Including Deaf/Hard-of-Hearing Cultures and Communities: Sensitivity to and Respect for an Individual Family's Characteristics
3. Language Acquisition and Communication Development: Typical Development, Communication Approaches Available to Children with Hearing Loss, and Impact of Hearing Loss on Access to Communication
4. Factors Influencing Infant and Toddler Development Technology: Supporting Development by Using Technology to Access Auditory, Visual, and/or Tactile Information
5. Collaboration and Interdisciplinary Models and Practices

INTRODUCTION

Early sensory experiences, which include auditory, visual, and kinesthetic stimuli, are crucial to the language and communication development of infants and toddlers. These experiences support the growth of brain synapses and pathways that map much of the neural circuitry providing the foundation for future linguistic and cognitive development (Eliot, 1999).

During the first year of life, the brain undergoes its most dynamic period of growth, making this period both critical and vulnerable for young children who are deaf or hard of hearing.

Caregiver participation stands as a powerful factor in early language development. Whether a family has chosen a listening and spoken language approach or an American Sign Language (ASL)/English Bilingual approach, consistent access to competent communication partners is needed. Thus, caregivers must provide interactions that establish communication, develop strong attachments, and set the basis for future linguistic and cognitive development. To this end, evidence-based practices support implementation of a family-centered approach to early intervention to ensure engagement and enhance caregiver–child communication. Interdisciplinary collaboration among early intervention professionals is essential to providing families with the information, guidance, support, and coaching they need to promote their child's early language acquisition.

Children who are deaf or hard of hearing represent a linguistically diverse population with individual abilities and learning needs. Technological advances in hearing aids and cochlear implants (CIs) as well as early age of implantation are increasing the number of children who are deaf or hard of hearing who can benefit from a listening and spoken language approach. Children who are deaf or hard of hearing vary in their abilities to access communication through auditory and visual modalities. Although some children, with the benefit of listening technologies, early access, and support, attain spoken language skills commensurate with their hearing peers, other children with similar supports acquire age-appropriate language visually, usually through a signed language, such as ASL. No two children who are deaf or hard of hearing are the same and their access to language and the means they use to express language vary along a continuum from fully visual using a signed language to fully auditory relying on hearing and spoken language in most situations. Through ongoing monitoring of progress and outcomes, professionals and family members can determine the most efficacious modalities for individual children.

This chapter will focus on the knowledge, skills, and dispositions early intervention specialists need to support families in the establishment of early learning environments that promote early communication, language, and cognitive development. The chapter will also address the role of assistive listening technologies and their potential benefit to the overall communication competence of young children. Collaboration and interdisciplinary models and practices will be emphasized to help early intervention specialists provide culturally and linguistically diverse families with the resources and support to fully consider all the options and opportunities available to them and their children.

EARLY COMMUNICATION AND BRAIN DEVELOPMENT

Mindy's family has received services since she was 6 months old. This places her at an advantage. In working with the family, Ms. Stevens has explained the importance that early stimulation has on Mindy's brain development and has worked to model ways in which the family can engage Mindy in activities that allow for repetition, create anticipation, and set up routines. During these times, Ms. Stevens consistently emphasizes the importance that sensory stimulation has on Mindy's brain development.

From a physiological standpoint, most children, whether they are deaf or hearing, possess the same neurological potential from birth (Marschark & Hauser, 2008). An infant's earliest experiences with the environment originate via auditory, visual, and kinesthetic input. This sensory input along with inferences made from context allows conceptual representation of familiar objects and routine events to develop. This gives way to the organization of the infant's world via the identification, discrimination, categorization, and recollection of the experiences occurring during their first year of life (Clark, 2004). Early experiences provide the cognitive basis onto which language will be mapped. In turn, the initial language mapping impacts further conceptual representation by allowing more specific categorization, complex thought, and the ability to distinguish both multiple perspectives and speakers' intent (Clark, 2004).

The presence and absence of early sensory input affect brain synapses and pathways. When stimulation occurs, these connections are retained, but when an infant is deprived, the brain resorts to rewiring or eliminating the unused connections (Hawley, 2000). As time passes, brain plasticity changes. Although some structures remain malleable, others are less responsive over time. Listening, seeing, and interacting with caregivers in their environment contribute to shaping and maintaining the brain's structures that serve as the foundation for language acquisition and all future learning (Hawley, 2000).

Sharma, Dorman, and Spahr (2002) state that "in the absence of normal stimulation there is a sensitive period of about 3.5 yr during which the human central auditory system remains maximally plastic" (p. 532). Because natural neurological pruning is related to the quality and quantity of early exposure to language, the situation for children who are deaf and receive linguistic input solely via the auditory channel without the benefit of appropriate listening technologies elicits concerns for the potential effects that reduced and inconsistent input has on their developing brain (Bavalier, Dye, & Hauser, 2006). This situation highlights the importance of providing complete access to language through the use of optimal listening technologies, the use of a natural signed language, or both.

CONTINUUM FOR PROCESSING AND USING LANGUAGE

When it comes to language access and use, children who are deaf or hard of hearing have been described on two continuums of expressive and receptive skills that range from the fully visual Signed Language user to the fully auditory spoken language user (see Figures 8.1 and 8.2; Nussbaum, Waddy-Smith, & Doyle, 2012). The combined use of spoken and signed languages and auditory and visual modalities spreads across two continuums to represent children who, for example, receive information visually but use a spoken language to express themselves. There are those children who are primarily spoken language users but can, in specific situations, use a visual language, as well as those who are fully bilingual and are able to code switch between the two languages as they see fit. Where a child falls on the continuum at any given time reflects the resources, opportunities, and options the child and the family have accessed.

Beyond the first few years of life, how signs are used in educational placements has a significant influence on the language use and development of children who are transitioning to more spoken language. Educational philosophies often guide a program's selection of communication options. These options include the use of a natural signed language (e.g., ASL); the use of a variety of invented signed systems also known as manually coded forms of English; or the use of Cued Speech, which is not a sign system but represents the phonology of a spoken language via handshapes and locations. Moeller (2006) proposed four ways to categorize how educational programs use signs with children who have cochlear implants. These included

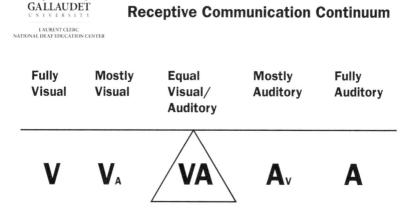

Nussbaum, D., Scott, S., Waddy-Smith, B., & Koch, M. (June, 2004). Spoken language and sign: Optimizing learning for children with cochlear implants. Paper presented at Laurent Clerc National Deaf Education Center, Washington, DC.

Adapted from McConkey -Robbins, Loud and Clear, Advanced Bionics, 2001

Figure 8.1 Receptive communication continuum. Reprinted with permission from Nussbaum, Waddy-Smith, and Doyle (2012).

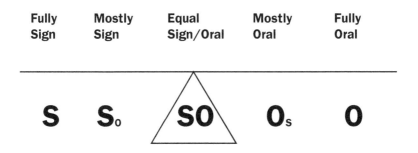

Nussbaum, D., Scott, S., Waddy-Smith, B., & Koch, M. (June, 2004). *Spoken language and sign: Optimizing learning for children with cochlear implants.* Paper presented at Laurent Clerc National Deaf Education Center, Washington, DC.

Figure 8.2 Expressive communication continuum. Reprinted with permission from Nussbaum, Waddy-Smith, and Doyle (2012).

foundational use, transitional use, differentiated/strategic use, and dominant use. With the exception of programs with a dominant use in which the emphasis was on visual communication, all others programs aimed to reduce or eliminate the use of signs in order to focus on developing the spoken language. Nussbaum et al. (2012) adapted Moeller's categories to describe the language use of the general population of children who are deaf or hard of hearing with and without cochlear implants and included a group of bimodal–bilinguals to represent individuals who become consistent users of both ASL and English, both spoken and written.

Families, professionals, and individuals who are deaf or hard of hearing use different languages (i.e., signed language, spoken language) and different modalities (e.g., visual, tactile, auditory, oral) to communicate. When communication modalities are used simultaneously, signing systems, rather than natural signed languages, are combined with a spoken language. This affects the clarity of production and diminishes the exposure the young child has to either language (Strong & Charlson, 1987; Swisher & Thomson, 1985).

Thus, this chapter focuses on two different pathways for Mindy that include the use of complete and natural languages, for example, a spoken language and a signed language. (See *Beginnings for Parents of Children Who Are Deaf or Hard of Hearing* in the Recommended Resources for a description of these different languages and communication modalities.)

Sociocultural and Environmental Considerations

Ms. Stevens consistently emphasizes the importance of providing a variety of interesting objects for Mindy to touch and smell and encourages her family to accompany all activities with descriptions, narratives, and natural dialogue related to objects and events in their environment. Introducing new words and/or signs (if the family has decided to sign with the child) for these activities and interactions allow Mindy and her family to communicate. Although infants possess the biological impetus for language acquisition, their environment provides the spark that ignites the process. The most important responsibility of caregivers is to ensure that Mindy has direct access to a natural language and communication partners. Natural languages, whether signed or spoken, are those used by the native communities of a respective country or region. With appropriate language models, most children acquire language following a predictably similar developmental timetable. This premise holds true for hearing children of hearing parents learning a spoken language as well as for deaf, hard-of-hearing, and hearing children of deaf parents acquiring a signed language (Mayberry, 2007; Petitto, 2009).

The most immediate environmental consideration for deaf or hard-of-hearing children occurs when the language (or languages) in their environment is either not *available* or not *accessible*. Varying ranges of hearing with and without amplification may create situations in which the spoken language that is readily *available* in a deaf infant's environment is not readily *accessible*. This environmental effect may be present, for example, when a family that does not know how to sign wants their deaf or hard-of-hearing infant to acquire a signed language. In that case, the signed language would be an *accessible* language when the child is attending visually, as it bypasses the auditory channel, but it is not readily *available* in the environment. A parallel example is a family that wants their child to acquire language through listening and speaking, however, is unable to ensure consistent use of the appropriate listening devices. The spoken language is *available* in the environment, but without the consistent use of appropriate listening devices it is not always *accessible*. In both cases, the language acquisition process for children who are deaf or hard of hearing differs as a result of a mismatch between the environment and the child's needs, and the child and adult must put additional effort forward to decrease the impact of this mismatch while enhancing the quality of their communication. The role of early intervention professionals and their ability to collaborate with others can make a significant difference in the early stages as professionals and families work together to gather information about the child's potential to access language through visual or auditory modalities.

Parental socioeconomic status has been known to impact language development (Hart & Risley, 1995). Differences in language and culture can lead to variable access to appropriate information about language and literacy that has an impact on the decisions parents of children who are deaf or hard of hearing make (Christensen, 2000; Sass-Lehrer, 2004; Young & Andrews, 2001). However, when early identification services are present and families are highly involved, children who are deaf or hard of hearing with normal cognitive abilities demonstrate advantages in language outcomes "regardless of communication mode, degree of hearing loss, socioeconomic status, gender, minority status, or presence of additional disabilities" (Moeller, 2000, p. 2). Research studies continue to support the notion that positive outcomes in language development are related to the age of identification, the provision of quality early intervention services (Yoshinaga-Itano, 2003), and family involvement (Calderon, 2000; Moeller, 2000).

COMMUNICATION IN THE FAMILY

Most children learn to communicate through interaction with family members (Kuhl, 2007; Topping, Dekhinet, & Zeedyk, 2013). Caregivers responsive to their infants' vocalizations, facial expressions, and gestures meet their communicative needs. Caregivers and infants typically develop strong attachment relationships that create an environment that supports communication development. Infants and toddlers who are developing typically acquire thousands of words and many rules of grammar during the first 3 years of life. Parents and other caregivers support the development of language skills through talking, singing, playing, and reading.

From birth to 6 months, babies primarily communicate through crying, cooing, and at around 6 months of age making other sounds. Between 6 and 12 months of age babbling begins, initially without a connection to objects; however, toward the end of this period the babbling is associated with objects or people in the environment. For infants with auditory access to spoken language the babble begins to resemble the speech of the family. During the 12-month to 18-month period children develop a vocabulary of about 20 words. For children who are deaf with signing deaf parents manual "babble" and early signs develop during the 6-month to 18-month period (Petitto & Marentette, 1991). See Alexander Graham Bell Listening and Spoken Language Ages and Stages and the Visual Language and Sign Language Checklist in Recommended Resources at the end of this chapter.

For all infants and toddlers the role of the family is crucial in facilitating the development of language and communication skills. The seminal work of Hart and Risley (1995, 1999) with 42 families and their young children proposed that the quantity and quality of child-directed speech dramatically influence language outcomes for young children. Their research showed that children who heard more words per hour and heard a higher ratio of encouragements to discouragements developed larger cumulative vocabularies. Their work also demonstrated that children whose parents provided more emphasis on the relationships between things and events, asked more questions, and were more responsive to their children's initiations had better language outcomes.

The Hart and Risley study also demonstrated that infants younger than 11 months heard an average of 700–800 utterances per hour. The researchers propose a model of conversational interaction consisting of three developmental stages. The first stage, from 11 months to 19 months of age, focuses on reciprocal interactions between the infant and caregivers. The second stage, from 20 months to 28 months, consists of intensive one-to-one conversations. The third stage, from 29 months to 36 months, shows the child as the primary speaker with caregivers listening and providing feedback and expansion. A key feature throughout is the emphasis on social interaction and reciprocity.

For infants and toddlers who are deaf, Moeller (2000) identified family involvement, including parent–child communication, as the most important factor in early language development. The impact of a variety of features of a caregiver's communication style has been demonstrated in several studies. Bergeson (2011) found that use of infant-directed speech registers by mothers interacting with infants with cochlear implants was even more pronounced than the infant-directed speech of mothers with hearing children and reflected the type of acoustic scaffolding used by parents of hearing children. The study also found an increased use of word and utterance repetition similar to mothers' speech to infants with normal hearing. These findings of mother–infant interaction support the concept that "mother and children must both be active participants in dynamic and reciprocal social exchanges to develop language and vocabulary skills" (Houston et al., 2012, p. 455). Daniel (2012) describes the features of child-directed speech and how this applies to auditory–verbal practice. These features, which include speech and language characteristics and following the child's lead, facilitate the development of conversational competence.

Research on infant-directed signing found that deaf mothers manipulated articulatory features of ASL when communicating with their infants by placing signs closer to the infant, changing palm orientation, and lengthening signs via expansion or repetition of its movement. Additionally, mothers directed the child's eye gaze during interaction and ensured that their faces and dominant signing hand were visible (Erting, Prezioso, & Hynes, 1994; Masataka, 1996). Parent–child interactions of these types not only encourage visual engagement and develop visual attention, they also support appropriate attachment (Enns & Price, 2013).

Access to Communication

Ms. Stevens guides and coaches Mindy's mother during weekly home visits that focus on communication development, social interactions, and cognitive activities through daily routines and engaging play. Infants and toddlers need access to language for communication to develop. Whether the infant is developing language through spoken or a natural signed language, such as ASL, the availability of a competent user of that language for a significant portion of the child's waking hours is essential. For optimal communication development, it is most beneficial that the competent language users are family members and caregivers who spend extensive periods of quality time with the child engaging in supportive and responsive interactions. For a young child who is developing spoken language consistent use of hearing aids and/or cochlear implants is required so that access to spoken language is maximized. The young child who is developing ASL or another signed language needs consistent access to skilled signed language users during daily routines.

Home Languages

Increasing numbers of children in the United States who are deaf or hard of hearing are growing up in homes in which English is not the only language used. The Gallaudet Research Institute (2011) reported that 18% of children who are deaf or hard of hearing are living in homes in which English is not used regularly.

Robbins (2007) uses a framework to describe three common types of bilingual families in which children who are deaf may be raised. Multilingual families are those in which the parents speak English and another language fluently. English as a new language describes families in which the parents or caregivers are just beginning to learn English or may not be fluent in spoken English. Extended family refers to families in which members such as grandparents may speak another language but English is spoken in the home most of the time. Early intervention services must be tailored to address the unique needs of children in different types of bilingual homes.

Douglas and Freutel's (2012) findings from several studies of children in auditory–verbal programs who are bilingual showed that the monolingual groups scored slightly higher on standardized measures of spoken English than the children in the bilingual group but did not show any significant differences in their ability to learn English. They describe supportive program features for children from homes in which spoken Spanish is the primary language such as weekly auditory–verbal sessions with a native Spanish-speaking practitioner, audiology services in Spanish, and a family language plan for providing support for Spanish and English input.

A family in which a signed language is the primary home language represents another type of bilingual environment. Early intervention specialists working with deaf families should be responsive to their values and draw on the language and cultural resources of the Deaf community. Specialists need to discuss the child's goals for bilingual development and provide strategies and materials parents and caregivers can use to support language and literacy development at home.

GUIDING FAMILIES TO SUPPORT THEIR CHILD'S LANGUAGE LEARNING

Ms. Stevens implements the recommendations of the Joint Committee on Infant Hearing [Joint Committee on Infant Hearing (JCIH), 2007] by providing access to resources, connecting the family with other families with deaf or hard-of-hearing children, and guiding Mindy's caregivers in providing opportunities for direct access to communication and language learning during daily routines. The JCIH Position Statement recommends that early intervention services include "a family-centered approach, culturally responsive practices, collaborative professional-family relationships and strong family involvement, developmentally appropriate practices, interdisciplinary assessment, and community-based provision of services" (p. 18). (See Chapter 4, *Legislation, Policies, and Role of Research in Shaping Early Intervention*, for more information about the JCIH Position Statement.)

Early intervention professionals support families as they foster their deaf or hard–of-hearing infants' and toddlers' communication development through guidance and coaching. Evidence-based practices for enhancing the development of parent–caregiver and child communication may be implemented through a family-centered approach to early intervention. (See Chapter 3, *Families: Partnerships in Practice.*) According to the American Speech-Language-Hearing Association (2005) the goal of evidence-based practice is to consider expert opinion based on experience, scientific evidence, and caregiver values to identify promising practices that will result in the highest quality services. In some cases, these communication-promoting evidence-based practices have been adapted from strategies used by parents of children who are not deaf or hard of hearing. In other cases, the strategies have been designed specifically for families of children who are deaf or hard of hearing.

Working closely with families to acquire skills that positively impact their child's communication abilities appears to be effective. Roberts and Kaiser (2011) reviewed 18 studies that evaluated parent-implemented intervention with children with delayed communication due to a variety of conditions. These studies found that parents were successful in learning and using new communication-promoting strategies designed to improve their children's communication skills. This research supports the value of family-centered early intervention and the effectiveness of guiding and supporting families in implementing communication-promoting behaviors with their children.

Compton and Niemeyer (2005) provide strategies for guiding families of infants who are deaf or hard of hearing in communication-promoting interactions including using eye contact, establishing joint attention, and observing the infant's communicative intent. They also provide recommendations for ways to interact with caregivers including establishing trust, demonstrating respect, listening to their perspective, and involving them in all decisions.

In 2013, the JCIH published a supplement to the 2007 position statement on newborn hearing screening. The supplement includes best practice guidelines, benchmarks, and a document on the essential knowledge and skills needed by early interventionists who are providing services to children who are deaf or hard of hearing and their families. The essential knowledge and skills include competencies for implementing strategies to support communication development. The supplement also includes checklists for self-monitoring of fidelity of intervention for both listening and spoken language, and ASL in Appendices 2 and 3 (JCIH, 2013).

Ms. Stevens has provided Mindy's family with access to a variety of electronic resources such as websites from the Alexander Graham Bell Association for the Deaf and Hard of Hearing, Beginnings for Parents of Children Who Are Deaf or Hard of Hearing, and the Laurent Clerc National Deaf Education Center among others. Mindy's parents participate in a parent group designed for families of infants and toddlers who are deaf or hard of hearing that is led by parents of a teenager who is deaf. Several resources, which provide support for professionals and families in the development of communication, are listed in the Recommended Resources section at the end of this chapter.

Lenihan and Daniels (2002) and Lenihan (2006) developed a set of 10 effective practices for early intervention with families of children who are deaf or hard of hearing based on the work of Rosetti (2001) and evidence from numerous studies. Table 8.1 represents an adapted version of the principles of effective practices to encourage early communicative interactions with young children who are deaf or hard of hearing.

During weekly home visits Ms. Stevens uses a family-centered approach. The format of each visit follows the rubric for a home visit (Moeller, Schow, & Whitaker, 2013; Stredler-Brown, Moeller, Gallegos, & Corwin, 2004; see Chapter 9, *Individualized Family Service Plans and Programming*). She often uses material from *Learn to Talk around the Clock* (Rossi, 2003) and from the SKI-HI curriculum (2004). Her work with the family reflects the principles of effective practice as described by Lenihan and Daniels (2002).

Keeping in mind the family's goal for Mindy to acquire a spoken language, the next section in this chapter describes two different journeys that

Table 8.1 *Effective Practices for Early Communicative Interactions*

Principles of Effective Practices	Indicators of Effective Practices
Involve both the child and his or her caregivers in interactions.	Involve caregivers in all communication and language activities. Ask open-ended questions about their child's development. Recognize caregivers' successful interactions. Provide resources for family.
Encourage turn taking, a critical skill and tool for early communication.	Establish and reinforce eye contact. Use facial expressions to reinforce the child's actions and vocalizations. Develop auditory/visual feedback by imitating the child's productions. Use phrases such as "my turn" and "your turn" in play.
Focus on functional communication skills and not language structure.	Observe ways in which the child uses language. Focus on the language that children most need. Engage in activities that are purposeful and playful. Ask caregivers to share communication goals for their children. Use activities that develop competencies in several areas.
Follow the child's lead and identify opportunities for spontaneous communication.	Attend to the child's eye gaze and gestures to determine the child's interest. Respond to the child's initiations. Observe the child's interests when playing freely. Prepare multiple materials and activities so that the child may choose.
Encourage caregivers to respond in ways that will enhance the child's language responses.	Repeat the child's vocalizations/signs and gestures. Use pauses and wait time to encourage the child to initiate. Use appropriate questions. Expand the child's utterances. Encourage positive interactions.

Table 8.1 *Continued*

Principles of Effective Practices	Indicators of Effective Practices
Arrange the environment and activities to encourage communicative interactions.	Offer choices and wait for the child to respond.
	Spend time in play with the child to set the stage for interactions.
	Omit a needed object from an activity; wait for the child to express the need.
	Use dolls, puppets, and toys to model and encourage vocalization.
	Plan activities that are developmentally appropriate for the child.
Use action-oriented activities to stimulate communicative exchanges.	Participate in action-oriented activities that are part of the child's daily life.
	Use pretend play.
	Use movement and music to develop language.
	Use games such as "peek-a-boo" and "so big."
Encourage parents to engage in natural conversations and activities with the child.	Use genuine daily routines as opportunities for communication.
	Encourage parents to include the child in family tasks and family fun.
	Use verbal (signed or spoken) routines.
	Share books daily.
Employ a variety of communication-eliciting techniques.	Establish modeling and imitating for developing new language.
	Reinforce the child's thoughts with language.
	Use songs, finger plays, and nursery rhymes to reflect the fun in language.
	Go beyond labeling objects.
	Introduce a question with a comment that establishes the topic and context.
Be alert to opportunities to expand communication skills to other settings and contexts.	Keep a developmental log that records language used in new settings.
	Brainstorm with caregivers the settings and contexts that may reinforce a new language skill.
	Involve the extended family and friends.
	Use naturalistic environments to increase generalization.

Mindy's family could take to achieve this goal. The first path describes an ASL/English bilingual approach to language development based on the use of American Sign Language alongside the auditory benefits Mindy receives from a listening device. The next path describes a listening and spoken language approach to language development based solely on the use of listening technologies and auditory–verbal practices.

ASL/ENGLISH BILINGUAL ACQUISITION

Evidence-Based Research Related to Communication Using a Signed and a Spoken Language

Like many hearing families, Mindy's family wants her to acquire a spoken language and opted for a cochlear implant in addition to signing. Ms. Stevens worked with the family toward this goal because she knows that early competence in a visual language can be effectively used to support and facilitate a child's spoken language development. Mindy's exposure to a visual language and age of implantation should also work in her favor. Although some professionals advocate for ASL (or another natural signed language) and *written* English (or another spoken language) as a form of bilingual development, the bilingual perspective discussed here includes the development of two languages and all their abilities, that is, receptive and expressive signing skills as well as spoken and written skills. Support for this approach is derived from the field of general bilingual education. Research evidence points to a positive transfer between the two, or more, languages a bilingual person uses with evidence of cognitive and communicative benefits (see Genesee, Lindholm-Leary, Saunders, & Christian, 2006, for a review of the bilingual literature).

Although spoken language bilingualism is seen as a positive attribute, misconceptions about signed languages have prevented some families from considering bilingualism as a viable option for their deaf or hard-of-hearing children. A prime example is the notion that using a signed language with young deaf or hard-of-hearing children in general, and children with cochlear implants in particular, precludes the development of spoken language. This idea has prevailed notwithstanding evidence to the contrary. In a study of 22 preschool children in Sweden who had cochlear implants and access to a signed language prior to implantation, the researchers reported that the children with the best oral skills also had a well-developed signed language (Preisler, Tvingtedt, & Ahlström, 2002). Yoshinaga-Itano (2006) found that the children in her study with access to signing prior to implantation achieved positive spoken language outcomes. Cochlear implant users with access to signing prior to implantation appear to exceed the performance of cochlear implant users who do not have this early access (Hassanzadeh, 2012; Yoshinaga-Itano, Sedey, & Uhler, 2008). Though more research evidence is needed with larger numbers of children, research studies have also demonstrated an overall positive relationship between early ASL skill and English literacy (Cummins, 2006), as well as cognitive benefits derived from bilingualism (Fish & Morford, 2012; Galambos & Goldin-Meadow, 1990).

Fish and Morford (2012) conducted a review of the literature on the benefits of bilingualism on cognition and language development including ASL/English bilingualism. As with spoken language bilinguals, simultaneous ASL/English bilinguals achieve language milestones at similar developmental timetables. Early bilingualism promotes language and literacy development and higher executive function control. Children placed in maintenance bilingual education exhibit heightened metalinguistic awareness, mental flexibility, creative thinking, and concept development (Bialystok, 2007; Grosjean, 2008).

Perhaps the most significant research finding to date that lends support to the viability of ASL/English bilingualism for deaf children comes from the neuroimaging research conducted with both deaf and hearing bilingual subjects. The research concluded that the human brain does not discriminate between a signed language and a spoken language (Petitto et al., 2001; Petitto, 2009). Because the brain does not detect modality (auditory or visual) in a language, it is equipped to initiate the language acquisition process with a spoken and/or a signed language as long as the input it receives is complete and accessible. This is an important point to consider because even with advances in technology that provide enhanced access to auditory input, the input is not equivalent to that of hearing children and some deaf children often need access to visual communication (Calderon, 2000; Moeller, 2000; Yoshinaga-Itano, 2003). The ASL/English bilingual approach is a viable option for children with varying access to auditory or visual stimuli and preferences for expressive and receptive language use. The type and degree of visual and auditory support needed often depend on the characteristics of the child (Nussbaum et al., 2012).

The interrelationship between cognition and language is established early in the child's life. Thus, a bilingual emphasis on early language development aims to ensure that children who are deaf or hard of hearing have two natural and accessible languages to support cognitive, linguistic, and social–emotional development (Gárate, 2011; Hassanzadeh, 2012; Mitchiner, Nussbaum, & Scott, 2012). As such, acquiring a signed language alongside the development of spoken language skills is seen as an asset that can lead to cognitive and communicative benefits (Fish & Morford, 2012; Gárate, 2012). Much like with first language acquisition, becoming a functional simultaneous bilingual is optimized when access to both languages is provided early in the child's life (Petitto, 2009). Families with infants and toddlers who are deaf or hard of hearing need information about ASL or the native sign language of their country and bilingual education as early as possible.

Research with sign–speech bilinguals has established that exposure to a signed and a spoken language from birth does not cause delays or confusion (Petitto & Kovelman, 2003). Instead, "the age of first bilingual exposure is a vital predictor of bilingual language and reading mastery" (Petitto, 2009, p. 1). Similarly, early access to a natural language, whether it is spoken or signed, is a predictor of positive spoken language outcomes for children who are deaf and use cochlear implants (Yoshinaga-Itano & Sedey, 2000). Mitchiner and Sass-Lehrer (2011) report on a study of Deaf mothers who chose cochlear implants for their children in order to support their children's bilingual development. With a strong foundation in ASL provided at home, access to auditory information through the use of the cochlear implant, and professional support for the development of spoken language, the children in this study were afforded "greater opportunities, independence, and access" to both languages and cultures (p. 90). In contrast, research finds that limited exposure to a complete language, incomplete or inconsistent access to a second language, and delayed introduction to literacy practices in either language have lasting linguistic, cognitive, and academic consequences for children who are deaf (Grosjean 2008; Mayberry, 2007; Petitto, 2009).

Facilitating Language Learning through Vision

Ms. Stevens, who knows how to sign, has taught the family simple signs during weekly visits and provided links to ASL story telling sites, Baby Signs DVDs, books, and sign videos from which the family can learn. She has also introduced Mindy's family to both deaf and hearing parents of deaf children who have opted to raise their children as bilinguals. In addition, Ms. Stevens put Mindy's parents in contact with the local Deaf Mentor program. (See Chapter 5, *Collaboration with Deaf and Hard-of-Hearing Communities.*)

Like all other sensory input, visual input has an important role in brain development, language comprehension, and learning in general. In hearing and deaf people alike, speech processing depends on both vision and audition. The input from both senses interacts and contributes to language comprehension (Morere, 2011a, 2011b). Vision also has a constant role for deaf children who depend on speechreading.

Learning through a visual language has cognitive, linguistic, and social benefits. Although research reports that a growing proportion of deaf children receiving a cochlear implant at an early age who are educated in oral communication programs achieve spoken language levels in receptive and expressive vocabulary within the average range of their hearing peers, the same research reports that "there were a number of children who did not reach age-appropriate levels of spoken language competence" (Geers, Moog, Biedenstein, Brenner, & Hayes, 2009, p. 383).

Early access to a visual language (e.g., ASL) initiates the language acquisition process during the critical period of brain development (Fish & Morford, 2012) preventing the delays that auditory stimulation alone may create. In the case of children who will receive a cochlear implant, learning a visual language can prevent cognitive delays by allowing infants to access information before, during, and after the implant. This access allows children to communicate and establish caregiver–child, child–adult, and child–child interactions that foster social–emotional development. Beyond the early years, maintaining the use of a signed language provides the child with communication options in specific situations (e.g., noisy environments, among all deaf or hard-or-hearing signers) or in the absence of their cochlear implant. Although it is too early to determine what quantity and quality of input Mindy will ultimately derive from her implant, the fact that she has been exposed to signing, and interacted with other signing infants and toddlers and their families, has already allowed Mindy's brain to map language pathways and to establish the basis for future symbolic learning. When Mindy begins to attend to spoken language, her brain will be ready to add new labels to the concepts she knows in sign and give way to bilingual development.

The next section describes Mindy's path to language acquisition via a listening and spoken language approach and the use of listening technologies and auditory–verbal practices.

LISTENING AND SPOKEN LANGUAGE ACQUISITION

At least 90% of children who are deaf or hard of hearing have parents who are hearing. This reality, coupled with advances in newborn hearing screening and listening technology, has led to increasing numbers of families choosing a listening and spoken language approach for their children (Alberg, 2011; Gallaudet Research Institute, 2002, 2011). For these families it is essential that their early intervention service providers possess the knowledge and skills needed to effectively support the child's early development of listening and spoken language. Most professionals working to support the development of listening and spoken language as the child's primary means of communicating and learning do not include a signed language in early intervention services. For most families choosing a listening and spoken language approach, a signed language is not used. In this section of the chapter, findings and strategies for developing listening and spoken language that do not include a signed language are discussed.

At 15 months of age, Mindy's parents met with the early intervention team including the service coordinator, Ms. Stevens, and Mindy's audiologist for a 6-month review. In this scenario, Ms. Stevens is a certified listening and spoken language specialist, auditory–verbal therapist who supports Mindy's use of listening to develop spoken language. Mindy demonstrates strong speech perception at the detection stage and is beginning to identify a number of sounds and common spoken utterances such as her name. Ms. Stevens and Mindy's parents noted that Mindy demonstrates appropriate communicative intent, uses two words (mama and bye-bye), and understands 10 words. Ms. Stevens noted that most of Mindy's receptive understanding consists of nouns and the team added an objective on her Individualized Family Service Plan (IFSP) related to more functional language.

Listening Technologies for Auditory-Verbal Practice

The emphasis on listening for the development of spoken language is a primary component of auditory–verbal practice. Ms. Stevens emphasized that in order for Mindy to maximize access to spoken language, optimal audiological technology must be used consistently. For certain levels of hearing, digital hearing aids provide the best quality of spoken language input. For severe-to-profound levels of hearing that are symmetrical, cochlear implants are usually the most effective listening technology. For a child with asymmetrical hearing levels, a cochlear implant for the severe-to-profound level and a hearing aid for the mild-to-moderate level are usually most effective in increasing access to spoken language. In addition to these personal listening devices, sound field and FM systems support listening in noise and at a distance in home, school, and childcare settings. A high level of knowledge and skill in listening technology is necessary for effective early intervention services. For detailed information about listening technologies for young children who are deaf or hard of hearing see Cole and Flexer (2015) in the Recommended Resources.

Evidence-Based Research on Communication
Using Listening and Spoken Language without Signs

The primary goal of a listening and spoken language approach is to develop communication through speech perception and speech production (Estabrooks, 2012; Spencer & Marschark, 2010). Several factors have been shown to positively impact the development of spoken language including age of early intervention services, age of implantation for children using cochlear implants, family involvement, and the type of early childhood intervention program (Geers & Nicholas, 2013; Moeller, 2000; Moog & Geers, 2010; Yoshinaga-Itano, Sedey, Coulter, & Mehl, 1998). Evidence documenting successful listening and spoken language comes primarily from two areas of study: auditory–verbal practice outcomes and the impact of cochlear implants on communication development.

Auditory–Verbal Practice

Early intervention specialists for children who are deaf or hard of hearing and their families often use an auditory–verbal approach, which does not include the use of a signed language. According to Estabrooks (2012), "auditory–verbal practice includes guidance, therapy, education, advocacy and family support. Auditory–verbal practice is the application and management of hearing technology in conjunction with strategies, techniques and conditions, which promote optimal acquisition of spoken language" (p. 2). The primary goals are for the child to learn to listen and talk with conversational competence and to be educated in general education settings. (See Estabrooks, 2012, and Rhoades & Duncan, 2010, for comprehensive descriptions of auditory–verbal practice.)

For early interventionists to use evidence-based practices it is important to be knowledgeable of the research supporting the use of auditory–verbal strategies. The following studies document the successful outcomes of auditory–verbal practice for the development of listening, language, speech, and academic achievement. Many of the children and families in these studies received family-centered early intervention services since a focus on coaching and guiding parents is a key component of auditory–verbal practice. Overall, this research demonstrates that with early identification, early access to spoken language through amplification or cochlear implantation, and early auditory–verbal services, most children will progress and maintain language development commensurate with their hearing peers without the use of sign language.

Children's expressive language development may be predicted by age of identification, by device fitting, by early intervention services, and by the teachers' expectations of the child (Wu & Brown, 2003). The 20 children in this study began auditory–verbal services between 4 and 54 months. Wu and Brown (2003) found that parents' expectation of the teacher's use of auditory–verbal practice was an additional factor predicting the children's receptive language development. In another study in England, Hogan, Stokes, White, Tyszkiewicz, and Woolgar (2008) found auditory–verbal therapy to be highly effective for accelerating spoken language development for all age groups and for children using different types of hearing technology. Hogan and colleagues assessed spoken language at the time of entry into an auditory–verbal program and at 6-month intervals.

Dornan, Hickson, Murdoch, and Houston (2009) studied the speech production and language of 25 children in an auditory–verbal therapy program in Australia over a 21-month period. The children in the study demonstrated improved speech perception skills, and their rate of progress for speech and language skills was similar to that of children with typical hearing. There was also significant improvement in scores for auditory comprehension, oral expression, total language, and articulation of consonants. At the final test point 84% of the children scored within the typical range for total language age, compared to 58.6% at the initial assessment.

Researchers studying 45 children who were identified early with a range of hearing levels and who received auditory–verbal early intervention services assessed the children's performance in speech production, vocabulary, and receptive and expressive language at ages 3 and 5 years (Fulcher, Purcell, Baker, & Munro, 2012). By 3 years of age, 93% of the children scored within normal limits for speech and 95% scored within normal limits for receptive and expressive language. By 5 years of age, 96% were within normal limits for speech and 100% within normal limits for language. (See Estabrooks, 2012, pp. 419–436, for a summary of additional research on auditory–verbal outcomes.)

Outcomes of Cochlear Implantation

When Mindy's parents met with the audiologist, she reminded them that Mindy's cochlear implant had only been turned on for 8 weeks and that Mindy was a very new listener. Children with hearing in the normal range listen for at least 9–12 months before using spoken words. She assured them that she would continue assessing Mindy's ability to access spoken language through listening during ongoing audiological visits and that Ms. Steven's would encourage and monitor her listening during weekly home visits.

"Without question, pediatric cochlear implantation has led to improved spoken language skills for deaf children, with the majority of those who receive a cochlear implant by age 2 years now scoring within a SD [standard deviation] of hearing age mates after a few years of use" (Geers & Nicholas, 2013, p. 643). In a study to determine if the language benefit of early age of implantation is maintained, Geers and Nicholas found that age-appropriate spoken language skills were more likely to continue into mid-elementary school for infants and toddlers who received implants before age 36 months. Multiple studies have demonstrated that children who receive a cochlear implant at the youngest ages tend to have improved outcomes in expressive language, receptive language and vocabulary as well as speech perception and production (Dettman, Pinder, Briggs, Dowell, & Leigh, 2007; Geers & Nicholas, 2013).

In a study of nine preschool children with cochlear implants, results showed that the children achieved spoken lexical skills within the average range when compared to children of the same age with normal hearing (Luckhurst, Lauback, & Unsterstein VanSkiver, 2013). The children with cochlear implants received services in a listening and spoken language program from an early age and the average age of cochlear implantation was 19.2 months. With this information, Ms. Stevens encouraged Mindy's family to continue to support the development of Mindy's listening skills.

Facilitating Language Learning through Listening

The principles of auditory–verbal practice (Estabrooks, 2012) emphasize the importance of early identification and services for infants and toddlers that focus on guidance and coaching of parents and other caregivers. Family-centered principles recognize parents and caregivers as the primary facilitators of their child's communication development and the importance of daily activities in creating environments that support communication development. The auditory–verbal practice principles include a focus on integrating listening and spoken language into all aspects of the child's life.

A foundational aspect of auditory–verbal practice is the emphasis on the development of listening skills. Cole and Gill (2012) state, "Maintaining auditory access and maximizing opportunities for the child to listen and talk need to remain the focus when the goal is to understand spoken language" (p. 277). Wilson (2012) describes a suggested framework for listening and spoken language that addresses levels of development including auditory awareness, auditory discrimination, and auditory memory among other listening and spoken language stages. The Model for Listening (Estabrooks, 2012, pp. 402–407) guides professionals and families in auditory skill development. Family-centered sessions include activities that provide rich auditory input such as sound–object association, songs, rhymes, shared book reading, play, and conversation. *Learn to Talk around the Clock* (Rossi, 2003) is an example of a curriculum that includes these activities for early intervention.

The purpose of developing listening skills is to enhance the auditory feedback loop and to develop speech production and spoken language. In addition to spoken language input, early interventionists encourage vocal play through responsiveness and communicative turn-taking and design activities that create a need for spoken communication (Winkelkotter & Srinivasan, 2012). Strategies such as waiting, sabotage, and arranging the environment to elicit communication are also used. See Table 8.1.

Early intervention sessions frequently include storytelling, shared book reading, and the use of children's literature as communication-promoting activities. Smith and Stowe (2012) describe storytelling with young children as an excellent way to build vocabulary, develop conversation, and grow creativity. Caleffe-Schenck (2012) provides examples of ways to use children's literature to develop listening skills including awareness, identification, memory, sequencing, and processing. Evans and Wilson (2012) identify strategies that caregivers of children who are deaf or hard of hearing can use daily in reading to their children.

Auditory–verbal sessions for infants and toddlers and their families are play-based and activities are designed to maximize the value that play brings to early learning (Laferriere & Rossi, 2012). Developmentally appropriate toys, games, and role plays provide opportunities for meaningful interactions among children, parents, and professionals.

As Mindy listens to the sounds and spoken language in her environment and makes connections between spoken language and the objects and actions of her daily routines she continues to develop communication skills. She consistently turns when her name is called and identifies when she hears meaningful sounds such as the garage door opening when her father returns from work. With consistent opportunities to interact with her family through listening and spoken language it is likely that she will make rapid growth in listening skills, receptive language, and expressive language. She will use age-appropriate functional language such as "uh-oh," "my turn," "all gone," and "no" and add spoken words and two-word utterances such as "my book," "Daddy car," and "more, please." With consistent use of her cochlear implant and effective early intervention services from Ms. Stevens, a listening and spoken language specialist, she will acquire language through listening and most likely develop spoken language commensurate with that of her hearing peers.

Effective Interdisciplinary Collaboration of Professionals and Family Members Using Either Listening and Spoken Language or ASL/English Bilingualism

When Mindy's mother reported that she had recently returned to work 3 days a week and that Mindy was receiving childcare from an aunt who had two young children, she noted that the aunt was still not confident about how to use the cochlear implant and often left it off for long periods of the day after Mindy's morning nap. The parents and professionals decided to begin providing early intervention services in the aunt's home once per week in addition to the weekly visit to Mindy's home. They agreed that Ms. Stevens would provide guidance to Mindy's aunt to ensure that the cochlear implant was used all waking hours and coach her in communication-promoting behaviors.

According to IDEA, Part C, and the JCIH (2007) collaboration is required to achieve the goals of early intervention. Professionals working in early intervention have increasingly complex responsibilities that require a team approach. Friend and Cook (2010) define collaboration as a style for direct interaction between at least two coequal partners voluntarily engaged in shared decision making as they work toward a common goal. Luckner and Rudolph (2009) describe the personal characteristics needed for effective collaboration including empathetic listening, honoring cultural differences, and maintaining confidentiality. Collaboration is at the core of family-centered practice and yet professional preparation programs are just beginning to focus on interdisciplinary learning and collaboration skill development (Lenihan & Rice, 2012; Trivette & Dunst, 2000).

The collaborative relationship of the family with professionals in audiology, speech-language pathology, and deaf education is essential in communication development. Evidence-based audiological assessment requires collaboration among the professionals and the family members (MacIver-Lux & Estabrooks, 2012). Shared observations, guidance, support, and ongoing communication are required to ensure that the child has optimal access to communication.

The team working with Mindy's family decided that in addition to continued family-centered early intervention services Mindy and her parents would attend a weekly program at a center for children who are deaf or hard of hearing with a small group of other families of toddlers facilitated by Ms. Stevens, and Mindy would enroll in the three morning a week toddler group that included children who are deaf as well and peers with typical hearing. Ms. Stevens and the teacher of the toddler group agreed to collaborate on assessment and planning to ensure that Mindy maintains age-appropriate progress in communication development.

SUMMARY

Infants and toddlers need early sensory experiences that stimulate communication, language, and cognitive development. Brain synapses and pathways that map linguistic neural circuitry depend on them. Caregivers who interact with their infants and toddlers establish the foundation for future linguistic and cognitive development. Children who are deaf or hard of hearing need consistent access to competent communication partners regardless of the pathway to language development they follow, that is, listening and spoken language or ASL/English Bilingual.

Working together to support the child and the family is the primary goal of the early intervention team. Of paramount importance is monitoring Mindy's language progress to ensure that the language(s) and modality(ies) used support the timely acquisition of language and minimize the possibility of language delay. Together they can create a communication and language plan describing the specific services, settings, family members, and professionals who will support Mindy's development. This communication plan will be attached to Mindy's Individualized Family Service Plan (IFSP) and include outcomes and strategies focused on promoting language learning throughout the day. Interdisciplinary collaboration and a family-centered approach increase the likelihood for success regardless of the chosen path to language acquisition. The next chapter will address the IFSP process and how communication and language goals are integrated into the early intervention programming for deaf or hard-of-hearing children.

SUGGESTED ACTIVITIES

1. Observe a family child session (e.g., home visit) and note the ways in which the professionals guide and coach the parents and other caregivers in communication development. If the child is using a listening and

spoken language approach, observe the ways the professionals maximize access to spoken language for auditory skill development, encourage vocalization and speech production, and integrate listening and spoken language. If the child is using an ASL/English bilingual approach, observe the ways the professionals encourage joint attention, direct eye-gaze for sign language development, and make associations between concepts in ASL and spoken English.

2. View videos of early intervention sessions such as "The Baby Is Listening" available from the Alexander Graham Bell Association for the Deaf and Hard of Hearing, https://netforum.avectra.com/eweb/shopping/shopping.aspx?site=agbell&webcode=shopping&shopsearchcat=merchandise&prd_key=96fb6b7e-d487-4506-96e1-5b6a3452eff1, and note strategies used to develop listening and spoken language.

3. View the video "Through Your Child's Eyes" available from the California State University–Northridge and the California Department of Education, http://www.csun.edu/~tyce/, and note the reasons these hearing families chose an ASL/English bilingual approach.

4. Interview early interventionists and parents and caregivers of young children who are deaf or hard of hearing to explore ways in which they have collaborated in developing communication.

5. Interview a deaf or hard-of-hearing parent who has chosen cochlear implants for his or her deaf child. Explore the reasons for the decision as well as plans for educational placement and services available for the child.

RECOMMENDED RESOURCES

1. Alexander Graham Bell Association for the Deaf and Hard of Hearing, Listening and Spoken Language Knowledge Center
   http://listeningandspokenlanguage.org/.
   Family resources for listening and spoken language including ages and stages of language development, assistive hearing technology, and language development resources.

2. Beginnings for Parents of Children Who Are Deaf or Hard of Hearing
   http://ncbegin.org.

Beginnings is an organization that helps families understand the diverse needs of children who are deaf or hard of hearing. Beginnings includes technical information on hearing and language, emotional support for families, and resources and referrals.

3. Bodner-Johnson, B., & Benedict, B. S. (2012). *Bilingual deaf and hearing families: Narrative interviews.* Washington, DC: Gallaudet University Press.

4. Boystown National Research Hospital

   http://www.babyhearing.org/.

   Resources for professionals supporting families including hearing and amplification and language and learning.

5. Cole, E., & Flexer, C. (2015). *Children with hearing loss: Developing listening and talking, birth to six* (3rd ed.). San Diego, CA: Plural Publishing.

6. Estabrooks, W. (Ed.). (2012). *101 Frequently asked questions about auditory-verbal practice: Promoting listening and spoken language for children who are deaf and hard of hearing and their families.* Washington, DC: AG Bell.

7. Laurent Clerc National Deaf Education Center

   http://www.gallaudet.edu/clerc_center.html.

   Information, training, and technical assistance for parents and professionals. See *Help for Babies 0 to 3*

   https://www.gallaudet.edu/clerc_center/information_and_resources/info_ to_go/help_for_babies_%280_to_3%29.html.

   A Good Start: Suggestions for Visual Conversations with Deaf and Hard of Hearing Babies and Toddlers

   https://www.gallaudet.edu/clerc_center/information_and_resources/ info_to_go/help_for_babies_%280_to_3%29/language_development_ for_babies/visual_conversations.html.

   Laurent Clerc Cochlear Implant Education Center (CIEC)

   https://www.gallaudet.edu/clerc_center/information_and_resources/ cochlear_implant_education_center.html.

8. National Center for Hearing Assessment and Management (NCHAM)

   http://www.infanthearing.org/.

   Research and training for newborn hearing screening and early intervention including *A Resource Guide for Early Hearing Detection and Intervention E-Book.*

9. Resources for Cochlear Implant Users

   Resources designed to support the listening and language development of children with cochlear implants; professional development webinars

> *Advanced Bionics: Tools for Schools*
> https://www.advancedbionics.com/com/en/support/tools_for_
>   schools.html.
> *Cochlear Americas: HOPE Cochlear (Re)habilitation Resources*
> http://hope.cochlearamericas.com/.
> *Med El: Bridge to Better Communication*
> http://www.medel.com/us/rehabilitation/.
>
> 10. Rhoades, E., & Duncan J. (2010). *Auditory-verbal practice: Toward a family-centered approach.* Springfield, IL: Charles C Thomas Publisher Ltd.
>   Snoddon, K. (2012). *American sign language and early literacy: A model parent-child program.* Washington, DC: Gallaudet University Press.
> 11. Visual Language & Visual Learning: Science of Learning Center
>   http://vl2.gallaudet.edu/research/research-briefs/
>   http://vl2parentspackage.org/
>   http://vl2.gallaudet.edu/resources/asl-assessment-toolkits/.
>   Research briefs on visual languages; Parent Package including tips for families, resources, ASL storytelling, and ASL assessment tools.
> 12. See Simms, L., Baker, S., & Clark, M. D. (2013). *Visual Language and Sign Language Checklist (VLSL).* Washington, DC: Gallaudet University Press for studies of sign language. The standardized Visual Language and Sign Language Checklist for signing children is a comprehensive checklist that can be used to set learning goals, identify gaps in learning, and develop appropriate materials to support development.
>   Also see Simms, L., Baker, S., & Clark, M. D. (2013). The standardized visual communication and sign language checklist for signing children. *Sign Language Studies, 14*(1) 101–124.

REFERENCES

Alberg, J. (2011). BEGINNINGS report: Change in communication choice over 10 years. FYI-First Years Info. Retrieved from http://firstyears.org/fyi/2011-summer.htm.

American Speech-Language-Hearing Association. (2005). *Evidence-based practice in communication disorders* [Position Statement]. Available from www.asha.org/policy.

Bavalier, D., Dye, M. W. G., & Hauser, P. C. (2006). Do deaf individuals see better? *Trends in Cognitive Science, 10,* 512–518.

Bergeson, T. (2011). Maternal speech to hearing-impaired infants in the first year of hearing aid or cochlear implant use: A preliminary report. *Cochlear Implants International, 12*(1), S101–104.

Bialystok, E. (2007). Cognitive effects of bilingualism: How linguistic experience leads to cognitive change. *International Journal of Bilingual Education and Bilingualism, 10*(3), 210–233.

Calderon, R. (2000). Parent involvement in deaf children's education programs as a predictor of child's language, early reading, and social-emotional development. *Journal of Deaf Studies and Deaf Education, 5*, 140–155.

Caleffe-Schenk, N. (2012). How do parents and practitioners use children's literature for auditory development? In W. Estabrooks (Ed.), *101 frequently asked questions about auditory-verbal practice: Promoting listening and spoken language for children who are deaf and hard of hearing and their families* (pp. 325–329). Washington, DC: AG Bell.

Christensen, K. (2000). *Deaf plus: A multicultural perspective.* San Diego, CA: Dawn Sign Press.

Clark, E. V. (2004). How language acquisition builds on cognitive development. *Trends in Cognitive Science, 8*(10), 472–478.

Cole, E., & Gill, E. (2012). Should a child with hearing loss be taught "baby sign"? In W. Estabrooks (Ed.), *101 frequently asked questions about auditory-verbal practice: Promoting listening and spoken language for children who are deaf and hard of hearing and their families* (pp. 275–278). Washington, DC: AG Bell.

Compton, M., & Niemeyer, J. (March, 2005). *Strategies to support communication development: Infants and toddlers with hearing loss.* Paper presented at the Early Hearing Detection and Intervention Conference, Atlanta, GA. Retrieved from http://www.infanthearing.org/meeting/ehdi2005/presentations.html.

Cummins, J. (2006, October). *The relationship between American Sign Language proficiency and English academic development: A review of the research.* Paper presented at the workshop Challenges, Opportunities, and Choices in Educating Minority Group Students, Hamar University College, Norway.

Daniel, L. (2012). What is child directed speech, and how does it apply to auditory-verbal therapy and education? In W. Estabrooks (Ed.), *101 frequently asked questions about auditory-verbal practice: Promoting listening and spoken language for children who are deaf and hard of hearing and their families* (pp. 193–119). Washington, DC: AG Bell.

Dettman, S., Pinder, D., Briggs, R., Dowell, R., & Leigh, J. (2007). Communication development in children who receive the cochlear implant younger than 12 months: Risks versus benefits. *Ear and Hearing, 28*, 11S–18S.

Dornan, D., Hickson, L., Murdoch, B., & Houston, T. (2009). Longitudinal study of speech perception, speech, and language for children with hearing loss in an auditory-verbal therapy program. *Volta Review, 109*(2/3), 61–85.

Douglas, M., & Freutel, J. (2012). How do children in auditory-verbal programs who are learning more than one spoken language perform on formal language measures? In W. Estabrooks (Ed.), *101 frequently asked questions about auditory-verbal practice: Promoting listening and spoken language for children who are deaf and hard of hearing and their families* (pp. 409–413). Washington, DC: AG Bell.

Eliot, L. (1999). *What's going on in there? The brain and mind development in the first five years of life.* New York, NY: Bantam Books.

Enns, C., & Price, L. (2013, June). *Family involvement in ASL acquisition.* (Visual Language and Visual Learning Science of Learning Center, Research Brief No. 9). Washington, DC.

Erting, C. J., Prezioso, C., & Hynes, M. (1994). The interactional context of deaf mother-infant communication. In C. J. Erting & V. Volterra (Eds.), *From gesture to language in hearing and deaf children* (pp. 97–106). Washington, DC: Gallaudet University Press.

Estabrooks, W. (Ed.). (2012). *101 frequently asked questions about auditory-verbal practice: Promoting listening and spoken language for children who are deaf and hard of hearing and their families.* Washington, DC: AG Bell.

Evans, M., & Wilson, K. (2012). How does the listening and spoken language professional guide and encourage parents to read aloud every day? In W. Estabrooks (Ed.), *101 frequently asked questions about auditory-verbal practice: Promoting listening and spoken language for children who are deaf and hard of hearing and their families* (pp. 330–333). Washington, DC: AG Bell.

Fish, S., & Morford, J. P. (2012, June). *The benefits of bilingualism* (Visual Language and Visual Learning Science of Learning Center, Research Brief No. 7). Washington, DC.

Friend, M., & Cook, L. (2010). *Interactions: Collaboration skills for school professionals* (6th Ed.). Boston, MA: Pearson.

Fulcher, A., Purcell, A., Baker, E., & Munro, N. (2012). Listen up: Children with early identified hearing loss achieve age-appropriate speech/language outcomes by 3 years-of-age. *International Journal of Pediatric Otorhinolaryngology, 76*(12), 1785–1794.

Galambos, S. J., & Goldin-Meadow, S. (1990). The effects of learning two languages on levels of metalinguistic awareness. *Cognition, 34*(1), 1–56.

Gallaudet Research Institute. (2002). *Regional and national summary report of data from 2000–01 annual survey of deaf and hard of hearing children and youth.* Washington, DC: Gallaudet University.

Gallaudet Research Institute. (2011). *Regional and national summary report of data from 2009-10 annual survey of deaf and hard of hearing children and youth.* Washington, DC: Gallaudet University.

Gárate, M. (2011). Educating children with cochlear implants in an ASL/English bilingual classroom. In R. Paludneviciene & I. W. Leigh (Eds.), *Cochlear implants: Evolving perspectives* (pp. 206–228). Washington, DC: Gallaudet University.

Gárate, M., (2012, June). *ASL/English bilingual education* (Visual Language and Visual Learning Science of Learning Center, Research Brief No. 8). Washington, DC.

Geers, A., Moog, J., Biedenstein, J., Brenner, C., & Hayes, H. (2009). Spoken language scores of children using cochlear implants compared to hearing age-mates at school entry. *Journal of Deaf Studies & Deaf Education, 14,* 371–385.

Geers, A., & Nicholas, J. (2013). Enduring advantages of early cochlear implantation for spoken language development. *Journal of Speech, Language and Hearing Research, 56,* 643–653.

Genesee, F., Lindholm-Leary, K., Saunders, W. M., & Christian, D. (2006). *Educating English language learners.* New York, NY: Cambridge University Press.

Grosjean, F. (2008). *The bilingualism and biculturalism of the deaf: Studying bilinguals.* Oxford, England: Oxford University Press.

Hart, B., & Risley, T. (1995). *Meaningful differences in the everyday experience of young American children.* Baltimore, MD: Brookes Publishing.

Hart, B., & Risley, T. R. (1999). *The social world of children learning to talk.* Baltimore, MD: Brookes Publishing.

Hassanzadeh, S. (2012). Outcomes of cochlear implantation of deaf children of deaf parents: Comparative study. *The Journal of Laryngology and Otology, 126,* 989–994. doi:10.1017/S0022215112001909.

Hawley, T. (2000) *Starting smart: How early experience affects brain development* (2nd ed.). Washington, DC: Zero to Three and the Ounce of Prevention Fund.

Hogan, S., Stokes, J., White, C., Tyszkiewicz, E., & Woolgar. (2008). An evaluation of auditory verbal therapy using the rate of early language development as an outcome measure. *Deafness and Education International, 10*(3), 143–167.

Houston, D. M., Beer, J., Bergeson, T. R., Chin, S. B., Pisoni, D. B., & Miyamoto, R. T. (2012). The ear is connected to the brain: Some new directions in the study of children with cochlear implants at Indiana University. *Journal of the American Academy of Audiology, 23,* 446–463.

Joint Committee on Infant Hearing. (2007). Year 2007 position statement: Principles and guidelines for early hearing detection and intervention
programs. *Pediatrics, 120,* 898–921. doi:10.1542/peds.2007-2333.

Joint Committee on Infant Hearing. (2013). Supplement to the JCIH 2007 position statement: Principles and guidelines for intervention after confirmation that a child is deaf or hard of hearing. *Pediatrics, 131*(4), e1324–1349.
doi:10.1542/peds.2013-0008.

Kuhl, P.K. (2007). Is speech learning "gated" by the social brain? *Developmental
Science, 10*(1), 110–120.

Laferriere, D., & Rossi, K. (2012). How can a young child receiving auditory-verbal
services learn effectively through play? In W. Estabrooks (Ed.), *101 frequently
asked questions about auditory-verbal practice: Promoting listening and spoken language for children who are deaf and hard of hearing and their families*
(pp. 363–367). Washington, DC: AG Bell.

Lenihan, S. (June, 2006). *Competencies of early interventionists.* Paper presented
at the Friedberger Cochlear Implant Symposium, Germany.

Lenihan, S., & Daniels, M. (June 2002). *Early intervention in deaf education: Providing high quality, research-based services.* Poster presented at the
2nd International Conference on Newborn Hearing Screening Diagnosis
and Intervention, Como, Italy.

Lenihan, S., & Rice, G. (March 2012). *Supporting collaboration in early intervention.* Paper presented at the Early Hearing Detection and Intervention
Annual Conference, St. Louis. Retrieved from http://ehdimeeting.org/2012/
schedule/griddetails.cfm?aid=665&day=MONDAY.

Luckhurst, J., Lauback, C., & Unsterstein VanSkiver, A. (2013). Differences in
spoken lexical skills: Preschool children with cochlear implants and children with typical hearing. *Volta Review, 113*(1), 29–42.

Luckner, J., & Rudolph, S. (2009). *Teach well, live well.* Thousand Oaks,
CA: Corwin.

MacIver-Lux, K., & Estabrooks, W. (2012). How can the child's professionals in
auditory-verbal practice and audiology work together? In W. Estabrooks
(Ed.), *101 frequently asked questions about auditory-verbal practice: Promoting
listening and spoken language for children who are deaf and hard of hearing
and their families* (pp. 14–18). Washington, DC: AG Bell.

Marschark, M., & Hauser, P. (2008). What we know and what we don't know
about cognition and deaf learners. In M. Marschark & P. C. Hauser (Eds.),
Deaf cognition: Foundations and outcomes (pp. 439–457). New York,
NY: Oxford University Press.

Masataka, N. (1996) Perception of motherese in a signed language by 6-month-old deaf infants. *Developmental Psychology*, *32*(5), 874–879. doi:10.1037/0012-1649.32.5.874.

Mayberry, R. I. (2007). When timing is everything: Age of first-language acquisition effects on second-language learning. *Applied Psycholinguistics*, *28*(3), 537–549.

Mitchiner, J., Nussbaum, D. B., & Scott, S. (2012, June). *The implications of bimodal bilingual approaches for children with cochlear implants* (Visual Language and Visual Learning Science of Learning Center, Research Brief No. 6). Washington, DC.

Mitchiner, J. C., & Sass-Lehrer, M. (2011). My child can have more choices: Reflections of deaf mothers on cochlear implants for their children. In R. Paludneviciene & I. W. Leigh (Eds.), *Cochlear implants: Evolving perspectives* (pp. 71–94). Washington, DC: Gallaudet University Press.

Moeller, M. P. (2000). Early intervention and language development in children who are deaf and hard of hearing. *Pediatrics*, *106*(3), e43. Retrieved from http://www.pediatrics.org/cgi/content/full/106/3/e43.

Moeller, M. P. (2006). Use of sign with children who have cochlear implants: A diverse set of approaches. *Loud & Clear!* *(2)*, 6–12. Retrieved from http://www.advancedbionics.com/content/dam/ab/Global/en_ce/documents/libraries/SupportLibrary/Newsletters/Loud%20and%20Clear/A%20Sign%20of%20the%20Changing%20Time%20Part%20II.pdf.

Moeller, M. P., Schow, R. L., & Whitaker, M. M. (2013). Audiologic rehabilitation for children: Assessment and management. In R. L. Schow & M. A. Nerbonne (Eds.), *Introduction to audiologic rehabilitation* (6th ed., pp. 305–375). Boston: Pearson.

Moog, J. S., & Geers, A. E. (2010). Early educational placement and later language outcomes for children with cochlear implants. *Otology & Neurotology*, *31*(8), 1315–1319.

Morere, D. (2011a). *Reading research and deaf children.* (Visual Language and Visual Learning Science of Learning Center, Research Brief No. 4). Washington, DC.

Morere, D. (2011b). Bimodal processing of language for cochlear implant users. In R. Paludneviciene & I. W. Leigh (Eds.), *Cochlear implants: Evolving perspectives* (pp. 113–141). Washington, DC: Gallaudet University Press.

Nussbaum, D., Waddy-Smith, B., & Doyle, J. (2012). Students who are deaf and hard of hearing and use sign language: Considerations and strategies for developing spoken language and literacy skills. *Seminars in Speech and Language*, *33*(4), 310–321.

Petitto, L. (2009). New discoveries from the bilingual brain and mind across the life span: Implications for education. *Mind, Brain and Education, 3*(4), 185–197.

Petitto, L. A., Katerelos, M., Levy, B. G., Gauna, K., Tetreault, K., & Ferraro, V. (2001). Bilingual signed and spoken language acquisition from birth: Implications for mechanisms underlying bilingual language acquisition. *Journal of Child Language, 28*(2), 1–44.

Petitto, L. A., & Kovelman, I. (2003). The bilingual paradox: How signing-speaking bilingual children help us to resolve it and teach us about the brain's mechanisms underlying all language acquisition. *Learning Languages, 8*(3), 5–18.

Petitto, L. A., & Marentette, P. (1991). Babbling in the manual mode: Evidence for the ontogeny of language. *Science, 251*, 1483–1496.

Preisler, G., Tvingstedt, A., & Ahlström, M. (2002). A psychological follow-up study on deaf preschool children using cochlear implants. *Child: Care, Health and Development, 28*(5), 403–418.

Rhoades, E., & Duncan J. (2010). *Auditory-verbal practice: Toward a family-centered approach.* Springfield, IL: Charles C Thomas Publisher Ltd.

Robbins, A. M. (2007). Clinical management of bilingual families and children with cochlear implants. *Loud and Clear!, 1.* Retrieved from http://amymcconkeyrobbins.com/PDF/Clinical_Management_of_Bilingual_Families.pdf.

Roberts, M., & Kaiser, A. (2011). The effectiveness of parent-implemented language intervention: A meta-analysis. *American Journal of Speech-Language Pathology, 20*, 180–199.

Rosetti, L. (2001). *Communication intervention: Birth to three.* Albany, NY: Delmar Publishing.

Rossi, K. (2003). *Learn to talk around the clock professional's early intervention toolbox.* Washington, DC: AG Bell.

Sass-Lehrer, M. (2004). Early detection of hearing loss: Maintaining a family-centered perspective. *Seminars in Hearing, 25*, 295–307.

Sharma, A., Dorman, M., & Spahr, T. (2002). A sensitive period for the development of the central auditory system in children with cochlear implants: Implications for age of implantation. *Ear and Hearing, 23*, 532–539. doi:10.1097/01.AUD.0000042223.62381.01.

SKI-HI Curriculum. (2004). North Logan, UT: HOPE Publishing.

Smith, J., & Stowe, D. (2012). Why is storytelling important in auditory-verbal therapy and education? In W. Estabrooks (Ed.), *101 frequently asked questions about auditory-verbal practice: Promoting listening and spoken language for children who are deaf and hard of hearing and their families* (pp. 316–319). Washington, DC: AG Bell.

Spencer, P., & Marschark, M. (2010). *Evidence-based practice in educating deaf and hard-of-hearing students.* New York, NY: Oxford University Press.

Stredler-Brown, A., Moeller, M. P., Gallegos, R., & Corwin, J. (2004). *The art and science of a home visit* (DVD). Boys Town, NE: Boys Town Press.

Strong, M., & Charlson, E. S. (1987). Simultaneous communication: Are teachers attempting an impossible task? *American Annals of the Deaf, 132*(5), 376–382.

Swisher, V. M., & Thomson, M. (1985). Mothers learning simultaneous communication: The dimension of the task. *American Annals for the Deaf, 130*(3), 212–217.

Topping, K., Dekhinet, R., & Zeedyk, S. (2013). Parent-infant interactions and children's language development. *Educational Psychology, 33*(4), 391–426.

Trivette, C. M., & Dunst, C. J. (2000). Recommended practices in family-based practices. In S. Sandall, M. McLean, & B. J. Smith (Eds.), *DEC recommended practices in early intervention/early childhood special education* (pp. 39–46). Longmont, CO: Sopris West.

Wilson, K. (2012). Are there specific curricula for auditory-verbal therapy and education? In W. Estabrooks (Ed.), *101 frequently asked questions about auditory-verbal practice: Promoting listening and spoken language for children who are deaf and hard of hearing and their families* (pp. 377–381). Washington, DC: AG Bell.

Winkelkotter, E. M., & Srinivasan, P. (2012). How can the listening and spoken language professional enhance the child's chances of talking and communicating during (versus) after the auditory-verbal session? In W. Estabrooks (Ed.), *101 frequently asked questions about auditory-verbal practice: Promoting listening and spoken language for children who are deaf and hard of hearing and their families* (pp. 14–18). Washington, DC: AG Bell.

Wu, M., & Brown, P. (2003). Parents' and teachers' expectations of auditory-verbal therapy. *Volta Review, 104*(1), 5–20.

Yoshinaga-Itano, C. (2003). From screening to early identification and intervention: Discovering predictors to successful outcomes for children with significant hearing loss. *Journal of Deaf Studies and Deaf Education, 8*(1), 11–30.

Yoshinaga-Itano, C. (2006). Early identification, communication modality, and the development of speech and spoken language skills: Patterns and considerations. In P. E. Spencer & M. Marschark (Eds.), *Advances in the spoken language development of deaf and hard of hearing children* (pp. 298–327). New York, NY: Oxford University Press.

Yoshinaga-Itano, C., & Sedey, A. (2000). Early speech development in children who are deaf or hard of hearing: Interrelationships with language and hearing. *The Volta Review, 100*(5), 181–211.

Yoshinaga-Itano, C., Sedey, A., Coulter, D., & Mehl, A. (1998). Language of early-and later-identified children with hearing loss. *Pediatrics, 100*(5), 1161–1171.

Yoshinaga-Itano, C., Sedey, A., & Uhler, K. (2008). *Speech piggybacks onto sign: Fast-mapping from sign to speech.* Paper presented at the Conference of Educational Administrators of Schools and Programs, Boulder, CO.

Young, A., & Andrews, E. (2001). Parents' experience of universal neonatal hearing screening: A critical review of the literature and its implications for the implementation of new UNHS programs. *Journal of Deaf Studies and Deaf Education, 6*, 149–160.

9 Individualized Family Service Plans and Programming

Rosemary Gallegos, Kristi Halus, and Jodee Crace

Sandra is an early childhood professional with specialized training and experience as an educator of children who are deaf or hard of hearing. She provides service coordination and early intervention services for Emily and her family. Emily is 24 months old and is deaf. Sandra is preparing for Emily's Individualized Family Service Plan (IFSP). Emily's family has been receiving early intervention services through their state's IDEA Part C program since Emily was 6 months old. Emily primarily communicates using sign language and is developing spoken language. Hearing aids provide her with access to some speech sounds. Emily is functioning at an 18-month level in all developmental areas. The interdisciplinary team, including Emily's parents, would like to focus on enhancing her language development and have concerns about her gross and fine motor development. Emily's parents have told Sandra that they would like the upcoming IFSP meeting to include the following: (1) a review of Emily's progress and update of the expected outcomes by the next 6 months, (2) a review and update of what the family wants to learn, and (3) an adjustment of services for both Emily and the family as needed based on progress they and

Emily have made toward their outcomes. The family would also like to begin discussing Emily's transition to preschool when she becomes 3 years old.

GUIDING QUESTIONS

1. What are the components of an IFSP and how do they support family-centered practice?
2. What information should the service coordinator and the interdisciplinary team gather in preparation for a review of the progress, outcomes, and services of a child who is deaf or hard of hearing?
3. How can early intervention professionals, community agencies, and the service coordinator collaborate to support the child and family?
4. How should professionals and families work together throughout the IFSP process?
5. What child and family characteristics should the interdisciplinary team consider when discussing possible services and opportunities for the child?

COMPETENCIES ADDRESSED IN THIS CHAPTER

1. Planning and Implementation of Services: Creating a Lesson Plan, Conducting a Home Visit, Developing the IFSP, and Using Appropriate Curriculums, Methods, and Resources
2. Collaboration and Interdisciplinary Models and Practices

INTRODUCTION

The Individual Family Service Plan (IFSP) is a process mandated in the United States by the Individuals with Disabilities Education Act Part C (IDEA, 2004) that strategically aligns family, community, and professional resources to provide effective services for a child and his or her family. Sandra, with her specialized training and experience as an early childhood educator and deaf educator, comes to the IFSP "table" with expertise in areas critical to understanding the development of young children who are deaf or hard of hearing. This chapter will concentrate on the application of specialized information about the development of a child who is deaf or hard of hearing within the framework of the IFSP process and the professional competencies of "Planning and Implementation of Services" and "Collaboration and Interdisciplinary Models and Practices" [Joint Committee on Infant Hearing (JCIH), 2013]. The chapter will provide (1) an overview of the IFSP process, (2) the development of child and family outcomes, (3) service delivery opportunities and environments that support the attainment of outcomes, including interdisciplinary planning, (4) effective home visits, (5) the transition from early intervention to preschool, and (6) special considerations for the IFSP team when a child is deaf or hard of hearing.

Emily's family has requested that the IFSP team review their child and family outcomes, include greater support for her language development and motor skills, and explore opportunities for preschools. Sandra's job is to prepare herself and the team to align the family's priorities with information from Emily's most recent assessments. She then needs to facilitate a dialogue among team members, including the family, to determine child and family outcomes that are most appropriate for the next 6–12 months. The team will also share their observations about how and in what settings Emily learns best and what outcomes can be achieved through family resources and daily routines; it will then develop a plan that is calculated to support Emily's continued development.

THE INDIVIDUAL FAMILY SERVICE PLAN (IFSP)

The Whole Child Approach

The development of an IFSP for deaf or hard-of-hearing infants and toddlers includes all the requirements of the United States federal and state regulations under Part C of the Individuals with Disabilities Education Act (IDEA). Emily's IFSP team will use a whole child approach [National Association for the Education of Young Children (NAEYC), 2009] when considering her development. This means that they will look at her over-all development within the domains of cognition, physical status (includ-ing vision, hearing, and health), communication, social and emotional skills, and adaptive development [34 CFR 303.344(a)] and how these areas of development influence each other.

The team will also consider the sequence of child development and Emily's individual learning style, strengths, and needs. They will integrate her family's priorities and consider how her learning is influenced and supported by her family culture, resources, and social contexts (NAEYC, 2009). What is unique to Emily as a child who is deaf is that the team must carefully consider her development of and access to language and communication and how this interacts with her overall development and learning. Acquisition of language occurs in the early years of life and is dependent on exposure to meaningful language and communica-tion. (See Chapter 8, *Collaboration for Communication, Language, and Cognitive Development*). Language development is influenced by quality interactions with others using a wide variety of vocabulary (Hart & Risely, 2003; Kovelman, Baker, & Petitto, 2008). The IFSP team must ensure that Emily's plan optimizes learning opportunities that are language and com-munication rich and accessible.

Family-Centered Practice

The IFSP is a vehicle for implementing family-centered practice. A major policy shift occurred in 1986 with amendments to Public Law 99-457 of the Education for All Handicapped Children Act that established ser-vices for children from birth to 3 years old. Recognizing the critical role of families in their child's development, services under this part of the law are provided to the family, not just the child, through the IFSP. Each state has a designated lead agency such as its Education Department or Department of Health that manages Part C services. These lead agencies develop state regulations and guidelines that are aligned with Federal Regulations and the spirit of family-centered practice. They also have a structure for funding services and oversight of early intervention providers.

Whereas the IFSP is unique to the United States, several other coun-tries have embraced principles associated with IDEA Part C and the IFSP. For example, the British Columbia Early Hearing Program in Canada has established an IFSP process that is similar in many ways to the process in the United States with some differences in the developmental domains and the assessment process. The United Kingdom has a technical assistance document for families and early intervention providers that mirrors the IFSP (National Children's Bureau, n.d.). Many early Interventionists in Germany are encouraged to provide family-centered services; however, there is no coordinated system similar to the IFSP throughout the coun-try (M. Hintermair, personal communication, December 6, 2013). Many early intervention programs in South Africa use family-centered and home-based principles modeled after the SKI-HI program (P. Pittman, personal communication, November 26, 2013).

The science of early intervention may be best known through the work of Dunst, Trivette, and Deal (1988) and Trivette, Dunst, and Hanby (2010) who describe a family-systems model. This approach focuses on the interrelationship of the family's concerns and priorities, family mem-bers' abilities and interests, the family's supports and resources, and capacity-building/help-giving practices of the interventionist. These con-cepts are reflected in Part C of the Individuals with Disabilities Education Act (IDEA), which requires the following:

> A family-directed assessment of the resources, priorities, and con-cerns of the family and the identification of the supports and services necessary to enhance the family's capacity to meet the developmen-tal needs of the infant or toddler [CFR 303.321(a)(ii)(B)]

> … the development, review, and implementation of an individual-ized family service plan or IFSP developed by a multidisciplinary team, which includes the parent (CFR 303.340).

The responsibility for implementing family-centered practices for young children who are deaf or hard of hearing is evident at both the state and family levels. At the state level it is the lead agency that cre-ates a system, guidelines, and networks and establishes a tone for quality family-centered practice as is the intent of and is prescribed by the policy set forth by IDEA Part C. At the family level, a service coordinator makes first contact with a family, organizes the team, and ensures that all components of the IFSP process have been addressed. The service coordinator should have specific and specialized information, experience, and knowledge regarding early development and learning including language and communication for young deaf or hard-of-hearing children (JCIH, 2013).

Requirements of the IFSP

Interdisciplinary IFSP teams must include required components and meet the specified timelines in the Federal Regulations for IDEA [CFR 303.342 (a) (b)]. Emily's family has gone through the annual IFSP process twice. The initial IFSP occurred within the required 45-day timeline after Emily was determined to be eligible for services. At the first IFSP meeting the family was mostly concerned about language and communication and family outcomes centered on gathering information and learning how to communicate with their daughter. The next IFSP meeting was 6 months later to review Emily's progress. At this meeting the team, including her family, commented that Emily was very attentive to visual information, and they agreed that language and communication outcomes using American Sign Language (ASL) should continue. Her parents noted that Emily was also beginning to notice sounds in the environment, and the team recommended increasing the time she wore her hearing aids. At their 1-year IFSP meeting, outcomes were revised and expanded to include increasing the family's skills in ASL, interacting more with signing deaf adults, and encouraging Emily's awareness of sound in her environment.

Individuals participating at Emily's IFSP meetings included all those required by the IDEA regulations (IDEA Early Intervention Program for Infants and Toddlers with Disabilities Regulations, 34 C.F.R. pt. 303 2011) and requested by her family. Present at the meeting were her parents, her grandmother (as requested by Emily's parents), Emily's service coordinator, who in this case is the early childhood educator for children who are deaf or hard of hearing, a physical therapist, and Emily's teacher from the play group at the school for the deaf that Emily has been attending. The physical therapist and Sandra, the early childhood educator and service coordinator, conducted Emily's initial evaluation and on-going assessments. Along with the family, service coordinator, and the provider(s) of the early intervention services, it is a requirement that the specialist(s) directly involved in the evaluations and assessments are included in the meeting to develop the initial IFSP and each subsequent annual meeting to review the IFSP [National Information Center for Children and Youth with Disabilities (NICHCY), 2014]. The content of an IFSP is outlined by IDEA (CFR 303.344 et seq.) and includes information about the child, family routines, outcomes, services, and transition. Special considerations for language and communication in IDEA Part C are not specifically described as they are in IDEA Part B for children who are school age, but it is clear that the law requires that necessary services must be provided to meet the unique needs of the child. It is incumbent on the IFSP team to consider what is unique about Emily who is a child who is deaf when developing her service plan. This means bearing in mind Emily's communication needs and opportunities for direct communication with peers and adults [American Speech-Language-Hearing Association (ASHA) and the Council on Education of the Deaf (CED) Joint Committee, 2006].

Additionally, the IFSP team and the service coordinator should be aware of related services and regulations in Part C of IDEA that influence how services are provided to children who are deaf or hard of hearing:

- Audiology services [34 CFR 303.13(b)(2)]
- Limitations on responsibility related to optimization of the cochlear implant [34 CFR 303.16 (c)(1)]
- Sign language and cued language services [34 CFR 303.13(b)(12)]
- Assistive technology device and service [34 CFR 303.13(b)(1)(i)(ii)]
- Native language including mode of communication for an individual who is deaf or hard of hearing [34 CFR 303.25 (a)(b)]
- Infant or toddler with a disability [34 CFR.21 (a)(1)(2)]
- Natural environments (34 CFR 303.26; 34 CFR 303.126)
- Qualified personnel [34 CFR 303.13(c)]
- Special instruction [34 CFR 303.13(b)(14)]

The requirements in the law provide a road map for the IFSP process. Emily's team has followed the IFSP guidelines and has applied the principles and practices of a family-centered approach. As a result, Emily's family knows the intended essence of an IFSP, which emphasizes family-determined outcomes in collaboration with an interdisciplinary team of knowledgeable professionals. Their process includes building a plan together that utilizes the resources available in Emily's family and community. Documentation of the IFSP process and review of their rights are important parts of the process. Emily's family is looking forward to a dynamic dialogue in which Emily's progress, next steps, and freshly crafted outcomes will highlight new benchmarks in her development.

THE IFSP PROCESS

Family and Child Outcomes

Initial concurrent steps in building child and family outcomes are illustrated in Figure 9.1. A "routines-based interview" with the family (McWilliam, 1992; McWilliam, Casey, & Sims, 2009) as part of the IFSP process gathers information about the family's daily life, family

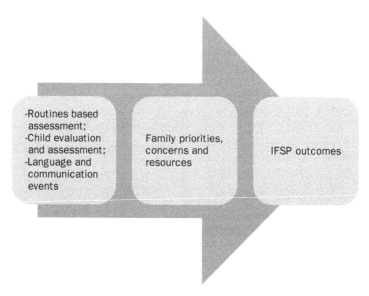

Figure 9.1 Initial steps for building child and family outcomes. Adapted from Jung and Grisham-Brown (2006).

and community resources, and circles of support (McWilliam, 2010). Access to language and communication is critical to the development of an infant or toddler who is deaf or hard of hearing. A dialogue with the family regarding when and what kind of communication is occurring during their daily routines will help the family take advantage of opportunities to include and connect the child with the family and other caregivers and facilitate language development. These "communication events" are essential to identifying meaningful language and communication outcomes and strategies for the child and family. The team will also gather and review current developmental information from assessment data that includes input from her family and other interdisciplinary team members. (See Chapter 7, *Developmental Assessment*.) The team will carefully consider her rate of progress across domains and whether it is sufficient given parental expectations and Emily's potential.

Collecting Family Information

Sandra, as the service coordinator, met with Emily's family prior to the IFSP meeting to review their priorities and collect additional family information. Emily's family identified the following priorities: (1) developing communication in both visual (ASL) and spoken language, (2) addressing concerns about Emily's motor development, (3) reviewing Emily's progress over the past 6 months, and (4) obtaining information about preschools. At the initial IFSP and as a review for this IFSP Sandra asked the family to update information about their everyday routines, activities, places, and people in their lives. In addition to family priorities, she also asked about their current concerns, what they were worried or wondering about, and what new resources, such as family, friends, and other services or organizations, they found helpful since the first IFSP meeting. She also revisited the routines-based interview [McWilliam, 1992; McWilliam, Casey, & Sims, 2009; New Mexico Family Infant and Toddler Program (NM FIT), 2011] they did together at the first IFSP meeting and asked the family how Emily's typical day or family routines have changed. (See Recommended Resources in this chapter for more information on the routine-based interview.)

Emily's family routines and resources changed since the first IFSP process, and they decided to update their illustration of their circles of supports (NM FIT, 2011). See Figure 9.2. Emily's parents drew themselves, Emily, and her brother in a circle at the center of the page. They drew an additional circle around them that included Emily's grandparents, neighbors, and friends. New to their illustration since the first IFSP were parents who have deaf children the same age as Emily, a playgroup at the school for the deaf, their audiologist, Emily's physical therapist, their Deaf Mentor, and Sandra. Emily's parents and Sandra discussed how this new information would be useful during the IFSP meeting.

Emily' parents and Sandra also discussed the language and communication events in Emily's and her family's daily routines and how they can continue to make these more accessible to Emily to support her language development. When Sandra used a routine-based assessment to obtain information about Emily's typical day, that is, who she interacts with, where, and what she does (McWilliam, 1992; McWilliam, Casey, &

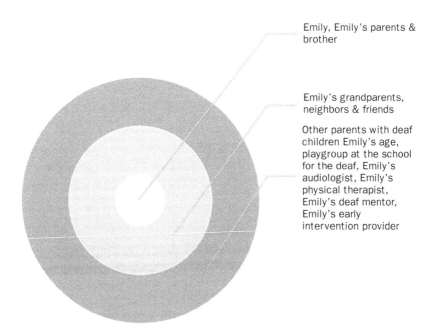

Emily, Emily's parents &
brother

Emily's grandparents,
neighbors & friends

Other parents with deaf
children Emily's age,
playgroup at the school
for the deaf, Emily's
audiologist, Emily's
physical therapist,
Emily's deaf mentor,
Emily's early
intervention provider

Figure 9.2 Emily's circles of support.

Sims, 2009; NM FIT, 2011), Sandra also asked what words and language concepts were connected to these events.

Emily's family also received services from a Deaf Mentor, another member of the interdisciplinary team. (See Chapter 5, *Collaboration with Deaf and Hard-of-Hearing Communities.*) The Deaf Mentor meets with Emily and her family on a weekly basis to share her experiences growing up and being a part of her own family's routines. These conversations have raised the family's awareness of how many language opportunities there are throughout the day and have helped them set high expectations and identify meaningful language outcomes for their family and for Emily.

Collecting Child Information

United States federal regulations under IDEA Part C require that the following developmental domains be addressed in a child's IFSP: (1) physical development (including vision, hearing, and health status), (2) cognitive development, (3) communication development, (4) social or emotional development, and (5) adaptive development. Some states may specify sensory motor, gross and fine motor skills as an additional required domain. (See Chapter 7, *Developmental Assessment.*)

Emily received an initial evaluation when she was referred to early intervention when she was 6 months of age and was determined to be eligible for Part C services. Since then, her team has been conducting assessments to track her progress and help determine outcomes. At each IFSP meeting, her team has considered her current developmental level in each of the required domains. Her levels are described functionally as strengths and needs in relation to what is working well and challenges related to her family's everyday routines and activities. Strengths describe what interests and motivates Emily and describe Emily's ability to navigate and participate in all aspects of her everyday life. Areas of needs that include situations that are challenging for Emily or her family are also noted.

For example, under the socioemotional domain, one of Emily's strengths is that she has a very outgoing personality and loves to interact with her cousins. Her parents report that Emily often grabs her cousin's toys causing the other children to become upset with her. Her family describes a need to improve their own communication skills and strategies to help Emily improve her play skills with other children. Although Emily's family knows that 2 year olds are still learning how to share, they recognized the advantage of having better ASL skills to explain why she cannot take another child's toy, redirect her, or help her learn to wait for her turn. In the communication and language domain, Emily's strength is that she uses a variety of one-word utterances in sign language to get what she wants. Under the needs section the family explains that when her family is not quite sure what she is trying to communicate to them, Emily becomes frustrated and throws a temper tantrum.

Emily's family is concerned that she has a 6-month delay in language. Through discussions with their service coordinator, Sandra, they are aware of the unacceptable history of low expectations for children who are deaf (National Agenda, 2005) and the research that shows that deaf children who are accessing specialized early intervention by 6 months of age can reach the same developmental trajectory as their hearing peers (Yoshinaga-Itano, Coulter, & Thomson, 2001). They are anxious to do everything they can to make sure that Emily reaches her potential in language development. Under the area of strengths on the IFSP, the team documents that Emily is using beginning ASL to communicate and has some resources to help her learn language. In the needs area, they mention their desire for Emily to have more access to language in ASL, as well as note their need for strategies to help Emily wear her hearing aids more consistently.

Emily's IFSP team is responsible for considering how Emily is doing in relation to state and federal requirements in three areas: (1) positive socioemotional skills (including positive social relationships), (2) acquisition and use of knowledge and skills (including early language/communication), and (3) use of appropriate behaviors to meet her needs. The United States federal government measures the effectiveness of early intervention and early childhood special education programs for children and families by collecting information on child progress through the "Early Childhood Outcomes (ECO)" process. See the Early Childhood Technical Assistance Center website under Recommended Resources. Emily's current abilities in the three areas mentioned above will be agreed on by families, caregivers, and the professionals working with Emily based on the results of assessments and observations of her progress. All identifying information will be confidential and will not shared outside of their state's Part C program.

Developing Outcomes

The team will pull together information obtained from the assessments that consider all areas of Emily's development, the information shared by her family, as well as observations of Emily by members of the interdisciplinary team, including the family. The family will prioritize its goals and concerns, describe, in its own words, what they would like to see for their family and child as a result of early intervention services over the next 6 months, and indicate how they will know that the outcomes have been met. Examples of outcome statements for Emily and her family might include the following:

- By December, Emily will use two words in ASL to tell us what she wants, like "ball + classifier (indicating size)," "two crackers," "duck book."
- By December, we (Emily's parents) will learn and use signs for helping Emily learn to share like "my turn, your turn," "where's your doll?", "wait 2 minutes," "I like how you share," "not yours," "waiting is hard."
- By Emily's third birthday, she will run without falling most of the time.
- By April, we (Emily's parents) will learn about the eligibility process for transition to public school preschool and opportunities for private preschools.
- In 3 months, Emily will increase the use of her hearing aids to all day before her nap and in 6 months to all waking hours.

STRATEGIES AND SERVICES

The team, including Emily's family, determined strategies for supporting progress toward Emily's outcomes. They decided who was the most appropriate person or persons to implement each identified strategy and when and where these activities would occur, such as during bath time, meals, or in the car (NM FIT, 2011). The team also decided which members of the interdisciplinary team would be responsible to help achieve the outcomes. Some examples of strategies that might appear in Emily's IFSP are listed below:

- The Physical Therapist (Maria) and the Early Childhood Educator (Sandra) will make joint home visits to work on Emily's running and add language that can be used during the running activities at her home or in the park nearby.
- The Early Childhood Educator (Sandra), the Deaf Mentor (Alana), and Emily's family will identify vocabulary and the related signs they need to help Emily learn to share; they will model these in play sessions with Emily's cousins at their home.
- The Early Childhood Educator (Sandra) and the Speech Language Therapist (Rebekah) will identify strategies for encouraging Emily to listen including identifying household sounds and encouraging her vocal word approximations.
- The Deaf Mentor (Alana) and the Speech Language Therapist (Rebekah) will visit the center-based program at the School for the Deaf to see what themes they are covering and help the family acquire new sign concepts and spoken words that Emily is using in her play group.
- The Deaf Mentor (Alana) and the Early Childhood Educator (Sandra) will model how to expand Emily's signed and spoken words to two-word sentences during snack and play time at home.

Natural Environments

Natural environments for infants and toddlers as described by Part C of IDEA "include the home, and community settings in which children without disabilities participate" [Sec. 632(4)(G),(H)]. IDEA also provides flexibility for services in other settings if the IFSP team and the family determine that a child's outcomes cannot be met in a "natural environment." An IFSP team should not be constrained to implement child outcomes in settings they believe will not support progress. Instead they should document and explain why certain services should be provided in other settings that may be more conducive to promoting the child's outcomes. In light of the discussion of Emily's language outcomes and what is known about the critical need for children who are deaf or hard of hearing to have access to language, it would be helpful to consider environments that allow Emily to fully participate and are natural to her.

Natural environments for infants and toddlers who are deaf or hard of hearing are settings in which the child has direct communication with peers and adults through the language and communication modality(ies) that is accessible to the child such as ASL or spoken English (Lederberg, Schick, & Spencer, 2013). This can occur in a range of settings in which there are adults who can fluently communicate in that language and in which peers are acquiring the same language (ASHA-CED Joint Committee, 2006). The ability to communicate fully with adults and peers in the language that is most accessible to the child facilitates language, cognitive, and socioemotional development. It is natural for a child to access the environment so that she can participate as a member, not a visitor, of her family and community (Antia, Stinson, & Gaustad, 2002). The phenomena of "relegated periphery" (Hopper, 2011) occurs when a child cannot access the conversations that are happening around her and without choice is on the outside of the events of her surroundings. A well-constructed IFSP will provide the resources and strategies to help Emily be a full participant in her everyday encounters with significant people in her life and have access to information and opportunities that all children need and deserve.

Emily's interdisciplinary team agreed that in order for Emily to reach the language outcomes identified in her IFSP and begin to narrow her language delay, she needed to interact more frequently with children and adults who use ASL. The family decided that in addition to services provided in the home by their interdisciplinary team, Emily should attend a playgroup at the school for the deaf four mornings each week in which all the teachers and children use ASL. They also noted that the speech and language specialist at the school would work closely with the teachers and Emily to support her developing listening and spoken language skills. The team documented this in the IFSP along with a justification.

Although Emily's IFSP team did not recommend more intensive spoken language support at this time, it is important to note that children who are deaf or hard of hearing and are developing listening and spoken language as their primary mode of communication rather than ASL may need a specialized setting in which the child has access to other children and adults who use spoken language and to trained facilitators of listening and spoken language.

Home Visits and Daily Routines

Home visits by one or more early intervention specialists provide opportunities to support family, primary caregivers, and child interactions and to promote other identified child outcomes in an environment that is both comfortable and familiar to the child and family. Some families prefer settings other than their home for family–child sessions such as the library, community, or childcare center. Visits with families can take place at the park, grocery store, or even Grandma's. The setting itself is less important than the family's comfort level and the opportunities the setting provides to help families develop the skills they need to embed learning goals into their family routines.

Because young children learn from experiences naturally embedded in their routines at home and in their community, the team considered opportunities for Emily's family to incorporate strategies for developing targeted skills into these environments. When a child is deaf or hard of hearing, communication access is a key consideration for all aspects of the child's life. Activities that happen many times a day in a toddler's life, such as eating, diapering, or getting ready to go somewhere, are natural opportunities for families to incorporate language-learning strategies such as expanding a child's utterance. Adults might use a strategy called "self-talk" that provides children with opportunities to see and/or hear adult thought processes. Other strategies that are easily incorporated into daily routines include expectant pauses and introducing new vocabulary and concepts. Expectant pauses are intentional pauses in conversation used by adults to encourage children to fill in words, to complete a sentence, or to give children time to process the language they see or hear and then respond. Daily activities such as cooking, cleaning, tidying up, laundry, and dishes are all opportunities to use strategies that promote language, cognitive, socioemotional, and motor development. Embedding outcomes in daily routines in the home make learning a natural part of the child's and family's everyday life rather than a separate additional activity.

Research and practice literature agree on four overarching components of the home visiting model that support child outcomes (Keilty, 2008). These are (1) context within family's routines, (2) child engagement in family activities, (3) caregiver engagement in home visits, and (4) caregiver competence and confidence. Keilty (2008) takes each of these components and suggests that early intervention specialists use guiding questions to regularly reflect on whether these characteristics are adequately incorporated in their interaction with families. The checklist poses questions such as "Does the home visit occur within the same routine activities where the caregiver will use the strategies between home visits?" and "Are home visits designed so that it depends on caregiver engagement for home visits to occur?" (Keilty, 2008, p. 37). Early intervention professionals might use a checklist such as the one created by Keilty (2008) to support their own reflective practice. They might also employ the support of a mentor or supervisor to provide feedback on their consistent use of these components to promote effective service delivery to families.

Families may benefit from services provided through video technology. Recently, tele-intervention, home visits conducted through video conferencing, has been explored as a way to offer more consistent specialized services for families and children who live far from available early intervention providers (Behl, Blaiser, White, & Callow-Heusser, 2013). Distance learning technologies have also been used successfully to provide families with access to sign language services and opportunities to connect with deaf and hard-of-hearing adults and other families with deaf children (Hopkins, Keefe, & Bruno, 2012).

Developmentally Appropriate Practice

Additional factors that impact the quality and effectiveness of home visits are Developmentally Appropriate Practice (DAP) and culturally responsive services [National Association for the Education of Young Children (NAEYC), 2009]. A provider who understands early stages of development and how to facilitate the next step in learning is key to partnering with families and guiding families in ways to use strategies that are appropriate to their child's age and developmental level (Knoche, Kuhn, & Eum, 2013). Knowing what is developmentally and individually appropriate for Emily helps her interdisciplinary team and her parents and caregivers select activities that are motivating and sufficiently challenging to keep Emily involved without frustrating her.

Programming for babies and toddlers ages birth to 3 years old is different than preschool because the developmental needs of babies and toddlers are unique and substantially different than those of preschool aged children. Emily's early intervention team has expertise in the development of infants and toddlers. Sandra and Alana, the deaf mentor, have specialized dispositions, knowledge, and skills for infants and toddlers who are deaf or hard of hearing. (See Chapter 1, *What Every Early Intervention Professional Should Know.*) This specialized training allows the team to draw on knowledge in areas such as contemporary infant development theory including brain development and bilingual development, infant bonding and mental health, infant and toddler development across domains, and the influence of culture on early development.

Specific to young children who are deaf or hard of hearing, there must be a service provider on the team who has expertise in understanding the role of auditory, visual, cross-modal perception and processing related to development (JCIH, 2013). Developmentally appropriate practices take into account what is known about child development and learning, what is known about the unique needs, strengths, and interests of each child, and what is known about the cultural and social environments in which each child lives (NAEYC, 2009).

Early intervention specialists must also be mindful and knowledgeable about how each child is nurtured within his or her family's culture and how early intervention services interact in this dynamic if they are to be effective within the context of the family's home and community. "The influence of culture on the rearing of children is fundamental and encompasses values, aspirations, expectations, and practices" (National

Research Council and Institute of Medicine, 2000). Providing culturally competent services requires commitment from the program leadership and informed specialists. Table 9.1 outlines examples of how the parent–infant child program at the New Mexico School for the Deaf operationalizes the five essential elements for a culturally competent system of care listed by Hepburn (2004).

Community-Based Resources

The interdisciplinary team will build on the resources and services that the family is already accessing and propose additional information that the family might consider pursuing to support the outcomes identified through the IFSP process. These may include (1) Deaf Mentor Programs, (2) family-to-family support, (3) family learning opportunities, (4) listening and spoken language services, and (5) play groups.

Deaf Mentor programs promote the family's understanding and appreciation of being deaf or hard of hearing. (See Chapter 5, *Collaboration with Deaf and Hard-of-Hearing Communities*.) Opportunities are available in some places in the form of Deaf Role Model Programs (Abrams & Gallegos, 2011) or Deaf Mentor Programs (SKI-HI, 2001). Families may be able to access ASL instruction or literacy instruction such as the Shared Reading Program. See the Shared Reading website at Gallaudet University in Washington, DC listed in the Recommended Resources in this chapter. If a formal Deaf Mentor program is not available in a family's community, the IFSP team can support the family in networking with members of the deaf community. State and private schools for the deaf are a valuable resource for deaf community gatherings and offer cultural events that are open to the public such as theater and sports activities.

Another important opportunity for families is meeting other families to observe their interactions with their children, obtain valued resources, and receive as well as provide socioemotional support. Emily's family included other families, both deaf and hearing, in their circles of support, reflecting the value they placed on these connections. Family-to-family interaction provides an avenue to reassurance and feelings of efficacy (Ainbinder et al., 1998). Similar to all families, those who are raising a child who is deaf or hard of hearing need other families to check in with,

Table 9.1 *Culturally Competent System of Care: Examples from the Parent–Infant Child Program at the New Mexico School for the Deaf*[a]

Essential Elements (Hepburn, 2004)	New Mexico Parent–Infant Child Program Strategies
Value, accept, and respect diversity	Develop the Individual Family Service Plan (IFSP) based on family routines, priorities, and resources.
	Incorporate a strengths versus a deficit approach when exploring family resources.
	Facilitate the leadership role of family members in making decisions for their child.
Have the capacity, commitment, and systems in place for cultural self-assessment	Collaborate with providers who serve a particular cultural/ethnic group or are of the same culture as the family and ask for guidance and feedback before and after a home visit or IFSP meeting.
Be conscious of the dynamics inherent when cultures interact	Use cultural brokers for initial meetings with family.
Have continuous expansion of institutionalized cultural knowledge	Hire providers that represent various cultural/ethnic groups.
	Participate in professional learning opportunities to increase cultural knowledge and appropriate practice.
Have developed service delivery models, modes, and adaptations to accommodate diversity	Provide early educators who speak the family's language.
	Provide interpreters at IFSP meetings.
	Provide written information in the family's language.
	Provide early educators who live in the family's community.
	Adapt home visit content to include cultural events and family traditions.

[a]Adapted from Hepburn (2004) by the New Mexico School for the Deaf. Used with permission.

to validate their thoughts about the best way to support their child, and to continue to build their circle of support. The IFSP team should explore the availability of formal parent-to-parent support programs. Informal networks can also be encouraged. (See Chapter 3, *Families: Partnerships in Practice.*)

In parent–child playgroups children learn with and from other children and families establish connections with specialists, deaf and hard of hearing adults, and other families. Playgroups may be started by families or be a formal service provided by the local school or program for deaf children or an early intervention agency. The playgroup Emily will be attending is at the school for the deaf where there will be many deaf and hard-of-hearing children and adults using ASL like Emily. There will also be children who are learning to listen and use spoken language. Emily will receive services to support both her development in ASL and to help her develop her listening and spoken language skills. Oral school programs that focus exclusively on the development of listening and spoken language skills are available in many communities and may provide parent–infant and center-based toddler and preschool programs (Option Schools Inc., n.d.).

Learning opportunities for families will vary from community to community but may include family conferences, sign language classes, and other events with guest speakers. Family organizations such as the Alexander Graham Bell Association for the Deaf and Hard of Hearing, American Society for Deaf Children, and Hands & Voices have websites that post learning opportunities and ways for families to connect with other families who have deaf or hard-of-hearing children.

Interdisciplinary Teams

At every stage of the process, eligibility, outcome development, service provision, and transition, interdisciplinary practice provides the necessary resources to develop and implement the IFSP and monitor progress. During Emily's first evaluation, Sandra, as the provider who has expertise in working with children who are deaf or hard of hearing, conducted her language and communication assessment while a speech language pathologist and a physical therapist looked for any additional characteristics that might impact her development. Collaboration across disciplines and early intervention agencies is critical in making the most of resources available to families and is especially important when a child has other developmental and/or medical concerns. About one out of three children, born deaf or hard of hearing, has additional single or multiple medical issues at birth (Chapman et al., 2011).

During the initial assessment of family priorities and concerns, Emily's family was concerned that Emily was not getting enough to eat, because she was not tolerating milk. Sandra brought in a nutritionist to further discuss these concerns with Emily's parents. If her family's primary concern had been health-related care or social services, Sandra might have suggested that the service coordinator be someone who has more expertise in one of those areas. Sandra would then have worked with the family and interdisciplinary team as the specialist for children who are deaf or hard of hearing.

Through collaboration, professionals learn which providers carry the specific expertise to best address each family's concerns and their child's unique needs. This also allows various programs and professionals to understand the best "match" between families, children, and specialists, and minimize confusion of roles or duplication of services. Through collaboration families are able to manage the number of visits by reducing the numbers of providers or requesting co-visits. Co-visits encourage providers with different areas of expertise to share strategies with each other and with families to support outcomes for children. For example, Emily's team agreed that the physical therapist and Sandra would visit the family together so that language strategies could be incorporated into her motor activity of running. A shared home visit and ongoing communication among providers and family members allow providers to learn from each other's specialized skills and integrate skill building in a natural way for the child.

Sandra maintains regular communication and has a strong working relationship with other educational, medical, and health care professionals involved in Emily's development. Sandra and Emily's audiologist work together to answer questions Emily's family has about her amplification, troubleshoot any problems with her hearing aids, and monitor her progress in listening skill development. Sandra also collaborates with the playgroup to help connect concepts for Emily between the playgroup and home.

Collaboration is crucial in facilitating the early referral of children who are deaf or hard of hearing to appropriate early intervention services. Effective relationships with community agencies helps experts such as Sandra raise awareness of the urgency to provide children who are deaf or hard of hearing with early and rich exposure to language.

TRANSITION PLANNING

Based on Emily's family's interest in exploring preschools, the team will consider what is available in their community and what Emily's parents believe would be the best preschool setting for Emily. They will also want to begin to discuss the transition and eligibility process for accessing services through Part B of IDEA services from the public schools when she is 3 years old.

At the beginning of their journey, Emily's parents thought that she would attend the same daycare as her older brother. But as they have learned more about preschool services and gained understanding about the importance of communication access from Sandra and the deaf adults they have met, their thinking has shifted. They are involved in a playgroup with other families of children who are deaf or hard of hearing. They understand that there are many opportunities in their community: in-home day care, private child care centers, Head Start, public school programs, the preschool program at their state school for the deaf, and combinations of these services. They are interested in visiting these programs with Sandra, and have created a list of questions and have a checklist (DeConde Johnson, Beams, & Stredler-Brown, 2005) to help them consider what types of support might be available to Emily in each of the settings, keeping in mind communication access, peers, specialized service providers, and Emily's individual learning style.

United States Federal regulations require that states have policies and procedures that ensure that a transition plan is in place not fewer than 90 days and not more than 9 months before a toddler's third birthday [CFR 303.209 (d) (2)]. Each state establishes guidelines to meet these minimum standards so it is important for providers to refer to their state regulations and procedures for direction. Emily's team is gearing up for her transition plan. It will include transition planning requirements such as informing her parents about preschool options, providing opportunities for them to visit and gather information about preschools, referring her to the Part B public school program, and setting up a transition conference.

SUMMARY

Professionals and families enter into a partnership when there is mutual respect and exchange of information and professionals view family members as experts on their children. Families with higher levels of self-efficacy experience better outcomes for their children (Dunst, Trivette, & Hamby, 2007). Emily's IFSP team is an example of an effective collaboration between professionals and family members that brings together the family's knowledge of their child, their community, and culture with the specialized knowledge and expertise of providers. This results in the implementation of an IFSP plan that utilizes resources in the community, reflects the family's priorities and concerns, and takes advantage of the specialists' knowledge of developmentally appropriate programming while addressing the unique needs of children who are deaf or hard of hearing

Emily's IFSP team is aware of best practices related to early intervention in general, and specifically for children who are deaf or hard of hearing (JCIH, 2013). Their lesson plans for home visits and family-centered play-based playgroups are guided by assessment, focused on next steps in language, literacy, and general developmental domains with specific adaptations for Emily's individual learning style and pace. They have revised their strategies and services in response to Emily's progress and her family's priorities and concerns. They have delved into what a natural learning environment is for Emily and have identified strategies that can be embedded in their family routines and utilized resources available through the community. As a result, Emily and her family have opportunities to work with and learn from Deaf adults, as well as other families who have children who are deaf or hard of hearing. They have been responsive to the family's values and beliefs and responded to the family's concerns about Emily's delay in language and their high expectations for her progress.

Because family circles of support are dynamic and evolve, the IFSP team, including the family, continues to seek a range of resources at various points in time. Collaboration among professionals and families is critical to quality service delivery and concomitant achievement of child outcomes. At every stage of the process, interdisciplinary practice will provide the necessary resources to develop the IFSP and to carry out the implementation of the plan.

To develop an appropriate IFSP and attain positive outcomes for both the child and family, it is essential that a service provider with specialized skills in working with infants and toddlers who are deaf or hard of hearing is on the interdisciplinary team. All specialists need to be familiar with the factors that constitute an appropriate early intervention program and best practices for implementation (JCIH, 2013). Every family deserves comprehensive information and support from the interdisciplinary team. Careful monitoring of the child's progress coupled with family-centered practices that honor family priorities and concerns guide professionals in ensuring the delivery of effective early intervention services.

SUGGESTED ACTIVITIES

1. Observe the amount and type of communication between a baby or toddler who is not deaf or hard of hearing and his or her family. Describe the amount of incidental and direct language exposure a child typically has and what strategies and services a child who is deaf or hard of hearing may need to access these same opportunities.
2. Practice conducting a routines-based interview with someone you know who has young children. Use a form required in your state's IFSP form. If your state does not provide such a form, access The Routines-Based Interview Report Form from The Early Childhood Technical Assistance Center http://www.siskin.org/downloads/RBI_Report_Form.pdf.

3. Describe what you learned from this interview process and reflect on how you would use this information for an IFSP with a deaf and hard-of-hearing infant or toddler.

4. Find out who the lead agency for Part C is in your state and review its website for resources, services, and guidelines in providing early intervention services including how they collaborate with the state school for the deaf and other programs that provide services for infants and toddlers who are deaf.

5. Use Keilty's (2008) Home Visiting Principles Checklist to reflect on your practice. If you are not seeing a family, arrange to observe a home visit. Identify a strength of your practice and an area that might be improved.

RECOMMENDED RESOURCES

1. Alexander Graham Bell Association for the Deaf and Hard of Hearing
   The Alexander Graham Bell Association has resources and information for families and professionals about developing listening and spoken language for individuals who are deaf or hard of hearing. http://listeningandspokenlanguage.org/Who_We_Are/.

2. American Society for Deaf Children (ASDC)
   ASDC is a "parent-helping-parent" network. Its quarterly publication features articles pertinent to families and providers working with infants and toddlers. *Words: A Passport to the World* (Fall 2010 Edition) summarizes language development and the importance of accessibility in the early years. http://deafchildren.org/join/endeavor-magazine/.

3. Boystown Press
   Boystown Press disseminates books, DVDs, and other material for families of children who are deaf, hearing, or hard of hearing. *The Home Team: Early Intervention Illustrated* DVD focuses on best practices for family involvement and family-centered early intervention. http://www.boystownpress.org/index.php/deaf-hard-of-hearing.html.

4. Early Childhood Technical Assistance Center (ECTA)
   The ECTA provides technical assistance, develops and disseminates professional development resources, and supports integration of outcome measures. http://ectacenter.org/eco/.

5. Early Intervention Strategies for Success Blog
   Early Intervention Strategies for Success Blog is a format for discussions about early intervention with strategies and information for implementing recommended practice.

http://veipd.org/earlyintervention/traditional-vs-collaborative-ei-visits-whats-the-difference/.

6. Hands & Voices

 Hands & Voices is a parent-driven organization supporting families of children who are deaf or hard of hearing. The Preschool/Kindergarten Placement Checklist for Children Who Are Deaf and Hard of Hearing was written to help parents when considering school placement opportunities for their child. http://handsandvoices.org/pdf/TransRevised0107.pdf.

7. HOPE Inc.

 The HOPE Company distributes material in English and Spanish for use in family-centered early intervention programs for children who are deaf or hard of hearing and deaf-blind. The SKI-HI Curriculum contains information and activity sheets to use with families. http://hopepubl.com/proddetail.php?prod=103.

 The Deaf Mentor Curriculum focuses on American Sign Language for families, early visual communication, and Deaf Culture.

 http://hopepubl.com/products.php?cat=5&pg=2.

8. The National Center for Hearing Assessment and Management (NCHAM)

 NCHAM is a National Resource Center for the implementation of effective Newborn Hearing Screening and Intervention systems. The section on early intervention provides resources and information to parents and professionals.

 http://www.infanthearing.org/earlyintervention/index.html.

9. Laurent Clerc National Deaf Education Center

 The Laurent Clerc National Deaf Education Center provides resources and information for parents and professionals on how to improve the quality of education of children who are deaf or hard of hearing throughout the United States. The Center is housed at Gallaudet University. http://www.gallaudet.edu/clerc_center/welcome.html.

10. Shared Reading Project

 The Shared Reading Project is designed to teach parents and caregivers how to read to their deaf and hard-of-hearing children using American Sign Language, and to use strategies to make book sharing more effective.

 http://www.gallaudet.edu/clerc_center/information_and_resources/info_to_go/language_and_literacy/literacy_at_the_clerc_center/welcome_to_shared_reading_project.html.

REFERENCES

Abrams, S., & Gallegos, R. (2011). Deaf role models making a critical difference in New Mexico. *Odyssey, 12*, 24–27.

Ainbinder, J. G., Blanchard, L. W., Singer, G. S., Sullivan, M. E., Powers, L. K., Marquis, J. G., & Santelli, B. B. (1998). A qualitative study of parent to parent support for parents of children with special needs. *Journal of Pediatric Psychology, 23*(2), 99–109.

American Speech-Language-Hearing Association (ASHA) and the Council on Education of the Deaf (CED) Joint Committee. (2006). *Fact sheet: Natural environments for infants and toddlers who are deaf or hard of hearing and their families.* Retrieved from http://www.asha.org/aud/Natural-Environments-for-Infants-and-Toddlers/.

Antia, S. D., Stinson, M., & Gaustad, M. (2002). Developing membership in the education of deaf and hard-of-hearing students in inclusive settings. *Journal of Deaf Studies and Deaf Education, 7*(3), 214–229.

Behl, D., Blaiser, K. M., White, K. R., & Callow-Heusser, C. A. (2013). *Using tele-intervention for children who are deaf or hard of hearing.* Retrieved from http://infanthearing.org/ti-guide/docs/Final-TI-Report-2013.pdf.

Chapman, D. A., Stampfel, C. C., Bodurtha, J. N., Dodson, K. M., Pandva, A., Lynch, K., B., & Kirby, R. S. (2011). Impact of co-occurring birth defects on the timing of newborn hearing screening and diagnosis. *American Journal of Audiology, 20*(2), 132–139. doi:10.1044/1059-0889(2011/10-0049).

DeConde Johnson, C., Beams, D., & Stredler-Brown, A. (2005). Preschool/kindergarten placement checklist for children who are deaf or hard of hearing. Retrieved from http://www.handsandvoices.org/pdf/PlacementChecklistR6-06.pdf.

Dunst, C. J., Trivette, C. M., & Deal, A. (1988). *Enabling and empowering families: Principles and guidelines for practice.* Cambridge, MA: Brookline Books.

Dunst, C. J., Trivette, C. M., & Hamby, D. W. (2007). Meta-analysis of family-centered help giving practices research. *Mental Retardation and Developmental Disabilities Research Reviews, 13*, 370–378.

Hart B., & Risley, T. R. (2003). The early catastrophe. *Education Review, 17*(1), 110–118.

Hepburn, K. (2004). *Building culturally & linguistically competent services to support young children, their families and school readiness.* Baltimore, MD: Annie E. Casey Foundation.

Hopkins, K., Keefe, B., & Bruno, A. (2012). Telepractice: Creating a statewide network of support in rural Maine. *Volta Review, 112*(3), 409–416.

Hopper, M. J. (2011). *Positioned as bystanders: Deaf students' experiences and perceptions of informal learning phenomena.* Unpublished doctoral dissertation, University of Rochester, Rochester, NY.

Individuals with Disabilities Education Act, Early Intervention Program for Infants and Toddlers with Disabilities Regulations, 34 C.F.R. pt. 303 (2011).

Individuals with Disabilities Education Improvement Act of 2004, 20 U.S.C. 33 § 1400 et seq. (2004). Reauthorization of the Individuals with Disabilities Education Act of 1990.

Joint Committee on Infant Hearing. (2013). Supplement to the JCIH 2007 position statement: Principles and guidelines for intervention after confirmation that a child is deaf or hard of hearing. *Pediatrics,131*(4), e1324–1349. doi:10.1542/peds.2013-0008.

Jung, L. A. & Grisham-Brown, J. (2006). Moving from assessment information to IFSPs: Guidelines for a family-centered process. *Young Exceptional Children*, 9, 2. doi: 10.1177/109625060600900201.

Keilty, B. (2008). EI home visiting principles in practice: A reflective approach. *Young Exceptional Children*, 11(2), 29–40.

Knoche, L. L., Kuhn, M., & Eum, J. (2013). More time. More showing. More helping. That's how it sticks. The perspective of early childhood coaches. *Infants & Young Children: An Interdisciplinary Journal of Special Care Practices*, 26(4), 349–365. doi:10.1097/IYC.ObO13e3182a21935.

Kovelman, I., Baker, S., & Petitto, L. (2008). Age of first bilingual language exposure as a new window into bilingual reading development. *Bilingualism: Language and Cognition*, 11, 203–223 doi:10.1017/S1366728908003386.

Lederberg, A. R., Schick, B., & Spencer, P. (2013). Language and literacy development of deaf and hard of hearing children: Successes and challenges. *Developmental Psychology*, 49(1), 15–30. doi:10:1037/a0029558.

McWilliam, R. A. (1992). *Family-centered intervention planning: A routine-based approach.* Tucson, AZ: Communication Skill Builders.

McWilliam, R. A. (2010). *Supporting young children and their families.* Baltimore, MD: Brookes Publishing Co.

McWilliam, R. A., Casey, A. M., & Sims, S. (2009). The routines-based interview: A method for gathering information and assessing needs. *Infants & Young Children*, 22(3), 224–233.

National Agenda: Moving Forward on Achieving Educational Equality for Deaf and Hard of Hearing Students. (April 2005). Retrieved from www.nedepnow.org.

National Association for the Education of Young Children. (2009). *Position statement: Developmentally appropriate practice in early childhood programs serving children from birth through age 8.* Washington, DC. Retrieved from http://www.naeyc.org/files/naeyc/file/positions/PSDAP.pdf.

National Children's Bureau, Early Support. (n.d.). *Our family, my life*. London, England, Retrieved from http://www.ncb.org.uk/media/1039041/our_family_my_life_resource.doc.

National Information Center for Children and Youth with Disabilities (NICHCY). (2014). *Building the legacy for our youngest children with disabilities: A training curriculum on part C of IDEA 2004*. Retrieved from http://www.parentcenterhub.org/repository/legacy-partc/.

National Research Council and Institute of Medicine, Board on Children, Youth, and Families, Commission on Behavioral and Social Sciences and Education. (2000). In J. P. Shonkoff & D. A. Phillips (Eds.), *From neurons to neighborhoods: The science of early childhood development*. Washington, DC.

New Mexico Family Infant and Toddler Program. (2011). *The individualized family service plan (IFSP)*. Retrieved from http://archive.nmhealth.org/ddsd/nmfit/Documents/IFSP%20TA%20Doc%20_Nov%202011_.pdf.

Option Schools Inc. (n.d.). Retrieved from http://optionschools.org/.

Public Law 99-457. (1986). Amendment to the Education for All Handicapped Children Act. Retrieved from http://uscode.house.gov/statutes/pl/99/457.pdf.

SKI-HI Institute. (2001). *Deaf mentor curriculum*. Logan, UT: HOPE Inc.

Trivette, C. M., Dunst, C. J., & Hamby, D. W. (2010). Influences of family-systems intervention practices on parent-child interactions and child development. *Topics in Early Childhood Special Education*, *30*, 3–19.

Yoshinaga-Itano, C., Coulter, D., & Thomson, V. (2001). Developmental outcomes of children with hearing loss born in Colorado hospitals with and without universal newborn hearing screening programs. *Seminars in Neonatology*, *6*(6), 521–529. doi:10.1053/siny.2001.0075

10 Early Intervention in Challenging National Contexts

Claudine Störbeck and Alys Young

S'du Moyo, a teenager in a rural village in Zimbabwe, recently gave birth to her first child, Senzeni. Given that she is young and healthy, S'du gave birth at home and the local women tended to her and the baby's needs. Once Senzeni was about 6 weeks old, S'du traveled to the nearest clinic for Senzeni to get her vaccination. Traveling long distances is a challenge, as vehicles are scarce and petrol prices have skyrocketed recently. S'du, her mother, and her infant had to leave home before dawn. They arrived at the clinic, joined the long queue, and were seen by the clinic sister by mid afternoon. S'du's mother told her that they were fortunate to have been seen before the vaccinations ran out. Because baby Senzeni was thriving and S'du herself was so young and healthy no one asked how her health had been during the pregnancy. Everyone at the clinic was enthralled by the beautiful engaging baby and said that S'du's family was truly blessed to have this special gift in their lives. But by the time Senzeni was nearing 12 months old S'du started to sense that there was something wrong. She was not babbling as much as the other babies in the village and she seemed to be less interested in story times and fireside songs as time went by.

S'du started to worry. She knew she needed to talk to someone and ask for advice, but she was very reluctant to do so. What if there was something "wrong" with Senzeni? Maybe she could not hear properly or maybe she had brain damage? Recently a cousin of hers had a baby with severe facial anomalies and developmental delays, and many community members started blaming her and saying that the ancestors had been angered and were punishing the family. Her husband left her as he was so ashamed and some people had started avoiding the family. Both her cousin and her parents were feeling guilty about somehow causing this "defect." If anyone discovered that her baby had "problems" she would be blamed in the same way and people would start avoiding her too. She knew it would also mean that her parents would lose their high standing in the community. On balance S'du thought it was better not to draw attention to Senzeni, but she had heard that the clinic that was offering vaccinations was now offering hearing screening too. Should she find out for sure if anything was wrong? But people with disabilities in her country were not readily respected or treated as equals. What benefit would it bring to know if Senzeni were deaf? After seriously considering all these concerns and issues she decided to leave it and wait and see what might happen as Senzeni grew up.

GUIDING QUESTIONS

1. What constitutes "low resource" or "developing world" national contexts and why might these be challenging for the implementation of early intervention?
2. In what ways can your practice in an early intervention program be impacted or improved through considering countries and contexts that are very different from your own?
3. How can the core principles and best practice guidelines for early intervention be adapted and implemented within these challenging environments without compromising either quality or cultural responsiveness?

COMPETENCIES ADDRESSED IN THIS CHAPTER

1. Socially, Culturally, and Linguistically Responsive Practices Including Deaf/ Hard-of-Hearing Cultures and Communities: Sensitivity to and Respect for an Individual Family's Characteristics
2. Professional and Ethical Behavior: Fundamentals of Early Intervention Practice, Legislation, Policies, and Research

INTRODUCTION

S'du lives in what is generally considered a developing nation. The category of "developing" nations and countries is defined by indices such as Gross National Income (GNI), degree of integration into the global financial system, life expectancy, and literacy, with 150 countries currently on this list (International Monetary Fund, 2012). The terms "resource-limited" or "low-income" countries are also commonly used. It is within these countries globally that the majority of deaf children are born and live today. Annually, there are 123 million births in developing nations (United Nations Population Fund, 2011). Of these, approximately 737, 000 children are born deaf or hard of hearing, or as described in the literature, "with a permanent congenital early-onset hearing loss" (PCHL) [Olusanya, 2012; United Nations Children's Fund (UNICEF), 2013]. This translates into 6 per 1,000 live births compared with 1.3–2 per 1,000 live births in developed countries (Olusanya, 2012; Olusanya & Newton, 2007). Overall, of the individuals identified as deaf or hard of hearing in the developing world 80% can attribute the deficit to preventable diseases in combination with the consequences of poverty, inadequate health care, and conflict (Kiyaga, 2011). As the most prevalent childhood sensory condition (Olusanya, Somefun, & Swanepoel, 2008) more than 90% of babies with PCHL reside in the developing world (Friderichs, Swanepoel, & Hall, 2012; Olusanya, Emokpae, Renner, & Wirz, 2009; Swanepoel & Störbeck, 2008).

This chapter considers the implications of early hearing detection and, more specifically, early intervention for deaf and hard-of-hearing children and their families in this context. We will describe how core principles in early intervention practiced in developed world countries can be realized differently in challenging national contexts. Furthermore, we will argue for the importance of not seeing differences as deficits in comparison with the baselines of the developed world. To do so fails to recognize the potential resources and strengths that may be contextually embedded in nation, culture, or tradition.

The chapter will also show how insights from early intervention in developing world contexts can help professionals within higher resourced contexts focus on the significance of cultural values and linguistic diversity as the starting point for the creation of effective services, rather than as variables requiring the adaptation of a standard approach.

CHALLENGING CONTEXTS

The priorities and practices of early hearing detection and intervention (EHDI) have been driven and developed in the national contexts in which only 10% of the world's deaf children reside. These economically rich countries can take for granted the existence of comprehensive health care, universal education, and a range of professional, skilled service providers as well as the infrastructures to ensure the delivery of care. Although in some cases equitable access to resources and professional expertise may pose challenges, the requirements for the provision of universal hearing screening and subsequent early intervention are present or obtainable. Hence it is with confidence that these resource-rich nations can set gold standards for the EHDI pathway: hearing of all infants screened by 1 month of age, a comprehensive audiological evaluation completed by 3 months, and referral to an early intervention program initiated within 2 days of the confirmation of hearing status, with all children receiving appropriate early intervention by no later than 6 months of age [Joint Committee on Infant Hearing (JCIH), 2007]. In some states and nations these standards are mandated by law (see Chapter 4, *Legislation, Policies, and Role of Research in Shaping Early Intervention*), and the principal challenge is merely to meet those standards and comply with national and professional guidelines. In total contrast, the majority of developing countries, such as the one in which S'du lives, do not yet recognize the importance of newborn hearing screening resulting in the early detection of deafness and therefore do not have national standards or legislation in place.

Although there is great diversity among countries known as developing nations, most lack, on a universal basis, the kinds and quality of infrastructures on which EHDI programs rely, for example, modern health care facilities, appropriate diagnostic technologies, assistive hearing technologies, and trained professional early interventionists (Cavalcanti & Guerra, 2012; Kamal, 2013). For this reason it is estimated that more than 90% of babies born in the developing world do not have the prospect of either hearing screening or early detection (Swanepoel, Störbeck, & Friedland, 2009). Furthermore, in many instances general infrastructures that enable access to early intervention, such as roads, family income to pay for services, literacy, and exposure to relevant public health information, are also missing (Kiyaga, 2011; Saadallah & Rashed, 2007; Yee-Arellano, Leal-Garza, & Pauli-Muller, 2006).

There are, however, pockets of provision. In some countries, such as in parts of South Africa, there are pilot hearing screening programs and some advanced audiological services, although not on a universal basis for all (Friderichs et al., 2012; Meyer & Swanepoel, 2011; Swanepoel, Ebrahim, Joseph, & Friedland, 2007; Theunissen & Swanepoel, 2008). In the absence of formal early intervention some organizations in various countries provide charitably funded early childhood education opportunities such as CLaSH (Children with Language, Speech, and Hearing Impairments) in Windhoek, Namibia, and Nzeve ("the ear") in Zimbabwe. In addition to philanthropic individuals, developing countries also attract the assistance of charitable development organizations such as CBM, The Christian Blind Mission (which is working toward improving Deaf Education in Madagascar with a growing interest in younger deaf children and infants), and lobbying organizations such as VSO (Voluntary Service Overseas). In the majority of cases, however, early intervention for deaf children and their families is being developed and practiced in conditions in which at least some of the resources critical for support, and often taken for granted in the developed world, cannot be assumed or relied upon.

In many of these developing countries life itself is precarious as a result of illnesses that are largely eradicated in the developed world, or as a result of war, famine, poverty, and political and economic instability. Consequently, a developmental intervention such as hearing screening and associated early intervention is often perceived as a nonessential service that does not take precedence over more urgent issues such as infant mortality, maternal health, lack of sanitation, and illnesses such as AIDS and tuberculosis (Olusanya, 2011a). The World Health Organization (WHO), which measures burden of disease by mortality or case fatality, has confirmed these priorities (Olusanya, 2007). For mothers such as S'du in our example, who have not had access to health education about hearing or language development, it is understandable that a condition that is immediately life threatening takes on a greater priority than something that cannot be "seen" and does not appear to be life threatening, such as being deaf.

In developed world countries all spheres of the community from families to national governments recognize the value of early hearing detection and high-quality early intervention in terms of optimal linguistic, socioemotional, and cognitive development for deaf or hard-of-hearing children. In some countries within the developing world, such optimization of an individual's potential is a luxury in comparison with the assurance of life itself (Kiyaga, 2011). It is well known that the consequences of limited hearing in infancy without access to early language developmental support are far reaching in terms of education, employment, citizenship, and economic independence (see Chapter 4, *Legislation, Policies, and Role of Research in Shaping Early Intervention*). In countries with low economic resources the negative consequences in adulthood resulting from failure to acquire a first language or achieve literacy may themselves be life threatening at the most basic of levels, such as the ability to earn and acquire food and shelter in order to sustain life (Olusanya, Ruben, & Parving, 2006). More generally the majority of deaf or hard-of-hearing people in the developing world still do not have the opportunity to achieve a quality of life equal to hearing peers, nor of accessing the means to equity in the first place through health, education, employment, and citizenship (Musengi, Ndofirepi, & Shumba, 2013).

ENTRY INTO "EARLY" INTERVENTION

In developed world countries, the focus on early intervention for deaf or hard-of-hearing children and their families did not arise as a result of universal newborn hearing screening. It has long been recognized that supporting deaf or hard-of-hearing infants and their families from the earliest days following identification would maximize developmental outcomes. The definition of "early," however, has changed with universal screening and confirmation of a child as deaf or hard of hearing routinely occurring in the first few months of life, rather than the first few years of life. Research evidence has made clear that there are significant differences in developmental opportunities between early and later identified infants provided that appropriate early intervention services begin by 6 months of age (Yoshinaga-Itano, 2003). Early identification without comprehensive early intervention will not ensure that the developmental gains available to deaf or hard-of-hearing children can be realized (JCIH, 2007).

However, in countries with low economic resources and health care services yet to be optimally developed, there is not necessarily a direct link between Universal Newborn Hearing Screening (UNHS) and early intervention, nor is there a logical necessity for "early" screening to mean from the time of birth. Within the majority of these developing world contexts the question of whether screening in the first few months of life makes a difference in the lives of deaf infants remains debatable and unresolved. "Universal" is not necessarily regarded as the most preferable screening option and the timing of screening is influenced by factors other than what might be regarded as developmentally optimal by first world standards.

For example, The Joint Commission on Infant Hearing (JCIH, 2007) and others (Olusanya, 2011b; Olusanya et al., 2009) have recommended that rather than universal newborn hearing screening, developing countries implement targeted newborn hearing screening (TNHS). This would include many of the high-risk factors (JCIH, 2007; Störbeck, 2012) as well as conditions such as the requirement for a bilateral referral, thereby excluding any unilateral referrals at screening. This is believed to be a more realistic goal that will increase the chances of identifying "high-risk" children earlier and directing scarce resources toward them. Yet in S'du's case, for example, targeted screening would not have led to the identification of Senzeni's deafness. She had been well all through her pregnancy, there was no family history, and Senzeni was not born with any physical features that might alert concern.

Even if a targeted program of newborn hearing screening were implemented by preference in countries of the developing world, ready access of babies for screening cannot be assumed. Serious consideration of both the timing and location of screening is needed in order to begin an early hearing detection program. Although screening in the developed world usually takes place in the hospital or clinic before the child is discharged from the hospital, fewer than 60% of babies born in developing countries are born in hospitals. Numbers drop to as low as 35% in South Africa and Nigeria and 15% in Somalia among others (Störbeck, 2012). Limiting hearing screening to only those babies born in hospitals would miss a significant number of babies born in developing countries. Nonetheless, novel and contextually coherent solutions are possible.

For example, to adapt to the significant shortage of ear-care professionals within the developing world, such as otolaryngologists or ear, nose, and throat doctors, and audiologists (Fagan & Jacobs, 2009; Olusanya, Luxon, & Wirz, 2004), the use of nurses (Friderichs et al., 2012; Meyer & Swanepoel, 2011; Moodley & Störbeck, 2012; Olusanya, 2011a) and even paraprofessionals for newborn hearing screening has been recommended (Olusanya et al., 2009). It has been demonstrated in a hospital-based service in a developing world context that "nonspecialist" staff can successfully screen newborns with an acceptable level of coverage and specificity (Olusanya, Wirz, & Luxon, 2008). However, the practice is yet to be readily accepted by audiologists even in contexts in which audiologists are a scarce resource. This in itself is a barrier to the development of widespread hearing screening programs. Yet in some developed world countries such as the United Kingdom, the training of lay people as hearing screeners is the preferred option to ensure universal and flexible screening coverage; audiologists' time is regarded as best used for more complex and specialized activities.

With regard to location, there have been various recommendations for community-based screening programs to be offered in immunization clinics in order to make use of current opportunities to interface with infants and caregivers (Swanepoel, Louw, & Hugo, 2007). Global immunization data demonstrate that 83% of the world's children under the age of 1 year have received their immunizations. The World Health Organization has identified a 2020 goal of each country achieving a 90% immunization coverage rate nationally (UNICEF, 2011). As the most consistent point of contact with parents in the developing world, immunization represents a significant point of opportunity for early detection of hearing ability. The point of mandatory BCG (Bacille Calmette-Guérin vaccine) inoculation in Côte d'Ivoire, for example, has been utilized for a pilot UNHS program (Tanon-Anoh, Sanogo-Gone, & Kouassi, 2010). In our example, S'du was prepared to travel a long distance in difficult circumstances to secure her baby's inoculations. Her presence at the clinic potentially provided a key opportunity, not just for hearing screening, but for support in coming to terms with the possibility that Senzeni was deaf, what it meant, and how to share the news with family and community.

The meshing of early hearing detection with preexisting infant health care programs provides developing countries with financially viable options as opposed to setting up new systems and processes. This approach also potentially enables hearing screening to be subsumed within systems that are socially accepted rather than being regarded as a separate and potentially stigmatizing event (Olusanya & Akinyemi, 2009).

There are significant questions surrounding the utility and ethics of early detection if there is no associated early intervention service for deaf or hard-of-hearing children and their families. What is the value of knowing if nothing or little can be done? For example, the provision of hearing aids, and just as importantly their continued maintenance (including changing ear molds as children's ears develop and a ready supply of batteries), is usually available only to the rich minority, not the poor majority. Even where access to hearing aids is possible they are not always targeted at those children for whom they might make the greatest difference in terms of audition (Kiyaga, 2011). Yet to debate the ethics of early intervention in terms of resources and practices associated with amplification, rehabilitation, and access to health care systems is perhaps to miss the point. As the whole of this book is committed to demonstrating, early intervention is a multifaceted process that fundamentally involves language, communication, the family, culture, and the developmental context. It is not narrowly defined.

In our example, S'du would benefit from information and interactions with knowledgeable and skilled others who can allay some of her fears about her child's future. At this point she does not know she has choices about how to support Senezi's language development and that she and her family can make a real difference. She has no answers to the false assumptions others might make about why her daughter is deaf. She has little means to combat the stigma she might acquire from her family and community. She has not met a deaf or hard-of-hearing adult who leads an independent life. Comprehensive early intervention in low resource countries must address these concerns (Bevilacqua, Alvarenga, Costa, & Moret, 2010), and yet, in many examples around the world, early hearing identification and intervention are defined far more narrowly as an issue of health and hearing.

There are significant problems with importing models and approaches of early intervention that have been tried and tested in the developed world into developing world contexts. Problems are not limited to the inherent differences between low resource and high resource countries. Fundamentally, early intervention practices must be culturally meaningful to be embraced in cultures and contexts far removed from the western ones in which they were developed. There is a range of normative assumptions that underpin early intervention with early identified deaf and hard-of-hearing children that potentially can be transformed within diverse cultural contexts. It is to some of these issues that we now turn.

CHALLENGING NORMATIVE ASSUMPTIONS

The early intervention component of the EHDI pathway, as practiced in developed world contexts, implies culturally embedded assumptions concerning, for example, who or what is "family," the usual expectations of parent–child early interaction practices, and the authority ascribed to professionals who provide early intervention services. Although there is increasing recognition of family and cultural diversity (e.g., Steinberg, Bain, Delgado, & Ruperto, 2003), the development of culturally sensitive early intervention services is usually regarded as an adaptation from the norm, however respectfully intended, or something special to achieve the same ends for those identified as "other" or "minority" or "different" [American Speech-Language-Hearing Association (ASHA), 2013; JCIH, 2013]. By contrast, a focus on early intervention practice in developing world contexts forces reflection on the very definition of some of the fundamentals that underpin the goals and practices of early intervention.

"Family" and "Parent"

Family-centered early intervention is a central touchstone of good practice as exemplified in this book and in recent international guidelines (Moeller, Carr, Seaver, Stredler-Brown, & Holzinger, 2013). But what and who counts as "family" needs to be routinely examined. In many cultures the notion of a nuclear rather than an extended family is alien, and the wider community might assume levels of care responsibility that would seem unusual from the perspective of many developed world cultures. Yet it is not necessarily correct to assume that what appears "different" from a developed world or majority culture perspective is a result of diversity in cultural values and norms. In many low-resource countries the nature of "family" is also fundamentally molded by material circumstance.

In the developing world a family can be anything from a child-headed household (due to parents lost to famine, violence, or AIDS) to a multi-generational family (of up to four to five generations in one home due to extreme poverty) in which it appears that the child has numerous "parents." In situations in which parents have either passed away or have had to migrate to city centers for scarce jobs, commonly children are "adopted" by neighbors who will either take them in or check on them daily. For example, in the township of Alexandra, South Africa local grannies, "goggos" who are not blood relatives, might take children into their homes and foster them informally as their own children. Who or what is "family" is contextually as well as culturally produced. It is not a given. Consequently the constituency of those engaged in family-centered approaches to early intervention must be negotiated. The family members available to support a deaf or hearing child's development in terms of "who" and in what "role" may be far richer than the European or North American notions of "family" routinely allow.

Child-Rearing Practices

Child-rearing practices vary widely on a global scale (Lloyd, Phoenix, & Woollett, 1991). Expected trajectories and norms of child development might be mediated by child-rearing practices that are far less common in the worlds in which "standard" approaches to supporting deaf children's language and social development have been created. For example, in communities in which children are to be seen and not heard, the language-learning process is passive and observational. Gaps in the language development and speech production of deaf and hard-of-hearing children are commonly not identified until later when the child has earned the right or reached the appropriate age to contribute to the conversation. In some communities such as the Wodaabe, parents are not allowed to speak to their first two children (Beckwith, 1983). In other communities, children are not encouraged to ask questions, one of the early developmental stages recognized in western child developmental charts. In our example, Senzeni's lack of enjoyment of fireside songs was a key trigger for her mother's concerns because it represented a *cultural* marker within normal child development that was not being reached.

These and other culturally normative practices associated with child development do not just make the early recognition of language delays more difficult, but also create a challenge for parents and families who wish actively to support their child's language development. Seemingly uncontroversial behaviors such as eye contact that have clear developmental benefits for children who are deaf or hard of hearing may require attitudinal shifts that are problematic for parents and caregivers in some communities. For example, in the Zulu culture, eye contact between a child and an adult can be seen as defiant and disrespectful and in many Asian and Latin American cultures sporadic eye contact is regarded as being more respectful than steady eye gaze. Another basic assumption underpinning early intervention practice is that parents and caregivers always communicate directly with their child, yet some cultures do not permit parents to communicate directly with their children.

Parents of children who are deaf or hard of hearing throughout the world and in many diverse cultural circumstances face the dilemmas and challenges of having to make changes for the sake of communicating optimally with their children. There is nothing special about developed world contexts in this respect. However, in some contexts there may be considerable social and cultural costs in making seemingly taken-for-granted adaptations such as those associated with foundations of preverbal language, for example, eye contact, parent–child interaction, social play, and touch. Adaptive behaviors may mark parents as culturally divergent within their own communities and represent significant transgressions of normative practices. The cultural imperative to conform may itself become a barrier to parents and families attempting to make changes that support their deaf or hard-of-hearing children's development. Families may risk cultural stigma in order to practice what they believe is best for their children.

UNDERPINNING CONCEPTS AND VALUES IN EARLY INTERVENTION

In developed world contexts, "quality," "effective," and "best practice" early intervention with deaf or hard-of-hearing children and their families are underpinned by some key concepts and values. These include parent–professional partnerships (Guralnick, 2000), family-centered practice (Moeller et al., 2013), and informed choice (Young et al., 2006). Guidelines supporting best practices advocate for the inclusion of deaf and hard-of-hearing people within policy and practice, equality for spoken and signed languages as potential options for families and children, and bias-free professionals who seek to empower not to persuade (JCIH, 2007, 2013; Moeller et al., 2013). Furthermore, early intervention practice no longer assumes a deficit model in which its purpose is to minimize the gap between deaf or hard-of-hearing children's development in comparison to their hearing peers. Rather the expectation is one of potentially normative growth in all developmental domains. The job of early intervention is to help deliver that goal.

In developing world contexts, some of these underpinning values and concepts are highly problematic. In part, this is a result of needing to consider the cultural equivalence of some of their components as our previous discussions concerning "family" and "child rearing" have illustrated. However, they are also problematic because of more macrolevel concerns such as the place of deaf or hard-of-hearing people in society and the economic realities of living in low resource nations.

For example, in some developed world countries, deaf or hard-of-hearing people still struggle for acknowledgment in the law of their equal rights to services. They might fight discrimination in employment, but would be unlikely to battle against a designation of being less than human. Yet in many countries, particularly those in sub-Saharan Africa as well as India, the status of deaf and hard-of-hearing people in society is considered so low that words used to refer to them deny both individuality and humanity. Kiyaga (2011) in discussing the countries of East Africa remarks:

> Deaf persons are never referred to by their personal name but instead are called *kasiru* in Luganda ["stupid one"]; *ebang* or *ebuubu ngon* in Iteso ["mad person or thing of no value"]; *kisiwi* in Kishwahili and *ikiragi* in Kinyarwanda both connote "a thing." (pp. 92–93, italics in original)

In circumstances in which stigma toward people who are deaf or hard of hearing is not merely attitudinal but structurally inscribed into language and social relations, notions of positive trajectories for the development for deaf or hard-of-hearing children are radical.

Another sociostructurally determined variable in the development of children who are deaf or hard of hearing in many countries concerns the gender of the child. In societies in which boys are more highly valued than girls, gender matters in the allocation of scarce resources, availability of education, and expectations of autonomy. In these circumstances. if a child is, in addition to being a girl, also deaf or hard of hearing, she is doubly disenfranchised. In some cases lack of equality extends to active abuse, including sexual abuse of deaf and hard-of-hearing girls (Kiyaga, 2011). Fundamental values of early intervention concerning equality of opportunity, treating all children equally, and seeking optimal developmental potential for children who are deaf or hard of hearing interact with deeply embedded social attitudes and expectations.

In the face of these and other macrolevel concerns, the central issue in early intervention shifts from its potential to release optimal development for a deaf or hard-of-hearing child to whether that potential might ever be realized in circumstances of extreme discrimination (regardless of the quality of the intervention).

Transforming Underpinning Concepts into Culturally Meaningful Practices

Despite the considerable, economic, cultural, and sociostructural challenges facing early intervention for children who are deaf or hard of hearing and their families, there are nonetheless some important examples of transformative practice in early intervention in challenging contexts. One such example is the HI HOPES early intervention service for deaf children and their families in South Africa (Störbeck & Pittman, 2008). HI HOPES is an acronym and stands for Home Intervention Hearing and Language Opportunities Parent Education Services. The service, funded by time-limited grants and donations, primarily from the business sector with recent support from provincial governments, is offered without bias and free of charge to any family with a deaf or hard-of-hearing child under the age of 3 years[a] who wishes to receive it.

One of its key principles is to "meet the family where they are." This is a familiar concept to many developed world early intervention programs and usually implies discovering where a family begins in its understanding of what it means for a child to be deaf or hard of hearing and tuning into the expectations, priorities, and values of the family in order to provide appropriate support. (See Chapter 3, *Families: Partnerships in Practice*.) Meeting a family where the family is takes on additional layers of consideration in low-resource settings and is a good example of the potential for transformative practice. This involves reconsideration of the meanings and implications of underpinning concepts in early intervention so as to be effective in culturally diverse and socioeconomically challenging contexts.

HI HOPES quite literally meets the family where they are in offering a home-based program. This is very rare in developing world contexts. HI HOPES has worked with adults, children, and families within home situations ranging from shacks, xenophobic temporary camps,[b] compounds and orphanages, to one bedroom back rooms for live in housekeepers and nannies to apartments and houses. It has provided a service to families living in townships, rural areas extending as far as 3 to 4 hours away from towns, and private dwellings in the wealthiest parts of cities. The home-based nature of the program eliminates the expense and travel time for families and, therefore, removes a potential barrier to participation. Providing services in the home is also vital because the home provides the primary context and physical and emotional resources to support the child's development.

For example, there is little point in an early interventionist working with a family in an overcrowded one room shack recommending developmental activities that rely on the acquisition of specific toys or materials

[a] Early Intervention is ideally offered from birth to 3 years, though when older children are referred to HI HOPES they are supported for shorter periods of time, as ethically it is felt that they cannot be turned away.
[b] Xenophobia is the act of intense dislike of foreigners often leading up to force and violence. During xenophobic attacks in South Africa in 2008, camps were set up to host foreigners and protect them from such attacks.

beyond the family's means. Being in the home enables an assessment of resources and strengths. Families can be shown how to utilize items such as stones, foods, tins, pots, and pans as well as the outside natural environment to help the child develop awareness of sound, play turn-taking games, build up signed vocabulary, develop early social skills, and so forth. This use of home-based resources is not only creative but fundamentally reinforces the adequacy of the circumstances in which the child is developing. At home, early interventionists (Parent Advisors in the HI HOPES program) can observe the adults and other children in context and identify positive family-specific resources that can be harnessed. For example, in some cultural contexts, interaction activities such as learning to listen that rely on silence and privacy might make little sense, but those that rely on the involvement of multiple people and quick exchanges of visual attention such as joint attention and rhymes or singing might work well.

The approach exemplified in HI HOPES is not an adaptation to limited circumstances but rather a deliberate exploitation of potential and resource. An approach emphasizing what is present rather than what is missing in the developmental environment also serves to destigmatize the "difference" or "problem" a deaf or hard-of-hearing child might bring to a family and reinforces the bonds of belonging.

CONCLUSIONS

As we end this chapter and indeed the book, readers may believe that they have learned a great deal about the developing world and might be quite relieved not to be working in such challenging contexts. If you believe that this chapter has provided a look at how the developing world works, then we have failed in what we have aimed to do, which is to provide you with some insight into your own contexts through this consideration and to challenge you to look past color, race, religion, dress, gender, language, accent, and socioeconomic status and see each family of a deaf or hard-of-hearing baby within the framework of the challenges and resources that the world holds for him or her. Becoming a culturally responsive and effective early intervention professional requires a daily acknowledgment of your biases, a continuous striving toward understanding each family's values and perspectives, and an appreciation that context and culture produce the conditions, resources, strengths, and values through which a deaf child will develop. Our challenge is to join in the production of assets that are grounded in what is normal for families, rather than to judge them or view them as divergent.

Early intervention with families with deaf or hard-of-hearing children is never about changing the context in which the child is developing, but is about working through it and learning from it. Importing any model, approach, or goal created and practiced in one societal context and seeking to impose it on another will not work. Transforming a model or approach through the families, contexts, cultures, and communities in which the child is being reared will work. Providing effective early intervention services in challenging contexts is not about being culturally sensitive and making adaptations; rather, it is about being transformative and growing best practice from within the worlds in which we seek to make a difference. It is the big lesson that attention to the developing world can teach us.

SUGGESTED ACTIVITIES

1. With reference to the vignette at the start of this chapter, what do you think that S'du should have done? Give reasons for and against her decision to wait and see what would become of Senzini. As a professional, but bearing in mind the cultural context of S'du's family, what could you have done?

2. List a few of the community groups and cultures you are currently working with as an early interventionist (if you are not yet working in the field of early intervention you can still do this for the area in which you live). How much do you know about these individual cultures? Be careful to differentiate between fact and assumptions or bias. How would you go about gaining more information about the traditions and beliefs of people in these communities and their cultures?

3. Read at least one of the articles in the following recommended resources list that addresses early intervention in a country, culture, or context with which you are unfamiliar.
4. Take some time for self-reflection: what are your own beliefs, opinions, assumptions, and biases regarding gender, race, language, culture, religion, and socioeconomic level?

RECOMMENDED RESOURCES

1. Kiyaga, N. B. (2011). Unique challenges related to the education of deaf and hard of hearing individuals in developing countries: Examples from East Africa. In D. F. Moores (Ed.), *Partners in education: Issues and trends from the 21st International Congress on the Education of the Deaf* (pp. 89–104). Washington, DC: Gallaudet University Press.
2. HI HOPES. http://www.hihopes.co.za.
3. Olusanya, B. O., & Akinyemi, O. O. (2009). Community-based infant hearing screening in a developing country: Parental uptake of follow-up services. *BMC Public Health, 9*, 66. doi:10.1.1186/1471-2458-9-66.
4. World Health Organization, UNICEF (2012). Early childhood development and disability: A discussion paper. http://www.who.int/disabilities/media/news/2012/13_09/en/index.html.

REFERENCES

American Speech-Language-Hearing Association. (2013). *Issues in ethics: Cultural and linguistic competence* [Issues in Ethics]. Retrieved from http://www.asha.org/Practice/ethics/Cultural-and-Linguistic-Competence/.

Beckwith, C. (1983). Niger's Wodaabe: "People of the Taboo." *National Geographic, 164*(4), 483–509. refdoc (ud4): 12254379.

Bevilacqua, M. C., Alvarenga, K. F., Costa, O. A., & Moret, A. L. M. (2010). The universal newborn hearing screening in Brazil: From identification to intervention. *International Journal of Pediatric Otorhinolaryngology, 74*, 510–515. doi:10.1016/j.ijporl.2010.02.009.

Cavalcanti, H. G., & Guerra, R. O. (2012). The role of maternal socioeconomic factors in the commitment to universal newborn hearing screening in the northeastern region of Brazil. *International Journal of Pediatric Otorhinolaryngology, 76*(11), 1661–1667. doi:10.1016/j.ijporl.2012.07.041.

CBM (Christian Blind Mission). Retrieved from http://www.cbm.org/Africa-252070.php.

CLaSH. Children with Language, Speech, and Hearing Impairments. Retrieved from http://www.clash-namibia.org/.

Fagan, J. J., & Jacobs, M. (2009). Survey of ENT services in Africa: Need for a comprehensive intervention. *Global Health Action, 2*, 1–7. doi:10.3402/gha.v2i0.1932.

Friderichs, N., Swanepeol, D. W., & Hall, J. (2012). Efficacy of a community based infant hearing screening programme utilising existing clinical personnel in Western Cape, South Africa. *International Journal of Pediatric Otorhinolaryngology, 76*(4), 552–559. doi:10.1016/j.ijporl.2012.01.015.

Guralnick, M. J. (2000). The early intervention system and out-of-home childcare. In D. Cryer & T. Harms (Eds.), *Infants and toddlers in out-of-home care* (pp. 207–304). Baltimore, MD: Brookes Publishing.

International Monetary Fund. (2012). *World economic outlook: Growth resuming, dangers remain.* Washington, DC. Retrieved from http://www.imf.org/external/pubs/ft/weo/2012/01/pdf/text.pdf.

Joint Committee on Infant Hearing. (2007). Year 2007 position statement: Principles and guidelines for early hearing detection and intervention programs. *Pediatrics, 120*, 898–921. doi:10.1542/peds.2007-2333.

Joint Committee on Infant Hearing. (2013). Supplement to the JCIH 2007 position statement: Principles and guidelines for intervention after confirmation that a child is deaf or hard of hearing. *Pediatrics, 131*(4), e1324–1349. doi:10.1542/peds.2013-0008.

Kamal, N. (2013). Newborn hearing screening: Opportunities and challenges. *Egyptian Journal of Ear, Nose, Throat and Allied Sciences, 14*(2), 55–58. doi:10.1016/j.ejenta.2013.01.002.

Kiyaga, N. B. (2011). Unique challenges related to the education of deaf and hard of hearing individuals in developing countries: Examples from East Africa. In D. F. Moores (Ed.), *Partners in education: Issues and trends from the 21st International Congress on the Education of the Deaf* (pp. 89–104). Washington, DC: Gallaudet University Press.

Lloyd, E., Pheonix, A., & Woollett, A. (Eds.). (1991). *Motherhood: Meanings, practices and ideologies.* London, England: Sage.

Meyer, M. E., & Swanepoel, D. W. (2011). Newborn hearing screening in the private health care sector: A national survey. *South African Medical Journal, 101*(9), 665–667.

Moeller, M. P., Carr, G., Seaver, L., Stredler-Brown, A., & Holzinger, D. (2013). Best practices in family-centered early intervention for children who are deaf or hard of hearing: An international consensus statement. *Journal of Deaf Studies and Deaf Education*, *18*(4), 429–445. doi:10.1093/deafed/ento34.

Moodley, S., & Störbeck, C. (2012). The role of the neonatal nurse in early hearing detection and intervention in South Africa. *Professional Nursing Today*, *16*(4), 28–31.

Musengi, M., Ndofirepi, A., & Shumba, A. (2013). Rethinking education of deaf children in Zimbabwe: Challenges and opportunities for teacher education. *Journal of Deaf Studies and Deaf Education*, *18*(1), 62–74. doi:10.1093/deafed/enso37.

Nzeve ("The Ear") Deaf Children's Center. Retrieved from http://www.nzeve.org/.

Olusanya, B. O. (2007). Addressing the global neglect of childhood hearing impairment in developing countries. *PLoS Medicine*, *4*(4), 626–630. doi:10.1371/journal.pmed.0040074.

Olusanya, B. O. (2011a). Highlights of the new WHO report on newborn and infant hearing screening and implications for developing countries, *International Journal of Pediatric Otorhinolaryngology*, *75*(6), 75–78. doi:10.1016/j.ijporl.2011.01.036.

Olusanya, B. O. (2011b). Making targeted screening for infant hearing loss an effective option in less developed countries. *International Journal of Pediatric Otorhinolaryngology*, *75*(3), 316–321. doi:10.1016/j.ijporl.2010.12.002.

Olusanya, B. O. (2012). Neonatal hearing screening and intervention in resource-limited settings: An overview. *Archives of Disease in Childhood*, *97*, 654–659. doi:10.1136/archdischild-2012-301786.

Olusanya, B. O., & Akinyemi, O. O. (2009). Community-based infant hearing screening in a developing country: Parental uptake of follow-up services. *BMC Public Health*, *9*, 66. doi:10.1.1186/1471-2458-9-66.

Olusanya, B. O., Emokpae, A., Renner, J. K., & Wirz, S. L. (2009). Costs and performance of early hearing detection programmes in Lagos, Nigeria. *Royal Society of Tropical Medicine and Hygiene*, *103*(2), 179–186. doi:10.1016/j.trstmh.2008.07.001.

Olusanya, B. O., Luxon, L. M., & Wirz, S. L. (2004). Benefits and challenges of newborn hearing screening for developing countries. *International Pediatric Otorhinolaryngology*, *68*(3), 287–305. doi:10.1016/j.ijporl.2003.10.015.

Olusanya, B. O., & Newton, V. E. (2007). Global burden of childhood hearing impairment and disease control priorities for developing countries. *Lancet*, *369*(9569), 1314–1317. doi:10.1016/S0140-6736(07)60602-3.

Olusanya, B. O., Ruben, R. J., & Parving A. (2006). Reducing the burden of communication disorders in the developing world: An opportunity for the millennium development project. *JAMA, 296*(4), 441–444.

Olusanya, B. O., Somefun, A. O., & Swanepoel, D. (2008). The need for standardization of methods for worldwide infant hearing screening: A systematic review. *Laryngoscope, 11*(10), 1830–1836. doi:10.1097/MLG.06013e31817d755e.

Olusanya, B. O., Wirz, S. L., & Luxon, L. M. (2008). Hospital-based universal newborn hearing screening for early detection of permanent congenital hearing loss in Lagos, Nigeria. *International Journal of Pediatric Otorhinolaryngology, 72*(7), 991–1001. doi:10.1016/j.ijporl.2008.03.004.

Saadallah, A. A., & Rashed, M. S. (2007). Newborn screening: Experiences in the Middle East and North Africa. *Journal of Inherited Metabolic Disorders, 30,* 482–489. doi:10.1007/s10545-007-0660-5.

Steinberg, A., Bain, L., Li, Y., Delgado, G., & Ruperto, V. (2003). Decisions Hispanic families make after the identification of deafness. *Journal of Deaf Studies and Deaf Education, 8*(3), 291–314. doi:10.1093/deafed/eng016.

Störbeck, C. (2012). Childhood hearing loss in the developing world. *International Journal of Child Health and Nutrition, 1*(1), 59–65. doi:10.6000/1929-4247.2012.01.01.07.

Störbeck, C., & Pittman, P. (2008). Early intervention in South Africa: Moving beyond hearing screening. *International Journal of Audiology, 47*(Suppl. 1), S36–S43. doi:10.1080/14992020802294040.

Swanepoel, D., Ebrahim, S., Joseph, A., & Friedland, P. L. (2007). Newborn hearing screening in a South African private health care hospital. *International Journal of Pediatric Otorhinolaryngology, 71*(6), 881–887. doi:10.1016/j.ijporl.2007.02.009.

Swanepoel, D. W., Louw, B., & Hugo, R. (2007). A novel service delivery model for infant hearing screening in developing countries. *International Journal of Audiology, 46*(6), 321–327. doi:10.1080/14992020601188583.

Swanepoel, D. W., & Störbeck, C. (2008). EHDI Africa: Advocating for infants with hearing loss in Africa. *International Journal of Audiology, 47*(Suppl. 1), S1–S2. doi:10.1080/14992020802300912.

Swanepoel, D. W., Störbeck, C., & Friedland, P. (2009). Early hearing detection and intervention in South Africa. *International Journal of Pediatric Otorhinolaryngology, 73*(6), 783–786. doi:10.1016/j.ijporl.2009.01.007.

Tanon-Anoh, M. J., Sanogo-Gone, D., & Kouassi, K. B. (2010). Newborn hearing screening in a developing country: Results of a pilot study in Abidjan, Cote d'Ivoire. *International Journal of Pediatric Otorhinolaryngology, 74*(2), 188–191. doi:10.1016/j.ijporl.2009.11.008.

Theunissen, M., & Swanepoel, D. (2008). Early hearing detection and intervention services in the public health sector in South Africa. *International Journal of Audiology, 47*(1), 23–29.

United Nations Children's Fund (UNICEF). (2011). *Expanding immunization coverage.* Retrieved from http://www.unicef.org/immunization/index_coverage.html.

United Nations Children's Fund (UNICEF). (May 2013). *The state of the world's children: Children with disabilities.* New York, NY: UNICEF.

United Nations Population Fund. (2011). *Delivering results in a world of 7 billion: 2011 Annual Report.* New York. Retrieved from http://www.unfpa.org/publications?title=&field_thematic_area_tid=All&field_publication_date_value%5Bvalue%5D%5Byear%5D=2011&field_type_of_publication_value=State+of+World+Population.

Voluntary Service Overseas (VSO). Retrieved from http://www.vsointernational.org/.

Yee-Arellano, H. M., Leal-Garza, F., & Pauli-Muller, K. (2006). Universal newborn hearing screening in Mexico: Results of the first 2 years. *International Journal of Pediatric Otorhinolaryngology, 70*(11), 1863–1870. doi:10.1016/j.ijporl.2006.06.008.

Yoshinaga-Itano, C. (2003). From screening to early identification and intervention: Discovering predictors to successful outcomes for children with significant hearing loss. *Journal of Deaf Studies and Deaf Education, 8*(1), 11–30. doi:10.1093/deafed/8.1.11.

Young, A. M., Carr, G., Hunt, R., McCracken, W., Skipp, A., & Tattersall, H. (2006). Informed choice and deaf children—underpinning concepts and enduring concerns. *Journal of Deaf Studies and Deaf Education, 11*(3), 322–336. doi:10.1093/deafed/enj041.

INDEX

Page numbers followed by "n" indicate footnotes. Page numbers in **bold** indicate chapter contributors.